# Revolutionary Patriots
### of
## Cecil County
### Maryland

Henry C. Peden, Jr.

HERITAGE BOOKS
2022

**HERITAGE BOOKS**
*AN IMPRINT OF HERITAGE BOOKS, INC.*

**Books, CDs, and more—Worldwide**

For our listing of thousands of titles see our website
at
www.HeritageBooks.com

Published 2022 by
HERITAGE BOOKS, INC.
Publishing Division
5810 Ruatan Street
Berwyn Heights, Md. 20740

Copyright © 1991 Henry C. Peden, Jr.

All rights reserved. No part of this book may be reproduced or transmitted in any form or by any means, electronic or mechanical, including photocopying, recording or by any information storage and retrieval system without written permission from the author, except for the inclusion of brief quotations in a review.

International Standard Book Number
Paperbound: 978-1-58549-184-1

FOREWORD

This book has been compiled for the purpose of serving as a finding list for patriots of Cecil County, Maryland who served in the Revolutionary War, 1775-1783, thus enabling descendants to join patriotic organizations such as the DAR and SAR. This book is more than a mere listing of names because many persons named herein also have dates of birth, death, marriage and other genealogical information included with their respective entries.

Many primary and secondary sources have been researched and information gleaned for this book. The compiler wishes to express his gratitude for the assistance of the staff and librarians at the Maryland State Archives and the Maryland Historical Society.

It is important to mention that many errors were found in the book by Mollie H. Ash that was published in 1940 and entitled "Cecil County, Maryland Signers of the Oath of Allegiance Sworn by County Justices, March 2, 1778." With all due respect to her efforts, a check of original lists uncovered many misspellings and omissions in her book and they have been corrected herein. Also, Capt. Henry Dobson was from Cecil County and was Captain of a Company in the 6th Maryland Line in 1780. It was not readily discernible which of his men were from Cecil County or other counties, so all were included here in order that no Cecil Countians were inadvertently omitted.

Each entry in this book has been documented, and a key to that documentation has been implemented within the text. A letter followed by a number is the code used for a source and the page within that source. For example, G-467 means that the source is "Archives of Maryland, Vol. 18, p. 467." There are some variations on this theme, and other sources not listed below have been incorporated into the text. The key to the coded source documentation is as follows:

A = Maryland Historical Society, Manuscripts Div. (MS.1146). Maryland State Archives Manuscripts (MdHR3218-1 to 18).

```
A-1    Oaths taken by Justice Elihu Hall
A-2    Oaths taken by Justice Thomas Bouldin
A-3    Oaths taken by Justice John Leach Knight
A-4    Oaths taken by Justice John Veazey
A-5    Oaths taken by Justice Samuel Miller
A-6    Oaths taken by Justice Richard Bond
A-7    Oaths taken by Justice Joseph Gilpin
A-8    Oaths taken by Justice Stephen Hyland
A-9    Oaths taken by Justice Timothy Kirk
A-10   Oaths taken by Justice James Maxwell
A-11   Oaths taken by Justice John Cox
A-12   Oaths taken by Justice John Ward Veazey
A-13   Oaths taken by Justice David Smith
A-14   Oaths taken by Justice John Ward
A-15   Oaths taken by Justice Tobias Rudulph
A-16   Oaths taken by Justice Amos Alexander
A-17   Oaths taken by Justice John Dockery Thompson
A-18   Oaths taken by Justice Samuel Glenn
```

B = Miller, Richard B. "Some Little Known Data Regarding Maryland Signers of the Oath of Fidelity, 1780-1781." MD Gen. Soc. Bulletin 27:1, Winter, 1986, pp. 101-124.

C = "Cecil County in the Revolutionary War, 1776-1783." Privately published by the Cecil Co. Bicentennial Committee.

D = Steuart, Rieman. The Maryland Line in the Revolutionary War, 1775-1783. Published by Society of the Cincinnati of Maryland, 1969.

E = Hodges, Margaret R. Unpublished Revolutionary Records of Maryland, Vol. I (Maryland Historical Society: Privately printed, 1941)

F = Wright, F. Edward and Clements, S. Eugene. Maryland Militia in the Revolutionary War. (Silver Spring, MD: Family Line Publications, 1987).

G = Archives of Maryland, Vol. 18, "Muster Rolls of Maryland Troops in the American Revolution, 1775-1783" (Published by the Maryland Historical Society, 1900).

H = Heitman, Francis B. Historical Register of Officers of the Continental Army During the War of the Revolution, 1775-1783 (Baltimore: Genealogical Published Co., reprint 1982, originally published in Washington, DC, 1914).

I = Papenfuse, Edward C. et al. Inventory of Maryland State Papers, Vol. I, "The Era of the American Revolution, 1775-1783" (Annapolis: Maryland Hall of Records, 1977).

J = Johnston, George. History of Cecil County, Maryland. (Baltimore: Genealogical Publishing Co., reprint 1989, originally published in Elkton, Maryland, 1881).

K = Calendar of Maryland State Papers, The Red Books, No. 4, Part 1 (Published by the Hall of Records Commission in 1950)

L = Calendar of Maryland State Papers, The Brown Books, No. 3 (Published by the Hall of Records Commission in 1948).

M = Cecil County Court Minutes, 1777-1784 (Original Records, Accession No. MdHR9260, at the Maryland State Archives).

N = Brumbaugh, Gaius M. Maryland Records, Vol. II, "Kilty's Law." (Baltimore: Genealogical Publishing Co., reprint 1985, originally published in Lancaster, PA in 1928).

O = Cecil County Marriage Licenses, 1777-1840 (Published by Capt. Jeremiah Baker Chapter, DAR, Elkton, MD, 1928).

P = Archives of Maryland, Vol. 11, "Journal and Proceedings of the Maryland Convention, July 26 to August 1, 1775."

Q = Newman, Harry Wright. Maryland Revolutionary Records. (Baltimore: Genealogical Publishing Co., reprint, 1980, originally published in Washington, DC, in 1938).

R = Barnes, Robert W. Maryland Marriages, 1634-1777. (Baltimore: Genealogical Publishing Company, 1975).

S = Original Manuscripts from the Maryland State Archives. (Accession Numbers indicated for the Hall of Records)

T = Original Manuscripts from the Maryland Historical Society Library Manuscript Division (MS.1814).

U = Maryland DAR Directory, 1892-1965 (Published by the Maryland Society, Daughters of the American Revolution in 1966).

V = Maryland DAR Directory, 1965-1980 (Published by the Maryland Society, Daughters of the American Revolution in 1985).

W = Archives of Maryland, Vol. 12, "Journal and Correspondence of the Maryland Council of Safety, July 7 to December 31, 1776."

Cecil County can well be proud of the many men she sent forth to serve in the American Revolution in the 2nd, 18th and 30th Militia Battalions, and in the Maryland Continental Line, as well as those who rendered material aid and signed the Oath of Allegiance. I trust that the descendants of these brave men and women whose names appear on the pages of this book are as equally as proud of their ancestors as their ancestors would be of them.

Henry C. Peden, Jr.<br>
Bel Air, Maryland<br>
January 1, 1991

REVOLUTIONARY PATRIOTS OF CECIL COUNTY, MARYLAND, 1775-1783

ABRAEM, RICHARD. Oath of Allegiance in 1778 (A-6).

ADAMS, WILLIAM. Oath of Allegiance in 1778 (A-7).

ADARE, JOHN. Took Oath of Allegiance in 1778 (A-2). John Adare married Elizabeth Sinno by license November 21, 1787 (O-9).

ADARE, WILLIAM. Oath of Allegiance in 1778 (A-2).

AGNEW, MICHAEL. Oath of Allegiance in 1778 (A-6).

AKEN, ROBERT. Oath of Allegiance in 1778 (A-5).

ALDRIDGE, FREDUS. Private in Capt. Stephen Hyland's Militia Company, September 8, 1775 (T-MS.1814). Took the Oath of Allegiance in 1778 (A-14). Fredus "Aldredge" married Catherine Cosden by license February 29, 1796 (O-16).

ALEXANDER, AMOS (1729-1780). He was one of the Justices who administered the Oaths of Allegiance in Cecil County in March, 1778 (A-16). Amos was born in New Munster, Cecil County, Maryland and married Sarah Sharpe. Their children were: Walter (born 1751); Priscilla (born 1753, married (1) Captain Isaac Alexander and (2) Robert Longworth; Rachel (born 1755); Jemima (born 1757, married Alexander Reed); Ruth (born 1759, married Andrew Wallace; Mary (born 1761, married John Evans); Dorcas (born 1763, married Henry McCoy); Amos, Jr. (born 1766, married Amanda Duffield); Sarah (born 1769, married Robert Hodgson); Mark (born 1772, married Elizabeth Gilpin); Margaret (born 1774, married James Alexander); and, James married Mary Clendennin (U-116). Amos served under Gen. Washington, was severely wounded, and left the Army in 1777. He is buried at Head of Christiana (C-70). (Source L-38 states that he was entitled to receive a military clothing allowance on March 6, 1779).

ALEXANDER, ARTHUR. Oath of Allegiance in 1778 (A-6). Private in Capt. Jeremiah Baker's Company, August 1, 1775, and in Capt. Baruch Williams' Company, March 3, 1776 (F-157).

ALEXANDER, CALEB. Private in Elk Battalion, October 1, 1778 (S-MdHR6636-12-37A). Oath of Allegiance in 1778 (A-7).

ALEXANDER, DAVID. Oath of Allegiance in 1778 (A-2).

ALEXANDER, EDWARD. Oath of Allegiance in 1778 (A-6). Private in Capt. Jeremiah Baker's Company, August 1, 1775, and in Capt. Baruch Williams' Company on March 3, 1776 (F-157). Edward Alexander married Susannah McCauley, January 16, 1786 lic. (O-8).

ALEXANDER, ELI. Oath of Allegiance in 1778 (A-2).

ALEXANDER, EZEKIEL. Private in Capt. Walter Alexander's Company, July 24, 1776 (C-86, G-62).

ALEXANDER, GEORGE. Oath of Allegiance in 1778 (A-16).

ALEXANDER, JAMES (Student). Oath of Allegiance, 1778 (A-16). James was a medical student at Nassau College, N.J. when the Revolution began. He returned home and enlisted as a Private and then Sergeant in 1776 in Capt. Alexander's Co. He was sick at Elkton and joined Capt. Evans' Co. until recovered, when he rejoined Capt. Alexander and served as Sergeant until discharged on December 1, 1776. He resumed his study of medicine and upon graduation he went to his father's home in North Carolina and offered his services as a surgeon on May 25, 1780. He served as Surgeon under Col. Davidson in Mecklenberg County, N.C. and left the service on March 1, 1781. He subsequently removed to Allen County, Kentucky where he applied for a pension in 1833, stating the above service and that he was born November 23, 1756 in Cecil County, Maryland in a house that stood on the Maryland-Pennsylvania line. He died March 11, 1839 and his widow Dorcas applied for a pension. James Alexander and Dorcas Garrison were married November 26, 1789 and had children Silas, Charles G., Mary S., Mark, Abigail, Hannah, James R., John G., and Dorcas R. (NGS Qtrly., Vol. 30, No. 2, pp. 52-53, 1942)

ALEXANDER, JAMES. Took the Oath of Allegiance in 1778 (A-16). Private in Capt. Walter Alexander's Company on July 24, 1776 (C-86, G-62).

ALEXANDER, JAMES JR. Oath of Allegiance in 1778 (A-16).

ALEXANDER, JOHN. Two men with this name took the Oath of Allegiance in 1778 (A-6, A-16). One was a Private in Capt. Edward Veazey's Company in 1776 (C-85). Received a military clothing allowance on March 6, 1779 (L-38). The other John Alexander (1714, Delaware - January 6, 1802, Cecil County, MD) married Rebecca Justice (1737-1793) in Cecil County, and their son James Alexander (1770-1826) married Julia Ann Hitchcock (1759-1823) in 1798 (Maryland Society, Sons of the American Revolution, application of descendant Frederick D. Reynolds, approved May 15, 1984, National No. 123999, State No. 2754).

ALEXANDER, JOHN JR. Private in Capt. Jeremiah Baker's Company, August 1, 1775, and in Capt. Baruch Williams' Company, March 3, 1776 (F-157).

ALEXANDER, JOHN McKNITT (1733-1817). Born in Cecil County, Maryland, he and older brother Hezekiah Alexander moved to Mecklenburg County, North Carolina circa 1754. They signed the famous Mecklenburg Declaration in May, 1775, declaring their independence from Great Britain. Their brother, Amos Alexander, remained in Cecil County and served in the Revolutionary War (C-69, C-70).

ALEXANDER, JOSIAH. Oath of Allegiance in 1778 (A-16).

ALEXANDER, MOSES. Oath of Allegiance in 1778 (A-2).

ALEXANDER, ROBERT. Although a native Cecil Countian, Robert resided in Baltimore prior to the American Revolution and represented Baltimore County in the provincial convention from June, 1774 to June, 1776 and was chosen to represent the State in the Continental Congress in 1776, but never took his seat as he was not in favor of independence, and he fled the state and reportedly had "gone to the British Army" by September 1, 1777 (J-336, K-121, S-MdHR4570-88).

ALEXANDER, WALTER (Of New Munster). Captain in the 30th Battalion, and 4th Battalion, Flying Camp, 1776 (C-86, G-62, D-49, I-18). He was the Captain "of a Company belonging to the Eastern Shore Battalion" on August 6, 1776 (W-174) and a Captain in the Elk or 2nd Battalion, 1777-1778, under Col. Hollingsworth (S-MdHR6636-12-37A). On July 29, 1776 he was paid 500 pounds to purchase arms and blankets for his company (W-134). Took the Oath of Allegiance in 1778 (A-16).

ALEXANDER, WILLIAM. Private in Capt. Walter Alexander's Company, July 24, 1776 (C-86, G-62). Recommended to the Council of Safety by Henry Hollingsworth, January 4, 1777 (I-82). William Alexander married Elizabeth Cruthers before 1776 (Q-109).

ALIE, BURNET. Private in Major Henry (Col. Harry) Lee's Partizan Corps (Legion) on February 17, 1780 (K-156).

ALLEN (ALLAN), ROBERT. Sergeant in the Maryland Line under Capt. Henry Dobson (C-82, J-322).

ALLIT, JOSEPH. Oath of Allegiance in 1778 (A-5).

ALMAN, JOHN. Oath of Allegiance in 1778 (A-4).

ANDERSON, HENRY. Oath of Allegiance in 1778 (A-13).

ANDERSON, JACOB. Oath of Allegiance in 1778 (A-6).

ANDERSON, JAMES. Oath of Allegiance in 1778 (A-12).

ANDERSON, JAMES (D.V.M.) Oath of Allegiance in 1778 (A-9).

ANDERSON, JNO. Oath of Allegiance in 1778 (A-9).

ANDERSON, JOHN. Two men with this name took the Oath of Allegiance in 1778 (A-6, A-13). One was 1st Lieutenant in Capt. Robert Porter's Co., 30th or Susquehanna Battn., September 9, 1778 (C-84, E-57, E-116). One was a Private in the Elk Battalion on Oct. 1, 1778 (S-MdHR6636-12-37A).

ANDREW, JAMES. Oath of Allegiance in 1778 (A-15).

ANDREWS, JAMES. Oath of Allegiance in 1778 (A-13). James Andrews married Martha Blake, July 14, 1777 lic. (O-2).

ANKRIM, JAMES. Oath of Allegiance in 1778 (A-9).

ARMSTRONG, ALEXANDER.  Oath of Allegiance in 1778 (A-6).  Private in Capt. John Oglevie's Company on July 14, 1776 (C-85, G-647).

ARMSTRONG, EDWARD SR.  Oath of Allegiance in 1778 (A-2).

ARMSTRONG, EDWARD JR.  Oath of Allegiance in 1778 (A-2).

ARMSTRONG, JOHN.  Two men with this name took the Oath of Allegiance in 1778 (A-15).  One was a Private in Capt. Henry Dobson's Company in the 6th Maryland Line in North Carolina in October, 1780 (G-348).

ARMSTRONG, WILLIAM.  Two men with this name took the Oath of Allegiance in 1778 (A-15).

ARNIT, ALEXANDER.  Oath of Allegiance in 1778 (A-5).

ARNO, WILLIAM.  Deserted, October 16, 1780 (G-346).

ARRANTS (ARRATS), HARMAN (Of Elk Neck).  Oath of Allegiance in 1778 (A-8).  Ensign in Capt. Abraham Cazier's Company, Elk Battalion, September 9, 1778 (S-MdHR4570-72), and 2nd Lieutenant in Capt. Walter Alexander's Company in the 4th Battalion, "an officer of a company belonging to the Eastern Shore Battalion." (W-174).  Served from August 3, 1776 through 1781 (C-86, D-51, E-2, E-55, H-76, K-116).  "Herman" Arrants md Francina Price, April 1, 1778 (O-3).

ARRANTS, JAMES.  Private in Continental Army in Col. Harry Lee's Partisan Cavalry, 1778-1780 (C-83, G-586, G-587).

ARRANTS, NATHAN.  Ensign in Capt. Stephen Hyland's Militia Company, September 8, 1775 (T-MS.1814) and commissioned Ensign again on May 23, 1776 (P-438).

ARRANTS, WILLIAM.  Oath of Allegiance in 1778 (A-7).  William Arrants married Susanna Latham, February 26, 1781 (O-4).

ARTHERGE, JOHN.  Oath of Allegiance in 1778 (A-4).

ASH, GEORGE.  Oath of Allegiance in 1778 (A-7).  George Ash married Barbary Smith by license April 11, 1788 (O-9).

ASH, NICHOLAS.  Oath of Allegiance in 1778 (A-7).

ASKIN, HENRY.  Oath of Allegiance in 1778 (A-6).

ASKIN, MICHAEL.  Oath of Allegiance in 1778 (A-6).  Private in Capt. John Oglevie's Co., July 25, 1776 (C-85, G-647).

ASPARAGOR, JOHANNES.  Oath of Allegiance in 1778 (A-8).

AVREN (AUREN), THOMAS.  Oath of Allegiance in 1778 (A-8).  Thomas Auren married Keesy Clark, Sept. 5, 1776 (R-6).

BAAL: See "Ball."

BADDERS, JOHN. Oath of Allegiance in 1778 (A-6).

BAILEY, JOHN. Private in Capt. Joshua George's Company, 18th Battalion, August 18, 1776 (C-84, G-61).

BAKER, JEREMIAH (1743-1814 or 1819). Son of Henry Baker II whose father Henry Baker I (Quaker) came to America in 1684 from Lancashire, England and settled in Philadelphia and subsequently near Charlestown, Cecil County. Jeremiah Baker was chosen Captain of Militia on August 1, 1775. On May 10, 1776 he requested a commission and became Captain in 30th or Susquehannah Battalion on July 6, 1776 (I-34, S-MdHR6636-9-93, P-419, P-553). He subsequently joined Captain John Mott's Company in the First Regiment of Hunterdon County, PA Militia (U-132, V-12). His first wife was Hannah Thackery, whom he married December 14, 1769 (R-7), and their children were: Marcie (born 1771, married first to George Simcoe and second to Christopher Little); Francis (born 1774- died c1813); Elizabeth (born 1776, married John Oglesby); Sarah (born 1778, married Isaac Watson); and, Henry (married Elizabeth June Adair). Jeremiah's second wife was Rebecca Mauldin (married 1794) and their children were Jeremiah (married Mary Campbell); Mary Ann (married James Beatty Herbert); and, Charlotte (married a Wingate). Jeremiah Baker is buried in the cemetery of St. Mary Ann's Church (C-47, E-57, F-157). The Cecil County Chapter of the Daughters of the American Revolution, Maryland Society, was named in his honor.

BAKER, JETHRO. Born circa 1701 in Bucks Co., Pennsylvania, married Ann Gonsen in 1765, and died in June, 1777, in Cecil County. He was appointed to gather blankets for the Army and from them contracted smallpox and died. Jethro's children were Nathan, Jethro, Siney and Lydia (U-132).

BAKER, JOHN. Two men with this name took the Oath of Allegiance in 1778 (A-5, A-6). One was a Private in Capt. Joshua George's Company in the 18th Battalion on August 18, 1776 (C-84, G-61).

BAKER, NATHAN. Oath of Allegiance in 1778 (A-5). One Nathan Baker married Joyce Yardley on January 12, 1736/7 (R-7).

BAKER, THOMAS. Private in Capt. W. Alexander's Company, enrolled July 4, 1776 by Ensign Hamilton (C-86, G-63). This or another Thomas was recruited in 1780 (G-345). "Thomans" Baker married Margaret Pheland in 1763 (R-7).

BALDIN, PETER. Oath of Allegiance in 1778 (A-16).

BALL (BAAL), GEORGE. Oath of Allegiance in 1778 (A-7). George "Baal" married Sarah Blew, May 9, 1766 (R-7). George "Ball" married Sarah Blue, May 9, 1766 (R-8). George "Ball" married Ann Kely, December 1, 1776 (R-8). George "Ball" married Ann Keely, December 1, 1777 (R-8). (Ed.: Additional research is required in order to determine which George rendered patriotic service.)

BALLINTINE, HUGH.  Oath of Allegiance in 1778 (A-5).

BANBURY, JOHN.  Recruit, October 16, 1780 (G-345).

BANKHEAD, JOHN.  Oath of Allegiance in 1778 (A-5).

BARCLAY, WILLIAM.  Oath of Allegiance in 1778 (A-13).

BARCLEY, JAMES.  Oath of Allegiance in 1778 (A-7). James "Barckley" married Margaret Finley by license dated December 21, 1778 (O-2).

BARCLEY, JAMES SR.  Oath of Allegiance in 1778 (A-9).

BARE, THOMAS.  Private in Capt. Henry Dobson's Company in the 6th Maryland Line in North Carolina in 1780 (G-348).

BARFORD, WILLIAM.  Oath of Allegiance in 1778 (A-7).

BARNABY, JOHN.  Oath of Allegiance in 1778 (A-7).

BARNES (BARNS), JAMES SR.  Oath of Allegiance in 1778 (A-9).

BARNES (BARNS), JAMES JR.  Oath of Allegiance in 1778 (A-9). James Barnes married Rozanna Johnson by license May 22, 1783 (O-5).

BARNES (BARNS), JOSEPH.  Oath of Allegiance in 1778 (A-9).

BARNES (BARNS), THOMAS.  Oath of Allegiance in 1778 (A-7).

BARNIT, JOHN.  Oath of Allegiance in 1778 (A-7). One John Barnett married widow Hannah Crouch ante 1823 (Q-110).

BARR, DAVID.  Oath of Allegiance in 1778 (A-7). Ensign in Capt. Scott's Company. Resigned August 23, 1781 (E-2).

BARR, JOHN.  Private in Capt. Stephen Hyland's Militia Company on September 8, 1775 (T-MS.1814). Took the Oath of Allegiance in 1778 (A-8).

BARR, ROBERT.  Took the Oath of Allegiance in 1778 (A-6). Robert Barr married Agnes Ferguson by license May 25, 1784 (O-6).

BARRETT, ANDREW.  Oath of Allegiance in 1780 (B-105).

BARRY, JOHN.  Oath of Allegiance in 1778 (A-9). Private in Capt. W. Alexander's Company, July 27, 1776 (C-86, G-62).

BARRY, THOMAS.  Private in Capt. Stephen Hyland's Militia Company on September 8, 1775 (T-MS.1814).

BASSETT, MICHAEL.  Oath of Allegiance in 1778 (A-4).

BASSETT, RICHARD.  Private in Col. Harry Lee's Partisan Cavalry (Lee's Legion), 1778-1780 (G-587, K-156).

BATEMAN, WILLIAM. Oath of Allegiance in 1778 (A-12). William Bateman married Sarah Pearce, March 14, 1780 lic. (O-3).

BAVINGTON, JOHN. Oath of Allegiance in 1778 (A-2).

BAXTER, JOS. Joseph Baxter was Colonel of the Susquehanna or 30th Battalion of Militia in 1777 (S-MdHR6636-9-93). He also took the Oath of Allegiance in 1778 (A-15).

BAY, KENNIDAY. Private in Capt. Walter Alexander's Company, July 24, 1776 (C-86, G-62).

BAYARD, BENJAMIN. Oath of Allegiance in 1778 (A-4). Benjamin Bayard married Rachel Lawrence by license dated April 20, 1781 (O-4).

BAYARD, JOHN JR. Oath of Allegiance in 1778 (A-4).

BAYARD, PETER. Oath of Allegiance in 1778 (A-4).

BAYARD, SAMUEL. Oath of Allegiance in 1778 (A-7). First Lieutenant in Capt. Samuel Veazey's Company in the 18th or Bohemia Battalion, 1777-78 (E-56, S-MdHR6636-9-93). Samuel Bayard married Ann Lawrence by license August 6, 1778 (O-2). Samuel "Byard," Jr. married Martha Scott by license June 2, 1789 (O-10).

BAYTHORN (BEYTHORN), JAMES. Oath of Allegiance, 1778 (A-7). He appears to have served because he is among those due a military clothing allowance on March 6, 1779 (L-38).

BEALL, EVAN. Oath of Allegiance in 1778 (A-18).

BEAN, WILLIAM. Oath of Allegiance in 1778 (A-9). Private in Capt. John Oglevie's Co. on July 25, 1776 (C-85, G-647).

BEARD, HUGH. Oath of Allegiance in 1778 (A-6).

BEARD, JAMES. Oath of Allegiance in 1778 (A-17).

BEARD, LAMBERT. Oath of Allegiance in 1778 (A-17).

BEARD, LEWIS. Oath of Allegiance in 1778 (A-17).

BEARD, WILLIAM. Oath of Allegiance in 1778 (A-9). Private in Capt. W. Alexander's Co., July 27, 1776 (C-86, G-62).

BEARE, LAWSON. Oath of Allegiance in 1778 (A-6).

BEASTIN, ANDREW. Oath of Allegiance in 1778 (A-4).

BEASTIN, GEORGE. Oath of Allegiance in 1778 (A-4).

BEASTIN, RICHARD. Oath of Allegiance in 1778 (A-4).

BEASTIN, ZEBULON. Oath of Allegiance in 1778 (A-4).

BEASTON, JEREMIAH.  Oath of Allegiance in 1778 (A-17).

BEASTON, JOSEPH.  Oath of Allegiance in 1778 (A-2).

BEATH (BATH), JOSEPH.  Private in Capt. Walter Alexander's Company, July 24, 1776 (C-86, G-62).

BEATY, SAMUEL.  Oath of Allegiance in 1778 (A-9).  Samuel Beaty married Ann Bryan, March 27, 1779 license (O-3).

BEAZLY, EDWARD.  Oath of Allegiance in 1778 (A-15).

BECK (BEEK), WILLIAM.  Oath of Allegiance in 1778 (A-8).  "William Beck" was a Private in Capt. Stephen Hyland's Militia Company, September 8, 1775 (T-MS.1814).  "William Beek" was a Private in Capt. Walter Alexander's Company, August 3, 1776 (C-86, G-63).

BECKELL (BECKETT), ISAAC.  Private in Capt. Henry Dobson's Co., 6th Maryland Line in N.C. in October, 1780 (G-347).

BEEDLE:  Also see "Biddle."  BEEDLE, HARMAN.  Oath of Allegiance in 1778 (A-17).

BEEDLE, HENRY.  Oath of Allegiance in 1778 (A-8).  "Henry Beedlee" was a Private in Captain Walter Alexander's Company, August 3, 1776 (C-86, G-63).

BEEDLE, HYLAND.  Oath of Allegiance in 1778 (A-8).

BEEDLE, JOHN.  Oath of Allegiance in 1778 (A-11).

BEEDLE (BEADLE), NOBLE.  Ensign in Capt. Thomas Bouldin's Company in the 30th Battalion, June 22, 1778 (E-57).

BEEDLE, PEREGRINE.  Oath of Allegiance in 1778 (A-11).

BEEDLE, RAMAN.  Oath of Allegiance in 1778 (A-17).

BEEDLE, SAMUEL.  Oath of Allegiance in 1778 (A-11).  Samuel Beedle married Rebecca Sappington by license dated August 24, 1785 (O-7), and another Samuel Beedle married Sarah Flinter by license dated February 8, 1790 (O-11).

BEEDLE, THOMAS (OF JOHN). Oath of Allegiance in 1778 (A-14).  Thomas Beedle married Rebecca Beedle by license dated December 7, 1784 (O-7).

BELEW, TILE.  Private in Capt. Joshua George's Company, 18th Battalion, August 18, 1776 (C-84).

BELL, JOHN.  Oath of Allegiance in 1778 (A-9).

BELL, ROBERT.  Oath of Allegiance in 1778 (A-9).

BENJAMIN, JOSEPH.  Born in England in 1748 and died circa 1825 in

Cecil County, Maryland. He was a shoemaker by trade in Virginia and served as a Trumpeter with Col. "Light Horse" Harry (Henry) Lee during the Revolution, subsequently receiving a pension. He married Elizabeth Winchester by license dated Apr. 17, 1779. (U-150, and data from Jon H. Livezey, Esq., a descendant, in 1988).

BENNET (BENNETT), JOHN. Private in Col. Harry Lee's Partisan Cavalry, 1778-1780 (G-586, G-587, K-156).

BENNET (BENET), NATHAN. Oath of Allegiance in 1778 (A-6). Private in Captain Walter Alexander's Company, enrolled on July 25, 1776, by Ensign Hamilton (C-86, G-63).

BENNETT, RICHARD. Oath of Allegiance in 1778 (A-5).

BERRY, JAMES. Private in Capt. Edward Veazey's Co. (C-85).

BETHELL, JOHN. Corporal in Capt. Henry Dobson's Company, 6th Maryland Line, in North Carolina in 1780 (G-347).

BEVERLY, JAMES. Private in Capt. Joshua George's Company, 18th Battalion, August 16, 1776 (C-84, G-61).

BIDDLE: Also see "Beedle."

BIDDLE, ANDREW. Oath of Allegiance in 1778 (A-2). Andrew "Beedle" married Mary Bouldin by license dated March 30, 1784 (O-6).

BIDDLE, NOBLE. Oath of Allegiance in 1778 (A-2). Second Lieutenant in Militia (C-87). See "Noble Beedle."

BIDDLE, STEPHEN. Oath of Allegiance in 1778 (A-17).

BIGGS, NATHAN. Oath of Allegiance in 1778 (A-4).

BILLIP, HARRY. Private in Capt. Henry Dobson's Company in the 6th Maryland Line in N. C. in October, 1780 (G-347).

BING, BETHEN. Oath of Allegiance in 1778 (A-7).

BING, JOHN. Oath of Allegiance in 1778 (A-6).

BING, OLIVER. Oath of Allegiance in 1778 (A-6). Private in Capt. John Oglevie's Company, July 25, 1776 (C-85, G-647)

BING, SAMUEL. Private in Capt. John Oglevie's Company, on July 25, 1776 (C-85, G-647).

BIRD, EMPSON. Oath of Allegiance in 1778 (A-8).

BIRD, GEORGE. Oath of Allegiance in 1778 (A-8).

BIRD, RICHARD. Commissioned an Ensign in Capt. Joshua George's Company, July 29, 1776 (C-84, G-62, W-157).

BIRD, THOMAS. 2nd Lieut. in Capt. John Leach Knight's Co., 18th or Bohemia Battn., 1777-78 (E-55, S-MdHR6636-9-93). Thomas Bird married Sarah Beedle by license, April 3, 1779 (O-3).

BITTLE, THOMAS. Oath of Allegiance in 1778 (A-2).

BITTLE, THOMAS JR. Oath of Allegiance in 1778 (A-2).

BLACK, DAVID. Oath of Allegiance in 1778 (A-2).

BLAKE, ISAAC. Oath of Allegiance in 1780 (B-105).

BLAKE, SOLOMON. Oath of Allegiance in 1778 (A-5). Solomon Blake married Mary Dougherty, November 2, 1778 lic.(O-2).

BLANEY, JOHN. Oath of Allegiance in 1778 (A-6).

BLANSFORD, JOHN. Oath of Allegiance in 1778 (A-18).

BLANSFORD, JOSEPH. Oath of Allegiance in 1778 (A-18).

BLUNDELL, CHARLES. Oath of Allegiance in 1778 (A-15).

BOGGS, ARCHIBALD. Oath of Allegiance, 1778 (A-15). Archibald Boggs md Sarah Sutton, November 4, 1777 lic. (O-1, R-16).

BOGGS, JAMES. Oath of Allegiance in 1778 (A-6). Ensign in Capt. John Oglevie's Company in the Elk or 2nd Battalion, from 1776 to at least October 1, 1778 (C-85, G-647, E-4, E-55, S-MdHR6636-12-37A, S-MdHR6636-9-93).

BOICE: See "Boyce."

BOING, ISAAC. Oath of Allegiance in 1778 (A-4).

BOLTERMON, JOHN. Oath of Allegiance in 1778 (A-12).

BOME, BARTLE. Private in Capt. Henry Dobson's Company, 6th Maryland Line in North Carolina in October, 1780 (G-349).

BOMGARDNER, GEORGE. Private in Capt. Henry Dobson's Company in the 6th Maryland Line in North Carolina, 1780 (G-349).

BOLTON, ROBERT. Oath of Allegiance in 1778 (A-5).

BOND, LEVI. Oath of Allegiance in 1778 (A-6).

BOND, RICHARD. One of the Justices who administered the Oaths of Allegiance in Cecil County in March, 1778 (A-6). He also made musket barrels for the state and requested a military exemption for gun welders in 1777 (C-70, I-129). Was a Justice of the Peace in Cecil County, 1779 (L-38), and applied to be Clothier General, Oct 12, 1779 (I-244).

BOND, RICHARD JR. Oath of Allegiance in 1778 (A-6). First

Lieutenant in Capt. Samuel Gilpin's Company of the Elk or 2nd Battn., 1777-78 (E-4, E-54, S-MdHR6636-9-93). Richard Bond Jr. married Mary Brumfield, May 18, 1784 lic. (O-6).

BOND, SAMUEL (QUAKER). Oath of Allegiance in 1778 (A-6).

BOND, SAMUEL JR. Oath of Allegiance in 1778 (A-6). One Samuel Bond married Elizabeth McVea by license April 7, 1778 (O-1).

BONNEDY, JOHN. Private in Major Henry (Col. Harry) Lee's Partizan Corps (Lee's Legion) on Feb. 17, 1780 (K-156).

BONSALL, ENOCH. Oath of Allegiance in 1778 (A-7).

BONDWICKE, WALTER. Oath of Allegiance in 1778 (A-7).

BONWICKE (BARWICKE), JAMES. Oath of Allegiance. 1778 (A-7).

BOON, JOSEPH. Oath of Allegiance in 1778 (A-5).

BOOTH, EBENEZER. Oath of Allegiance in 1778 (A-7).

BOOTH, EDWARD. Sergeant in Capt. Henry Dobson's Company, 6th Maryland Line, in N.C. in Oct., 1780 (G-347). Edward Booth married Rachel Reynolds c1780 in Cecil Co. (Q-110).

BOOTH, JONATHAN. Oath of Allegiance in 1778 (A-7). Captain in the Elk or 2nd Battalion, under Col. Hollingsworth, April 21, 1778 (E-4, E-55, I-160, S-MdHR6636-12-37A).

BOOTH (BEETH), JOSEPH. Oath of Allegiance in 1778 (A-16).

BORLAND, JAMES. Oath of Allegiance in 1778 (A-9).

BORLAND, JOHN. Oath of Allegiance in 1778 (A-9).

BORRIS, EDWARD. Oath of Allegiance in 1778 (A-5).

BOUCHALL, S. G. Oath of Allegiance in 1778 (A-3).

BOUCHELL, JOHN. Oath of Allegiance in 1778 (A-4).

BOUCHELL, SLYTER. Private in Capt. Joshua George's Company, 18th Battalion, Aug. 16, 1776 (C-84, G-61). Commissioned Second Lieutenant in Capt. John Ford's Company, 18th or Bohemia Battalion, June 22, 1778 (E-56). One "Sluyter" Bouchell married Mary Bayard, May 25, 1738 (R-18).

BOUCHELL, SLYTER JR. Oath of Allegiance in 1778 (A-4).

BOUCHELL, THOMAS. Oath of Allegiance in 1778 (A-4).

BOULDIN, LEWIS. Oath of Allegiance in 1778 (A-2).

BOULDIN, RICHARD (1720-1803). Married Mary N.----- and had

children: Jane; Tamar (married Tobias Beetle in 1815); Herman (married Margaret Stephenson in 1798 and Sophia McIntire in 1807); Samuel (married Ruth Roberts in 1824); Reuben; William (married Margaret Taylor in 1803); Andrew (married Frances Ford in 1814); Richard (married Dorcas Boulden in 1808 and Mary Ann Harrington in 1825). Richard and wife Mary died on same day, December 6, 1803 (V-27). Richard took the Oath of Allegiance in 1778 (A-2). (Ed.: It seems that several of the marriage dates are too many years apart for these people to be in the same generation especially since Richard Bouldin was born in 1720 and had children getting married as late as 1824. More research is needed to document the relationships in this family.)

BOULDIN, THOMAS. Took the Oath of Allegiance in April 23, 1779 (U-166). (Ed.: That same source indicates he was born in 1706 in Cecil County, Maryland and died in Charlotte County, Va on May 1, 1777. If such was true, then he could not have taken the Oath in 1779.) Thomas married Ann (Nancy) Clark in 1733. Their children were James (born 1734, married Sally Watkins); Thomas (married Martha Moseley); Joseph (married Nancy Cheetham); Wood (born 1742, married Joanna Tyler); Richard (born 1744, married Betty Moseley); Mary (married Thomas Cox); Ephraim; William; and, Francina (U-166, U-167).

BOULDIN (BOULDEN), THOMAS JR. (1728-1783). One of the Court Justices who administered the Oaths of Allegiance in 1778 (A-2). Married Augustina Bouldin in 1764 and had a son John (born 1765), who married (1) Sarah Richardson, (2) Ann Faries, and (3) Margaret Faries. First Lieutenant in Capt. T. Brevard's Company, 18th or Bohemia Battalion in 1777, and Captain in the Sassafrass Battalion of Militia on April 21, 1778 (C-87, E-56, S-MdHR6636-9-93, U-166).

BOULDIN (BOULDEN), THOMAS SR. 2nd Lieut. in Capt. Brevard's Company, 18th Battalion, 1777-78 (E-56, S-MdHR6636-9-93).

BOWARD, LEONARD. Private in Capt. Henry Dobson's Company, 6th Maryland Line, and suffering from fatigue at Camp Hillsborough, North Carolina in October, 1780 (G-349).

BOWEN, JONATHAN. Oath of Allegiance in 1778 (A-8). Jonathan Bowen married Mary Hall by license July 19, 1786 (O-8).

BOWEN, THOMAS. Two men with this name took the Oath of Allegiance in 1778 (A-2, A-4).

BOWERS, GEORGE. Private in Capt. Henry Dobson's Company in the 6th Maryland Line in N. C. in October, 1780 (G-348).

BOYCE, ALEXANDER. Oath of Allegiance, 1778 (A-8). Alexander "Boys" married Margaret Robertson by license October 18, 1780 lic. (O-4).

BOYCE, FRANCIS. Oath of Allegiance in 1778 (A-8).

BOYCE (BOICE), GEORGE. Oath of Allegiance in 1778 (A-8). "George Boice" was a Private in Continental Army in Col. Harry Lee's

Partisan Cavalry, April 7, 1778 to June 12, 1783 (C-83, G-586, G-587, G-588, K-156). "George Boyce" was a Private in Capt. Joshua George's Company, 18th Battalion, August 16, 1776 (C-84, G-61).

BOYD, ALEXANDER. Two men with this name took the Oath of Allegiance in 1778 (A-9).

BOYD, FRANCIS. Oath of Allegiance in 1778 (A-13). First Lieutenant in Capt. Edward Daugherty's Company in 1777, and in Capt. Philip Cole's Company, Susquehanna or 30th Battalion, on September 9, 1778 (E-57, S-MdHR6636-9-93).

BOYD, JOHN. Oath of Allegiance in 1778 (A-6). One John Boyd was "a recruit, who deserted a few days after he enlisted" for military service on Oct. 16, 1780 (G-346). "John Boyed" md Mary McBurney, May 24, 1778 lic. (O-2).

BOYD, NATHAN. Oath of Allegiance in 1778 (A-6).

BOYD, ROBERT. Oath of Allegiance in 1778 (A-4).

BOYLE, JOHN. He fled the state, "supposed to be gone to the British Army," September 1, 1777 (K-121, S-MdHR4570-88).

BOYLES, ADAM. Oath of Allegiance in 1778 (A-3).

BOYLES (BAYLES), JOHN. Oath of Allegiance in 1778 (A-16).

BOYLES, ROBERT. Oath of Allegiance in 1778 (A-3).

BOYLES (BOYLS), TIMOTHY. Oath of Allegiance in 1778 (A-8).

BRADDOCK, JOHNSON. Private in Capt. Joshua George's Company, 18th Battalion, August 16, 1776 (C-84, G-61).

BRADLEY, CORNELIUS. Oath of Allegiance in 1778 (A-6).

BRADLEY, GEORGE. Oath of Allegiance in 1778 (A-7).

BRADLEY, NEAL. Oath of Allegiance in 1778 (A-7).

BRAZIER, W. F. Oath of Allegiance in 1778 (A-17).

BREVARD, BENJAMIN. Represented Cecil County at the Maryland Convention that met on August 14, 1776 (J-322).

BREVARD, THOMAS, CAPT. Oath of Allegiance in 1778 (A-2). Captain, Elk Battalion. Resigned June 22, 1778 (E-56).

BRICEN (BRISON): See "Bryson."

BRIDGE, DANIEL. Oath of Allegiance in 1778 (A-14).

BRIGHLEY, JOAKIM. Oath of Allegiance in 1778 (A-13). "Joackin Brackley" married Martha Hagar by license December 31, 1782 (O-5).

BRIND, ISAAC. Oath of Allegiance in 1778 (A-4).

BRISLAND, WILLIAM. Private in Capt. John Oglevie's Company, July 25, 1776 (C-85, G-647).

BRISON: See "Bryson."

BRISTOW, JOHN. Oath of Allegiance in 1778 (A-2). One John Bristow married Rachel Thackery, March 7, 1784 lic. (O-6)

BRISTOW, JOHN JR. Oath of Allegiance in 1778 (A-8).

BRISTOW, WILLIAM. Oath of Allegiance in 1778 (A-15).

BROCKELL, RICHARD. Private in Capt. Henry Dobson's Company in 6th Maryland Line, 1780, and hospitalized in Annapolis in October, 1780 (G-349).

BROOKINGS, CHARLES. Oath of Allegiance in 1778 (A-4).

BROOKS, THOMAS. Private in Capt. Stephen Hyland's Militia Company, September 8, 1775 (T-MS.1814).

BROOM (BROOME), ABRAHAM. First Lieutenant in Militia (C-87). On May 10, 1777, he was recommended by Henry Hollingsworth for a commission to manufacture munitions (I-104). Took Oath of Allegiance in 1778 (A-7). Abraham Broom married Elizabeth Rumsey, May 19, 1784 lic. (O-6).

BROOM (BROOME), THOMAS. Private in Continental Army in Col. Harry Lee's Partisan Cavalry, from June, 1778 on (C-83, G-586). Sergeant on rolls of February 17, 1780 K-156). Was granted leave of absence on March 20, 1784 (G-588).

BROWN, DANIEL. Oath of Allegiance in 1778 (A-7).

BROWN, JACOB. Oath of Allegiance in 1780 (B-106).

BROWN, JAMES (1753-1781). Married Catherine McCormick in 1770 and had children: Joshua (born 1771, married Mary Lee); Catherine (born 1773/4); George (born 1775, married Ann McDowell). Private in Capt. Joshua George's Company, 18th Battalion, August 16, 1776 (C-84, G-61, U-180). This or another James Brown was recruited on October 16, 1780 (G-345). Also, James Brown was a Private in Major Henry (Harry) Lee's Partizan Corps, February 17, 1780 (K-156).

BROWN, JESSEE. Oath of Allegiance in 1780 (B-106).

BROWN, JOHN. Two men with this name took the Oath of Allegiance in 1778 (A-6, A-7). One John Brown was "a recruit, who deserted same day he enlisted" for military service on October 16, 1780 (G-346). One John Brown married Rebecca Neilar, February 18, 1789 lic. (O-10). Another "Capt. John Brown" married Mrs. Jane Thompson, widow of John Thompson, on January 23, 1752 (R-22).

BROWN, JOSEPH JR. Oath of Allegiance in 1778 (A-9).

BROWN, MESSER. Oath of Allegiance in 1778 (A-9).

BROWN, WILLIAM. Two men with this name took the Oath of Allegiance in 1778 (A-14, A-15). One married Mary Brown by license dated February 21, 1778 (O-1). Another William Brown married Rebecca Hendrickson, May 8, 1779 lic. (O-3)

BROWNE, HUGH. Oath of Allegiance in 1778 (A-7).

BRUMFIELD, DANIEL. Oath of Allegiance in 1778 (A-5).

BRUMFIELD, FRANCIS. Oath of Allegiance in 1778 (A-15).

BRUMFIELD, JAMES. Oath of Allegiance in 1778 (A-5).

BRUMFIELD, JOHN. Oath of Allegiance in 1778 (A-5). John Brumfield married Elizabeth Gibson in Aug., 1767 (R-24).

BRUMFIELD, NATHAN. Oath of Allegiance in 1778 (A-5). Nathan Brumfield married Ann Foster on December 5, 1774 (R-24).

BRUMFIELD, WILLIAM. Oath of Allegiance, 1778 (A-5). William Brumfield married Mary Brunfield on Dec. 25, 1765 (R-24).

BRYAN, AUGUSTINE. Oath of Allegiance in 1778 (A-18).

BRYSON, DANIEL. Oath of Allegiance in 1778 (A-8). Private in Capt. Jeremiah Baker's Company, August 1, 1775, and in Capt. Baruch Williams' Company, March 3, 1776 (F-157).

BRYSON, RICHARD. Oath of Allegiance in 1778 (A-4).

BRYSON (BRISON, BRICEN), THOMAS. Oath of Allegiance in 1778 (A-8). "Thomas Bricen" was a Private in Capt. Walter Alexander's Company, August 3, 1776 (C-86, G-63).

BRYSON (BRISON), WILLIAM. Private in Capt. John Oglevie's Company, July 25, 1776 (C-85, G-647). William "Brison" married Mary Reynolds, November 11, 1782 lic. (O-5).

BUCHANAN, JAMES. Oath of Allegiance in 1778 (A-7).

BUCHANAN, ROBERT. Oath of Allegiance in 1778 (A-7).

BUCHANAN, WILLIAM. Ensign in Capt. Andrew Miller's Company, Elk Battalion, April 21, 1778 (E-54) and October 1, 1778 (S-MdHR6636-12-37A). Took Oath of Allegiance, 1778 (A-7).

BUCKWORTH, SAMUEL. Oath of Allegiance in 1778 (A-4).

BULTEEL, HENRY. Oath of Allegiance in 1778 (A-6).

BURK, JAMES. Private in Capt. Henry Dobson's Company, 6th Maryland Line, in North Carolina in Oct., 1780 (G-349).

BURK, RICHARD. Oath of Allegiance in 1778 (A-15). Richard Burk married Grace Farrier on August 10, 1766 (R-26).

BURKE, WILLIAM. Oath of Allegiance in 1778 (A-6). Received a certificate for flour on January 17, 1780 (I-262).

BURLEY, NEAL. Private in Capt. Jeremiah Baker's Company, on August 1, 1775, and in Capt. Baruch Williams' Company, on March 3, 1776 (F-157).

BURNHAM, THOMAS. Oath of Allegiance in 1778 (A-4). Thomas Burnham married Mary Nurner on August 21, 1729 (R-26).

BUTLER, JOHN. Oath of Allegiance in 1778 (A-5).

BUTLER, RICHARD. Oath of Allegiance in 1778 (A-7).

BYERS, STANLY. On July 15, 1776 he was recommended to the Council of Safety by Henry Hollingsworth for a naval position (I-43).

CACKEY, HECTOR. Private in Capt. Henry Dobson's Company in the 6th Maryland Line, in N.C. in October, 1780 (G-348).

CAHOE, THOMAS JR. Drum and Fifer in Capt. Henry Dobson's Company in the 6th Maryland Line, in N.C., 1780 (G-347).

CAHOE, THOMAS SR. Private in Capt. Henry Dobson's Company in the 6th Maryland Line. On Guard in N.C., 1780 (G-349).

CALDWELL, ROBERT. Oath of Allegiance in 1778 (A-9). Robert Caldwell md Jean Patton by license Nov. 21, 1789 (O-10).

CALHOUN, WILLIAM. Oath of Allegiance in 1778 (A-9).

CALWELL, JAMES. Oath of Allegiance in 1778 (A-5).

CALWELL, WILLIAM. Oath of Allegiance in 1778 (A-5).

CAMERON, JOHN. Oath of Allegiance in 1778 (A-5). Private in Capt. Jeremiah Baker's Company, August 1, 1775, and in Capt. Baruch Williams' Company, March 3, 1776 (F-157).

CAMPBELL, ALEXANDER. Two men with this name took the Oath of Allegiance in 1778 (A-6, A-7). Iliander (Alexander?) Campbell married Ann Simpers, April 30, 1778 lic. (O-1).

CAMPBELL, ARCHIBALD. Oath of Allegiance in 1778 (A-6).

CAMPBELL, GEORGE. Oath of Allegiance in 1778 (A-6). "George Harvey Campbell" married Margaret Riely by license dated July 10, 1779 (O-3).

CAMPBELL, HENRY. Private in Capt. Joshua George's Company, 18th Battalion, August 16, 1776 (C-84, G-61).

CAMPBELL, JAMES. Born March 16, 1748, son of John and Jane Campbell, in Smithsborough, County Monaghan, Ireland, and married Sarah Rutter, January 11, 1764 in Cecil County, Maryland (R-28). Took Oath of Allegiance in 1778 (A-15). Either this or maybe another James Campbell married Mary Morrice Tiledon by license dated Sept. 21, 1779 (O-3).

CAMPBELL, JAMES JR. Oath of Allegiance in 1778 (A-5).

CAMPBELL, JOHN. Three men with this name took the Oath of Allegiance in 1778 (A-5, A-6, A-7). One was a Private in Capt. Walter Alexander's Company, July 27, 1776 (C-86, G-62). Another John Campbell was recruited on October 16, 1780 and sent to Chester Town (G-345). And another was a Private in Capt. Henry Dobson's Company in the 6th Maryland Line, 1780 (G-348). One John Campbell married Mary Allen by license dated March 25, 1788 (O-10), and another married Polly Evans by lic. May 16, 1792 (O-13).

CAMPBELL, JOHN JR. Oath of Allegiance in 1778 (A-6).

CAMPBELL, JOHN SR. Oath of Allegiance in 1778 (A-6).

CAMPBELL, JOSEPH. Oath of Allegiance in 1778 (A-6).

CAMPBELL, THOMAS. Private in Capt. Joshua George's Company, 18th Battalion, August 16, 1776 (C-84, G-61).

CAMPBLE, HENRY. Oath of Allegiance in 1778 (A-4).

CAMPBLE, JAMES. Oath of Allegiance in 1778 (A-13).

CAN, AUGUSTEEN. Private in Capt. Joshua George's Company, 18th Battalion, August 16, 1776 (C-84, G-61).

CAN, JOHN. Two men with this name took Oath of Allegiance in 1778 (A-7, A-17). One John "Cann" married Rachell Dormett on January 2, 1740 (R-28).

CANN, ROBERT. Oath of Allegiance in 1778 (A-12).

CANNON, MOSES. Oath of Allegiance in 1778 (A-5).

CANTWELL, PATERSON. Oath of Allegiance in 1778 (A-2).

CARAVELL, JOHN. Oath of Allegiance in 1778 (A-13).

CARBERRY, PETER. Recruited on October 16, 1780 (G-345).

CARITHERS: See "Caruthers."

CARITHERS, JAMES. Oath of Allegiance in 1778 (A-9).

CARITHERS, ROBERT. Oath of Allegiance in 1778 (A-9).

CARLIN (CARLON), GEORGE. Private in Capt. Walter Alexander's Company, July 27, 1776 (C-86, G-62).

CARMOTHAN, JAMES. Oath of Allegiance in 1778 (A-1).

CARPENTER, VALENTINE. Took Oath of Allegiance, 1778 (A-2). He married Mary Barneby by license April 18, 1778 (O-1).

CARRIL, DANIEL. Oath of Allegiance in 1778 (A-6).

CARRIL, JOHN. Oath of Allegiance in 1778 (A-6).

CARSON, JOHN. Oath of Allegiance in 1778 (A-7).

CARSON, ROBERT. Oath of Allegiance in 1778 (A-7).

CARSWELL, JOHN. Private in Capt. Jeremiah Baker's Company, August 1, 1775, and in Capt. Baruch Williams' Company, March 3, 1776 (F-157).

CARTER, NOAH. Drum and Fifer in Capt. Henry Dobson's Co. in the 6th Maryland Line, in N. C. in October, 1780 (G-347).

CARTY, JOHN. Oath of Allegiance in 1780 (B-107). John Carty married Elizabeth Nowland by lic. October 6, 1790 (O-11).

CARUTHERS: See "Carithers."

CARUTHERS, FRANCIS. Oath of Allegiance in 1778 (A-16).

CARUTHERS, JOHN. Oath of Allegiance in 1778 (A-16). John Caruthers married Elizabeth Beard by license December 7, 1787 (O-9).

CARUTHERS, WALTER. Oath of Allegiance in 1778 (A-16).

CARUTHERS, WILLIAM. Oath of Allegiance in 1778 (A-13).

CASHIRE (CASHNE?), WILLIAM. Private in the Militia on October 1, 1778 (S-MdHR6636-12-37A).

CASSADY, WILLIAM. Oath of Allegiance in 1778 (A-13).

CASSE, ROBERT. Oath of Allegiance in 1778 (A-7).

CASWELL, RICHARD. Born in 1729 in Cecil County, Maryland, married (1) Mary McElwain (1731-1756) and had children: William and Mary; married (2) Sarah Heritage and had children: Richard, Sarah, Winston, Anne, Calpam, John, Susannah, and Christian (V-48). He was a Brig. General, President of the Provincial Congress in 1776, and first Governor of North Carolina, where he died in 1789 (V-48).

CATHCART, DAVID. Oath of Allegiance in 1778 (A-9).

CATHER, DAVID.  Oath of Allegiance in 1778 (A-13).

CATHER (COTHER), GEORGE.  Oath of Allegiance in 1778 (A-13). Private in Capt. Jeremiah Baker's Co,, August 1, 1775, and in Capt. Baruch Williams' Co., March 3, 1776. Became a First Lieutenant in Capt. Jeremiah Baker's Co., 30th Battalion, 1777 (E-57, F-157, S-MdHR6636-9-93). George "Cother" married Margaret McCluar, March 3, 1778 (O-1).

CATHER (COTHER), ROBERT.  First Lieutenant in Capt. Samuel Miller's Company, 30th Battalion, in 1777 and on rolls of Sept 9, 1778 (E-57, K-116, S-MdHR6636-9-93, MdHR4570-72). Robert "Cather" married Hannah White, Mar 31, 1778 (O-1).

CATTO (CATO), GEORGE.  Oath of Allegiance in 1778 (A-7). An order to pay him half pay of a Private for his military services was passed on February 19, 1819 (N-327).

CAUGHEY, PATRICK.  Oath of Allegiance in 1778 (A-9).

CAULK, THOMAS W.  Oath of Allegiance in 1778 (A-11).

CAVINDER, JAMES.  Private in Capt. Walter Alexander's Company, July 24, 1776 (C-86, G-62).

CAVINDER, JOHN.  Oath of Allegiance in 1778 (A-6).

CAZIER:  See "Cozier."

CAZIER (COZIER), ABRAHAM.  Oath of Allegiance in 1778 (A-4). 1st Lieutenant in Capt. Thomas Savin's Co. in 1777 and Captain in the Elk (or 2nd) Battalion, 1778-1781 (C-87, E-7, E-55, K-116, N-326, S-MdHR6636-9-93, MdHR4570-72). Abraham "Cazier" married Elizabeth Crockett by license dated August 10, 1783 (O-6). Abraham Cazier married Mary Currier by license dated July 11, 1786 (O-8).

CHAMBERS, JOHN CAMPBELL.  Oath of Allegiance in 1778 (A-7). First Lieutenant in Capt. Andrew Miller's Company, Elk or 2nd Battalion, 1777-1778 (E-8, E-54, S-MdHR6636-12-37A, S-MdHR6636-9-93). "John Chambers" married Hannah Taylor by license dated March 31, 1791 (O-12).

CHAMBERS, JONAS.  Oath of Allegiance in 1778 (A-7).

CHAMBERS, NICHOLAS.  Oath of Allegiance in 1778 (A-2).

CHAMBERS, WILLIAM.  Private in Capt. Henry Dobson's Company in the 6th Maryland Line, 1780 (G-348).

CHANDLEE, BENJAMIN.  Oath of Allegiance in 1780 (B-107).

CHANDLEE, BENJAMIN JR.  Oath of Allegiance in 1780 (B-107).

CHANDLER, THOMAS.  Oath of Allegiance in 1778 (A-5).

CHAPPELL, JOHN. Oath of Allegiance in 1778 (A-17). John Chappell md Mary Sappington by lic. June 29, 1784 (O-6).

CHESNEY, WILLIAM. Oath of Allegiance in 1778 (A-7).

CHESNUT (CHISNUT), WILLIAM. Private in Col. Harry Lee's Partisan Cavalry, 1779-1780 (G-586, G-587).

CHESTNUT, BENJAMIN. Private in Major Henry (Harry) Lee's Partizan Corps on February 17, 1780 (K-156).

CHICK, NATHANIEL. Oath of Allegiance in 1778 (A-2).

CHICK, PEREGRINE. Oath of Allegiance, 1778 (A-2). Peregrine Chick married Margaret Turner by lic. May 6, 1790 (O-11).

CHILDS, NATHANIEL. Took Oath of Allegiance in 1778 (A-11). Nathaniel Childs md Mary Hungard, August 23, 1737 (R-33).

CHURCH, ABRAHAM. Private in Capt. Henry Dobson's Company in the 6th Maryland Line, May 30, 1778, for 3 years (G-348).

CHURCHMAN, ELIJAH. Oath of Allegiance in 1780 (B-107).

CHURN, MICHAEL. Oath of Allegiance in 1778 (A-2).

CITELY (CEITLY, KITLEY, KEITLY), THOMAS. Of Elk Neck. "Thomas Citely" was a Private in Captain Walter Alexander's Company, August 3, 1776 (C-86, G-63).

CLARK, JAMES FINLEY. Oath of Allegiance in 1778 (A-16).

CLARK, JOHN. Two men with this name took the Oath of Allegiance in 1778 (A-6, A-13).

CLARK, JOHN BEARD. Oath of Allegiance in 1778 (A-13).

CLARK, MICHAEL. Oath of Allegiance in 1778 (A-15).

CLARK, ROBERT. Recruited on October 16, 1780 (G-345).

CLARK, SAMUEL. Oath of Allegiance in 1778 (A-15). First Lieutenant in Capt. James Dougharty's Company, in the 30th or Susquehanna Battalion, April 21, 1778 (E-58).

CLARK, THOMAS. Oath of Allegiance in 1778 (A-9).

CLAYTON, JOSHUA DR. (1744-1798). Married in 1767 to Rachael Bassett McCleary and had children: James Lawson (born 1769, married Elizabeth Polk); Richard (born 1774, married (1) Mary Richardson, (2) Mary Laurenson, and (3) Araminta Lewis); Thomas (born 1777, married Jeanette Macomb). Joshua was Second Major on January 6, 1776 and then Lieutenant Colonel in the 18th or Bohemia Battalion in 1778 (C-87, E-55, S-MdHR6636-9-93). Participated in the Battle of Brandywine, at which time he was Surgeon and aide to General

Washington. He became Governor of Delaware and U.S. Senator after the war. He died on August 11, 1798 (H-159, J-323, J-326, U-216).

CLAYTON, RICHARD. Oath of Allegiance in 1778 (A-6).

CLEAVER, BENJAMIN. Private in Capt. Henry Dobson's Company in the 6th MD Line; Artificer in Roanoak in 1780 (G-349).

CLENDENIN, JAMES. Drummer (a lad) in Capt. John Oglevie's Company, July 25, 1776 (C-85, G-647).

CLENDENIN, JOHN. Oath of Allegiance in 1778 (A-6).

CLENEHAN, ROBERT. Private in Capt. Henry Dobson's Company in6th Maryland Line, in N.C. in October, 1780 (G-348).

CLENSHEY, JAMES M. Private in Capt. John Oglevie's Company, July 25, 1776 (C-85, G-647).

CLOOSE (CLEESE), JOHN. Oath of Allegiance in 1778 (A-7).

CLOOSE (CLEESE), PETER. Oath of Allegiance in 1778 (A-7).

CLOWARD, WILLIAM. Oath of Allegiance in 1778 (A-7).

COALE, PHILIP. Oath of Allegiance in 1778 (A-5).

COARD, JAMES. Oath of Allegiance in 1778 (A-9).

COARD, WILLIAM. Oath of Allegiance in 1778 (A-9).

COCH (COCK), JAMES. Oath of Allegiance in 1778 (A-7).

COCHRAN, JAMES. Oath of Allegiance in 1778 (A-16). Private in Capt. Walter Alexander's Company, July 24, 1776, and Ensign in 1777 and then 2nd Lieutenant in Capt. Hezekiah South's Company in the Elk Battalion on April 21, 1778. (C-86, G-62, E-7, E-54, S-MdHR6636-9-93). James Cochran married Sarah Fulton by lic. dated Feb. 18, 1792 (O-12).

COCHRAN (COHRAN), JOHN. Oath of Allegiance in 1778 (A-6). Ensign in Capt. Henry Dobson's Company on April 10, 1776 (P-320) and an Ensign in Capt. Samuel Gilpin's Company in the Elk Battalion on April 21, 1778 (S-MdHR6636-12-37A, S-MdHR6636-9-93, E-8, E-54).

COCHRAN, MOSES. Oath of Allegiance in 1778 (A-4).

COCHRAN, PATRICK. Oath of Allegiance in 1778 (A-4).

COCHRAN (COHRAN), ROBERT. Oath of Allegiance in 1778 (A-6).

COCHRAN, WILLIAM. Oath of Allegiance in 1778 (A-16).

COHOUND, WADLEY. Oath of Allegiance in 1778 (A-5).

COLE, ELIJAH. Born 1760, and died in New Castle County, Delaware circa 1831. He married Sarah Ford Boulden (died 1795) on December 22, 1784 and had four children: Sarah, Mary, Hannah and Abigail F. (1794-1865, married Oliver Mitchell (1780-1867) on October 24, 1810 (V-59, O-7, MD Society, Sons of the American Revolution, application of descendant Joseph McMonagle, National No. 130160, State No. 2945, approved November 4, 1987). He took the Oath of Allegiance in Cecil County in 1778 (A-7). Commissioned a First Lieutenant in Capt. John Oglevie's Company in Cecil County Militia on April 10, 1776 (C-85, G-647, P-320).

COLE, PHILIP. Captain in 30th or Susquehannah Battalion under Colonel Stephen Hyland, April 21, 1778 (E-57).

COLE, WILLIAM. Private in Capt. Henry Dobson's Company in the 6th Maryland Line; joined October 3, 1780 (G-348). William "Coale" md Elizabeth Reed, Sept 14, 1792 (O-13).

COLLINS, EDMOND. Private in Capt. Henry Dobson's Company in the 6th Maryland Line, in N. C. in October, 1780 (G-348).

COLLINS, JOHN. Oath of Allegiance in 1778 (A-5).

COLLINS, SOLOMON. Private in Capt. Walter Alexander's Company, July 27, 1776 (C-86, G-62).

COLLINS, TIMOTHY. He was reported "supposed to be gone to the British Army" by Sept 1, 1777 (K-121, S-MdHR4570-88).

COMEGYS, ALPHONSO. Oath of Allegiance in 1778 (A-12).

COMEGYS, JESSE. Oath of Allegiance in 1778 (A-12). Private in Capt. Joshua George's Company, 18th Battalion, August 16, 1776 (C-84, G-61). 2nd Lieutenant in Capt. John W. Veazey's Co., Sassafras Battn., June 22, 1778 (E-56). Jesse "Comegyes" married Mary Everyt, Dec. 8, 1777 (O-1).

COMEGYS, JONATHAN. Private in Capt. Joshua George's Company, 18th Battalion, August 16, 1776 (C-84, G-61).

CONCAU (CORCAU?), JOHN. Oath of Allegiance in 1778 (A-7). "John Corcoa" married Jane Kincaid, June 9, 1779 (O-3).

CONNALLY, CORNELIUS. Oath of Allegiance in 1778 (A-7).

CONNELLY, GUSTAIN. Oath of Allegiance in 1778 (A-7).

CONNELLY, JAMES. Oath of Allegiance in 1778 (A-5).

CONNELLY, JEREMIAH. Oath of Allegiance in 1778 (A-7).

CONNELLY, JOHN. Oath of Allegiance in 1778 (A-5).

CONNELLY, MICHAEL. Oath of Allegiance in 1778 (A-6). Private in Capt. Henry Dobson's Company in the 6th Maryland Line, in N. C. in October, 1780 (G-349).

CONNELLY, SAMUEL. Oath of Allegiance in 1778 (A-7).

CONNOLEY, JOHN. Oath of Allegiance in 1778 (A-11).

CONNER, CORNELIUS. Oath of Allegiance in 1778 (A-7).

CONNER, JAMES. Oath of Allegiance in 1778 (A-6). Private in Capt. Joshua George's Company, 18th Battalion, August 16, 1776 (C-84, G-61). James Conner married Ann Johnson by license dated March 6, 1778 (O-1).

CONNER (CONNOR), JAMES. Private in Capt. Walter Alexander's Company, July 27, 1776 (C-86, G-62).

CONNOR, JAMES. Private in Capt. John Oglevie's Company, July 25, 1776 (C-85, G-647).

CONWAY, WILLIAM. Private in Capt. Walter Alexander's Company, July 24, 1776 (C-86, G-62).

COOPER, EPHRAIM. Private in Capt. Joshua George's Company, 18th Battalion, August 16, 1776 (C-84, G-61).

COOPER, HEZEKIAH. Oath of Allegiance in 1778 (A-4).

COOPER, JOHN. Two men with this name took the Oath of Allegiance in 1778 (A-8, A-17). One John Cooper married Ann Kankey by license dated January 31, 1781 (O-4).

COOPER, JONAS. Oath of Allegiance in 1778 (A-8).

COOPER, THOMAS. Oath of Allegiance in 1778 (A-17). Second Lieutenant in Capt. James Porter's Company in the 18th Battalion, 1777-1778 (E-56, S-MdHR6636-9-93). Thomas Cooper married Rebecca Kankey by lic. May 15, 1784 (O-6).

CORBALLY, RICHARD. Oath of Allegiance in 1778 (A-2).

CORBET (CORBITT), DAVID. Oath of Allegiance in 1778 (A-5). Ensign in Capt. James Pritchard's Co., Susquehanna or 30th Battn., 1777, and 2nd Lieutenant in Capt. Samuel Miller's Co., 1778 (E-58, S-MdHR6636-9-93, MdHR4570-72). David "Corbit" md Ester Corbit, June 12, 1770 (R-40).

CORBET, JOSEPH. Oath of Allegiance in 1778 (A-5).

CORBET, WILLIAM. Oath of Allegiance in 1778 (A-5). Second Lieutenant in Capt. Samuel Miller's Company, Susquehanna or 30th Battalion in 1777 and on rolls of September 9, 1778 (E-57, S-MdHR6636-9-93).

CORD, THOMAS.  Oath of Allegiance in 1778 (A-5).

CORLET, JOHN.  "A deserter, deserted" Oct. 16, 1780 (G-346).

COSDEN, JAMES.  Oath of Allegiance in 1778 (A-12). Ensign in Capt. James Porter's Company, 18th Battalion in 1777 and on rolls on September 9, 1778 (E-56, S-MdHR6636-9-93).

COSDEN, THOMAS.  Oath of Allegiance in 1778 (A-8).

COTHER:  See "Cather."

COSNER, DANIEL.  Oath of Allegiance in 1778 (A-7).

COULSON, NATHANIEL.  He was reported "supposed to be gone to the British Army" by Sept 1, 1777 (K-121, S-MdHR4570-88).

COULTER, SAMUEL.  Oath of Allegiance in 1778 (A-5). Second Lieutenant in Capt. James Pritchard's Company, 30th Battalion, 1777-1778 (E-58, S-MdHR6636-9-93). Samuel Coulter md Sarah Foster by license Nov. 18, 1778 (O-2).

COWEN, JOHN.  Oath of Allegiance in 1778 (A-15).

COX, JOHN (1713-1785).  Married Rebecca----- in 1736 and had children: John, Benjamin, Thomas, Samuel, George, Sophia, Rebecca, Alice and Elijah (U-238) .Representative to the Maryland Convention on May 16, 1775 (K-2) and on July 26, 1775 (P-3). He was a Justice who administered the Oath of Allegiance in March, 1778 (A-11). Commissioned a Captain in the 18th Battalion in 1777 and in the Elk Battalion on April 21, 1778 (E-55, S-MdHR6636-9-93). John Cox received a certificate for wheat on January 20, 1780 (I-264).

COX, JOHN.  Private in Capt. Joshua George's Company, 18th Battalion, August 16, 1776 (C-84, G-61).

COX, WILLIAM.  Oath of Allegiance in 1778 (A-14).

COZIER:  See "Cazier."

COZIER (CAZIER), JAMES.  Private in the Maryland Line (C-82).

COZIER (CAZIER), JOHN.  Private in the Maryland Line (C-82). John "Cazier" married Martha Ford, Feb. 20, 1793 (O-13).

CRABSON (CRABSTON), MOSES.  Took Oath of Allegiance in 1778 (A-6). "Moses Crabstein" was a Private in Capt. Jeremiah Baker's Company, August 1, 1775, and in Capt. Baruch William's Company, March 3, 1776 (F-157).

CRAGE, JAMES.  Oath of Allegiance in 1778 (A-7). James "Craig" md Gertrude Eliason by lic. Jan. 27, 1787 (O-8).

CRAIG, ROBERT CAPT.  An inhabitant of Cecil County and the owner of a well-fitted Brigantine in the Sassafras River, Robert Craig was "a person of property and by his conduct appears to be well attached to the American cause, and from his long experience at sea is well acquainted with foreign ports, is recommended for importing arms and ammunition." Signed for the Committee of Safety by John Veazey, Jr. and John D. Thompson, Jan. 29, 1776 (P-121).

CRAIGE, GEORGE. Oath of Allegiance in 1778 (A-2). George "Crage" md Elizabeth Taylor by lic. May 26, 1781 (O-4).

CRAIGE, JOHN. Oath of Allegiance, 1778 (A-4). John "Craig" married Mary Bryan by license dated April 5, 1778 (O-1). John Craig md Rebecca Manley by lic. Mar. 27, 1785 (O-7).

CRAIGE, WILLIAM. Took the Oath of Allegiance on January 13, 1779 before Court Justice John Veazey (J-36).

CRAIGIE, JAMES. Oath of Allegiance in 1778 (A-4).

CRAIGIE, JAMES JR. Oath of Allegiance in 1778 (A-4).

CRAMAR, PHILIP. Oath of Allegiance in 1778 (A-15).

CRASBY (CROSBY), JESSE. Bugler in Continental Army in Col. Harry Lee's Partisan Cavalry, from 1778 on (C-83, G-586, G-587, K-156). Granted leave on June 28, 1783 (G-588).

CRAWFORD (CRAFORD), JAMES. Oath of Allegiance in 1778 (A-9). Ensign in Capt. William Ewing's Co., 30th Battalion, on April 21 and Sept 9, 1778 (E-58, K-116, S-MdHR4570-72).

CRAWFORD, JOHN. Oath of Allegiance in 1778 (A-9).

CREAIGHTON (CREAGHTON, CREATON), WILLIAM. Private in Capt. Walter Alexander's Company, July 27, 1776 (C-86, G-62).

CRESWELL, JAMES. Recruiting Officer in 1780 (G-345). James "Criswell" md Elizabeth Dean by lic. Apr. 30, 1778 (O-1).

CRIME, MICHAEL. Private in Capt. Henry Dobson's Company in the 6th Maryland Line, in N. C. in October, 1780 (G-348).

CROCKIT (CROCKETT), SAMUEL. Oath of Allegiance in 1778 (A-5). Second Lieutenant in Capt. Edward Daugherty's Co., in 1777 and in Capt. Philip Cole's Company, 30th Battn., June 22, 1778 (E-57, S-MdHR6636-9-93). Samuel "Crockett" md Elizabeth Jackson by license dated May 14, 1778 (O-1).

CROMBERS, JONAS. He appears to have served because he was due a military clothing allowance, March 6, 1779 (L-38).

CROMWELL, JOHN. Oath of Allegiance in 1778 (A-1). John Cromwell married Ann Johnson by lic. Feb. 23, 1779 (O-2).

CROOKSHANKS (CRUCKSHANKS), WILLIAM. Oath of Allegiance in 1778

(A-5). Private in Major Henry Lee's Partizan Corps on February 17, 1780 (K-156). On April 23, 1787, the Auditor General's Office certified that there was due to the administratrix of William Crookshanks the amount of 15 lbs., 12 sh. and 6 p. for his pay as a Trooper in Col. Lee's Legion from August 1, 1780 to Jan. 1, 1781 (G-590).

CROSBY, HUGH. Oath of Allegiance in 1778 (A-5).

CROSBY, NATHANIEL. Oath of Allegiance in 1778 (A-15).

CROSS, JOHN. Oath of Allegiance in 1778 (A-6). He appears to have served because he is listed among those who were due a military clothing allowance, March 6, 1779 (L-38).

CROUCH, ISAAC. Took the Oath of Allegiance in 1778 (A-8). Isaac Crouch married Ann Johnson, May 3, 1760 (R-44).

CROUCH, JAMES. Private in Capt. Stephen Hyland's Militia Company, September 8, 1775 (T-MS.1814). Took the Oath of Allegiance in 1778 (A-8). James Crouch married Mary Jones by license dated August 18, 1781 (O-5).

CROUCH, JOHN. Private in Capt. Stephen Hyland's Militia Company, September 8, 1775 (T-MS.1814). Took the Oath of Allegiance in 1778 (A-8). John Crouch married Sarah Hull by license dated November 20, 1777 (O-1). John Crouch married Mary Hart by lic. dated Apr. 16, 1783 (O-5). John Daw Crouch md Mary Dollison by lic. June 8, 1790 (O-11). John Crouch md Cornelia Chrisfield Sept. 22, 1791 (O-12).

CROUCH, ROBERT. Born 1759. Took the Oath of Allegiance in 1778 (A-7). Private in Col. Harry Lee's Partisan Cavalry from April 7, 1778 through June 12, 1783 (C-83, G-586, G-587, G-588, K-156). Robert Crouch married Sarah Chew by license dated August 29, 1789 (O-10). Robert Crouch married Hannah Cleeves, November 19, 1800 (Q-17, Q-112).

CROUCH, WILLIAM. Private in Capt. Stephen Hyland's Militia Company, September 8, 1775 (T-MS.1814). Took the Oath of Allegiance in 1778 (A-8). One William "Couch" married Margaret Hollingsworth by license Nov. 24, 1789 (O-10). William Crouch md Ann Crockett, Dec. 21, 1791 lic.(O-12).

CROW, ANDREW. Oath of Allegiance in 1778 (A-18).

CROW, ANDREW JR. Oath of Allegiance in 1778 (A-18). "Andrew Crow" md Susannah Laurenceson, Mar. 22, 1780 lic. (O-4).

CROWL, ALEXANDER. Oath of Allegiance in 1778 (A-16).

CROWLEY, JOHN. Oath of Allegiance in 1778 (A-5).

CROZEN, ROBERT. Oath of Allegiance in 1778 (A-2).

CROZIER, JAMES. Recruited on October 16, 1780 (G-345).

CULLEY, GEORGE. Oath of Allegiance in 1778 (A-6).

CUMMINGS, JAMES. Two men with this name took the Oath of Allegiance in 1778 (A-6, A-9). "James Cumming" was an Ensign in Capt. James Maxwell's Co., 30th Battalion, in 1777 and rolls of Apr. 21, 1778 (E-57, S-MdHR6636-9-93).

CUMMINGS (CUMMINS), JOHN. Oath of Allegiance in 1778 (A-8). "John Cummins" was a Private in Continental Army in Col. Harry Lee's Partisan Cavalry in June, 1778 (C-83, G-586).

CUMMINGS, SAMUEL. Two men with this name took the Oath of Allegiance in 1778 (A-6, A-9).

CUNNINGHAM, CARBERY. Private in Capt. John Oglevie's Company, July 25, 1776 (C-85, G-647).

CUNNINGHAM, GEORGE. Private in Capt. John Oglevie's Company, July 25, 1776 (C-85, G-647).

CUNNINGHAM, HUGH. He was reported "supposed to be gone to the British Army" by Nov 15, 1777 (K-121, S-MdHR4570-88).

CUNNINGHAM, JAMES. Oath of Allegiance in 1778 (A-5).

CUNNINGHAM, JOHN. Two men with this name took the Oath of Allegiance in 1778 (A-5). One John Cunningham, age 23 in 1776 and a Labourer born in Charlestown, served as a Matross in the Artillery of the Maryland Line as shown on its rolls of January 24 to February 3, 1776 (T-MS.1814, C-82). Another or possibly the same John Cunningham served as a Private in Capt. Walter Alexander's Company in the Susquehanna or 30th Battalion, enrolled July 25, 1776 (C-86, G-63). John Cunningham married Elizabeth Cadwell by license dated November 18, 1777 (O-1, R-45).

CUNNINGHAM, WILLIAM. Oath of Allegiance in 1778 (A-2).

CURRANT, JAMES. Oath of Allegiance in 1778 (A-2).

CURRIER, BENONI (BENOMI). Private in Capt. Joshua George's Company, 18th Battalion, August 16, 1776 (C-84, G-61).

CURRIER (CURRER), SAMPSON. Oath of Allegiance, 1778 (A-15).

CURRIER (CURRER), WILLIAM. Representative to the Maryland Convention on May 16, 1775, August 10, 1775 and June 21, 1776 (K-2, K-28, P-13). A Signer of the Declaration of Freemen of Maryland in 1775 (J-322) he also took the Oath of Allegiance in 1778 (A-8). William Currier married Mary Bird, dau of Empson and Susanna, on July 17, 1774 (R-45).

CUSICK, CHRIS. Private in Capt. Henry Dobson's Company in the 6th Maryland Line, in N. C. in October, 1780 (G-347).

DAGG, JAMES. Oath of Allegiance in 1778 (A-9).

DALEY, DANIEL. Private in Capt. Joshua George's Company, 18th Battalion, August 16, 1776. (C-84, G-61).

DANLEY (DONLEY), EDWARD. Oath of Allegiance in 1778 (A-15).

DANUEL, JOHN. Oath of Allegiance in 1778 (A-4).

DAUGHERTY: See "Dougherty."

DAUGHERTY, EDWARD. Captain in 30th Battalion of Militia under Col. Joseph Baxter in 1777 (S-MdHR6636-9-93).

DAUGHERTY, ROGER. Private in Capt. Walter Alexander's Company, July 27, 1776 (C-86, G-62).

DAVIDSON, JAMES. Oath of Allegiance in 1778 (A-16).

DAVIDSON, JAMES JR. Oath of Allegiance in 1778 (A-16).

DAVIDSON, JOHN. Oath of Allegiance in 1778 (A-16). Private in Capt. W. Alexander's Co., July 24, 1776 (C-86, G-62).

DAVIDSON, WILLIAM. Oath of Allegiance in 1778 (A-16).

DAVIDSON, WILLIAM JR. Oath of Allegiance in 1778 (A-16).

DAVIS, AMOS. Recruited on October 16, 1780 (G-345).

DAVIS, HENRY. Private in Capt. Henry Dobson's Company in the 6th Maryland Line, 1780 (G-348).

DAVIS, JOHN. Two men with this name took the Oath of Allegiance in 1778 (A-7, A-12). One John Davis married Elizabeth Stogden by license February 19, 1784 (O-6).

DAVIS, MORRIS. Oath of Allegiance in 1778 (A-17).

DAVIS, ROBERT. Private in Capt. Henry Dobson's Company in the 6th MD Line, April 28, 1778, for 3 years. Serving in Hillsborough, North Carolina in October, 1780 (G-348).

DAVIS, SAMUEL. Private in Capt. Walter Alexander's Company, in the 30th Battn., enrolled July 18, 1776 (C-86, G-63).

DAVIS, WILLIAM. Oath of Allegiance in 1778 (A-2).

DAWSON, JOSEPH. Oath of Allegiance in 1778 (A-16). Private in Capt. W. Alexander's Co., July 24, 1776 (C-86, G-62).

DAWSON, NATHANIEL. Took Oath of Allegiance in 1778 (A-4). Private in Capt. Joshua George's Company, 18th Battalion, August 16, 1776 (C-84, G-61). Nathaniel Dawson married Ann Beaston by license dated October 29, 1787 (O-8).

DAWSON, WILLIAM. Passed, November session, 1810, that the "Treasurer pay to William Dawson, of Cecil County, late a meritorious soldier in the Revolutionary War, or order, quarterly payments, a sum of money equal to half pay of a Private, as a provision to him in his indigent situation, now advanced in life, and as a further remuneration to him for those services by which his country has been so essentially benefitted." (N-334). William Dawson married Elizabeth Graves by license dated Dec. 29, 1780 (O-4).

DAY, GEORGE. Oath of Allegiance in 1778 (A-9). Private in Capt. John Oglevie's Company, July 25, 1776 (C-85, G-647).

DEATH, JACOB. Oath of Allegiance in 1778 (A-9). Commissioned Ensign in Capt. Robert Porter's Co., Susquehanna or 30th Battn., Sept 9, 1778 (C-84, E-57, K-116, S-MdHR4570-72).

DEATH, RANDLE. Oath of Allegiance in 1778 (A-9). "Randall Death" married Honour Kersy in 1733 (R-49).

DENNEY, JOHN. Private in Capt. Walter Alexander's Company, July 24, 1776 (C-86, G-62).

DENNIS, JOHN. Private in Capt. Joshua George's Company, 18th Battalion, August 16, 1776 (C-84, G-61). John Dennis married Arramantha Harvey(?) by lic. Aug. 26, 1783 (O-6).

DENOON, JOHN. Drum and Fifer in Capt. Henry Dobson's Company, 6th Maryland Line, in N. C. in 1780 (G-347).

DEVERICKS, JAMES. Private in Capt. Henry Dobson's Company in the 6th Maryland Line, in N. C. in 1780 (G-348).

DEVLIN, JAMES. Oath of Allegiance in 1778 (A-7).

DICKSON, STAFORD. Oath of Allegiance in 1778 (A-6).

DICKSON, THOMAS. Two men with this name took the Oath of Allegiance in 1778 (A-4, A-13).

DIXSON, THOMAS. Private in Capt. W. Alexander's Company, in the 30th Battalion, enrolled July 25, 1776 (C-86, G-63).

DOBSON, ADAM. Oath of Allegiance in 1778 (A-7). Adam Dobson married Tamor Chiles by license April 4, 1788 (O-9).

DOBSON, HENRY (1755-1781). Grandson of Richard Dobson and Abigail Hollingsworth. Resided between Elkton and North East on the west side of Little Elk Creek. Commissioned First Lieutenant in Flying Camp, 4th Battalion, under Capt. Samuel Evans, on September 28,

1776 (W-306). He marched to Philadelphia in October, 1776. Served as a Captain in the 6th Maryland Line from December 10, 1776 through 1780 (G-346). He received a military clothing allowance on March 6, 1779. He was promoted to Major in the 3rd Maryland Line on June 1, 1781. Major Dobson was wounded at the Battle of Brandywine and killed at Eutaw Springs, South Carolina on September 8, 1781 (C-82, G-73, G-74, D-73, D-74, J-323, L-38, L-102).

DOMINICK, BENJAMIN. Private in Capt. Henry Dobson's Company in the 6th Maryland Line, in N. C. in Oct., 1780 (G-348).

DONAGAN (DOMAGAN), WILLIAM. Oath of Allegiance, 1778 (A-6).

DONAHO, JOSHUA. Oath of Allegiance in 1778 (A-7).

DONALDSON, DAVID. Oath of Allegiance in 1778 (A-13).

DONN, JOHN. Oath of Allegiance in 1778 (A-5).

DONNELEY, PATRICK. Private in Capt. John Oglevie's Company, July 25, 1776 (C-85, G-647).

DONNOLLY (DONOLY), EDWARD. Private in Capt. W. Alexander's Company, enrolled August 3, 1776 (C-86, G-63).

DONNOLLY (DONOLY), CALEB (CALAB). Oath of Allegiance in 1778 (A-8). Private in Capt. Walter Alexander's Company, August 3, 1776 (C-86, G-63). Private in Capt. Henry Dobson's Company in the 6th Maryland Line in 1780, but named on List of Defectives, June 8, 1780 (G-348, G-414).

DONOVAN, JOHN. Oath of Allegiance in 1778 (A-5).

DOOGAN, JAMES. Private in Capt. Walter Alexander's Company, 30th Battalion, enrolled July 18, 1776 (C-86, G-63). One "James Dogan" (or Dugan) was a Private in Capt. Jeremiah Baker's Company, August 1, 1775, and in Capt. Baruch Williams' Co., March 3, 1776 (F-157).

DORAN, PATRICK. Sergeant in Capt. Henry Dobson's Company in the 6th Maryland Line, in N. C. in October, 1780 (G-347).

DOROUGH, JOHN. Private in Capt. Henry Dobson's Company in the 6th Maryland Line, in N. C. in October, 1780 (G-348).

DOUGHERTY, JAMES. Two men with this name took the Oath of Allegiance in 1778 (A-9, A-15). "James Dougharty" was Captain, 30th Battalion, 1777 and "James Daugherty" was Captain, 1778 (E-58, S-MdHR6636-9-93). "James Daugherty" married Mary Glasgow by lic. dated October 7, 1781 (O-5).

DOUGHERTY, MICHAEL. Took Oath of Allegiance in 1778 (A-5). Private in Capt. Jeremiah Baker's Company, August 1, 1775 and in Capt. Baruch Williams' Co., March 3, 1776 (F-157).

DOUGLAS, GRAY. Oath of Allegiance in 1778 (A-16).

DOWDLE, WILLIAM. Private in Col. Harry Lee's Partisan Cavalry in 1780 (G-586, G-587). He was granted leave of absence on March 30, 1784 and paid in 1785 (G-588, 590).

DOWLIN, ROGER. Private in Capt. Henry Dobson's Company in 6th Maryland Line. Sick at Albany in Oct., 1780 (G-349).

DOWNEY, PATT. Private in Capt. Walter Alexander's Company, 30th Battalion, enrolled July 17, 1776 (C-86, G-63).

DOYAL, PATRICK. Oath of Allegiance in 1778 (A-1).

DOYL, THOMAS. Private in Capt. Walter Alexander's Company, July 24, 1776 (C-86, G-62).

DUFF, SAMUEL. Oath of Allegiance in 1778 (A-6).

DUFFIELD, WILLIAM. Private in Capt. John Oglevie's Company, July 25, 1776 (C-85, G-647).

DUFFY, JOHN. Private in Capt. Walter Alexander's Company, July 27, 1776 (C-86, G-62). John "Duffey" married Martha Hance by license dated August 12, 1790 (O-11).

DUGIN, JAMES. Private in Capt. Stephen Hyland's Militia Company, September 8, 1775 (T-MS.1814). (See "Doogan.") James Dugin married Sarah Auren, January 11, 1775 (R-55).

DUNBARR, ANDREW. Oath of Allegiance in 1778 (A-9).

DUNN, WILLIAM. Name appeared on a List of Defectives from the Maryland Line on June 8, 1780 (G-414).

DURBIN, SAMUEL. Oath of Allegiance in 1778 (A-5).

DURHAM, WILLIAM. Private in Capt. Henry Dobson's Company in the 6th Maryland Line, in N. C. in October, 1780 (G-348).

DUVALL, RICHARD. Private in Capt. Henry Dobson's Company in the 6th Maryland Line. On Guard in N. C. in 1780 (G-349).

EAKIN, JAMES. Oath of Allegiance in 1778 (A-10).

EDGE, WILLIAM. Oath of Allegiance in 1778 (A-2). William Edge married Catharine Connor, April 6, 1779 lic. (O-3).

EDMISTON, DAVID. Oath of Allegiance in 1778 (A-10).

EGAN, PATRICK. Private in Capt. Henry Dobson's Company in the 6th Maryland Line, in N. C. in October, 1780 (G-347).

EKEY, PETER (PETTER). He appears to have served because he was due military clothing allowance, Mar. 6, 1779 (L-38).

ELEXSON, CHARLES. Private in Capt. Joshua George's Company, 18th

Battalion, August 18, 1776 (C-84, G-61).

ELLERY, JOHN. Private in Capt. Henry Dobson's Company in the 6th Maryland Line, in N. C. in October, 1780 (G-348).

ELLIOTT (ELLIOT), JAMES. Oath of Allegiance in 1778 (A-7).

ELLIOTT (ELLIET), JOHN. Oath of Allegiance in 1778 (A-15). Private in Capt. Henry Dobson's Company in the 6th Maryland Line in 1780 (G-348).

ELLIOTT, JOSEPH. Oath of Allegiance in 1778 (A-16). Private in Capt. Henry Dobson's Co., 6th Maryland Line, in North Carolina in October, 1780 (G-347).

ELLIOTT, WILLIAM. Oath of Allegiance in 1778 (A-7).

ELLIS, RICHARD. Oath of Allegiance in 1778 (A-4). He was recommended to the Governor by Col. Henry Hollingsworth to be Cecil County Surveyor on March 31, 1780 (I-280).

ELSBERRY (ELSBUREY), LAMBERT. Took the Oath of Allegiance in 1778 (A-4). Ensign in Capt. John Leach Knight's Co., in the 18th Battalion, 1777-1778 (E-55, S-MdHR6636-9-93).

ELWOOD, JOHN. Oath of Allegiance in 1778 (A-4).

ELWOOD, RICHARD. Oath of Allegiance in 1778 (A-8).

ELWOOD, RICHARD FORD. Oath of Allegiance in 1778 (A-4). "Richard F. Elwood" was Private in Capt. Joshua George's Company, 18th Battalion, August 18, 1776 (C-84, G-61).

EMMITT, ABRAM. Oath of Allegiance in 1778 (A-16).

EMMITT, DAVID. Private in Capt. Walter Alexander's Company, 30th Battalion, enrolled July 18, 1776 (C-86, G-63).

EMMITT, JOHN. Private in Capt. Walter Alexander's Company, 30th Battalion, enrolled July 25, 1776 (C-86, G-63).

ENGLAND (ENGLANG), GEORGE. Oath of Allegiance in 1778 (A-8).

ENGLAND, RICHARD. Oath of Allegiance in 1778 (A-15).

ENSOR, AUGUSTEEN H. Private in Capt. Stephen Hyland's Co. of Militia on September 8, 1775 (T-MS.1814). Private in Capt. Joshua George's Company in the 18th Battalion n August 18, 1776 (C-84, G-61).

ETHERINGTON, BARTHOLOMEW SR. Took the Oath of Allegiance in 1778 (A-12).

ETHERINGTON, BARTHOLOMEW JR. Took the Oath of Allegiance in 1778 (A-12). Bartholomew Etherington married Sarah Beedle by license dated December 1, 1784 (O-6).

ETHERINGTON, BENJAMIN. Oath of Allegiance in 1778 (A-11).

ETHERINGTON, JOHN. Took Oath of Allegiance in 1778 (A-12). Private in Capt. Joshua George's Company, 18th Battalion, August 18, 1776 (C-84, G-61). John Etherington married Sarah Ware by license dated February 4, 1779 (O-2).

ETHERINGTON, THOMAS. Oath of Allegiance in 1778 (A-11).

ETHERINGTON, THOMAS JR. Oath of Allegiance in 1778 (A-14).

EVANS, JAMES SR. Oath of Allegiance in 1778 (A-10). Served as a Judge of Elections on November 8, 1776 (K-55).

EVANS, JAMES JR. Oath of Allegiance in 1778 (A-10). James Evans md Catherine Porter by lic. June 11, 1784 (O-6).

EVANS, JOHN. Son of Robert Evans. Oath of Allegiance in 1780 (B-110). Lieutenant in the Militia (C-70). Brother of Robert Evans. The family originated in Wales (C-87). John Evans married Mary Alexander of New Munster (J-487).

EVANS, ROBERT. Son of Robert Evans. Oath of Allegiance in 1778 (A-10). Private in Capt. Walter Alexander's Company, 30th Battalion, enrolled July 24, 1776 (C-86, G-62). Was commissioned a Second Lieutenant in Capt. James Maxwell's Company of Militia in the 30th Battalion on April 21, 1778, but fell from his horse and died before he could serve (C-70, E-57, J-487, S-MdHR6636-9-93).

EVANS, SAMUEL. Commissioned a Captain in the Maryland Line September 28, 1776 (C-82, W-306). Marched to Philadelphia in October, 1776 (G-73, G-74, J-322). Captain in the 4th Battalion, 1776 to 1778 (S-MdHR6636-12-37A, D-79, E-13, E-54, S-MdHR6636-9-93). Oath of Allegiance, 1778 (A-16).

EVERTSON, EVERT. Oath of Allegiance in 1778 (A-14). He was Sub-Sheriff of Cecil County on September 7, 1778 (I-187). "Everet Everson" md Susanna Ward by lic. April 5, 1782 (O-5). "Everd Everdson" md Annacart Plow in 1731 (R-60).

EVERTSON, JACOB. 2nd Lieutenant in Capt. C. Heath's Company of the 18th Battalion, 1777-1778 (E-56, S-MdHR6636-9-93). Jacob "Everdson" married Hester Vanhorn, daughter of Nicholas, by license dated December 30, 1742 (R-60).

EWING, HENRY. Oath of Allegiance in 1778 (A-6).

EWING, MOSES. Oath of Allegiance in 1778 (A-5).

EWING, NATHANIEL. On December 15, 1775 he sent a request to Matthew Tilghman, President of the Maryland Convention, concerning his desire to serve the province (I-6).

EWING, PATRICK. He was elected a delegate to the Maryland Provincial Convention on May 16, 1775 and was also a representative on June 21 and August 14, 1776. (C-31, I-2, I-33, J-321, J-322, K-2, K-28). Patrick Ewing married Elizabeth Porter by lic. July 16, 1789 (O-9).

EWING, PETER. He was elected a delegate to the Maryland Provincial Convention on May 22, 1775 (C-31).

EWING, ROBERT. Took Oath of Allegiance in 1778 (A-6). One Robert Ewing married Isabella Lissey by license March 24, 1784 (O-6) and one Robert Ewing married Peggy Ewing by license March 23, 1793 (O-13).

EWING, THOMAS. Oath of Allegiance in 1778 (A-5).

EWING, WILLIAM. Oath of Allegiance in 1778 (A-10). Captain in the 30th (or Susquehanna) Battalion, on September 9, 1778 (E-58, K-116, S-MdHR6636-9-93, S-MdHR4570-72).

EYANSON, JOHN. Born January 23, 1750 in Cecil County, MD, he married Anna Eddy (born 1755 in Chester County, PA) and had a daughter Ann (born 1798, married Dan Wetzler). John served in the 3rd Battalion of Minuteman in Salem, New Jersey and reenlisted at Chester, Pennsylvania and fought at Brandywine and was at Valley Forge. He died in Lebanon, Pennsylvania on May 31, 1831 (V-93).

FAIRBROTHER, FRANCIS. Paid for freight of linen from Edward Parker's factory in Cecil County on July 3, 1776 (P-545).

FALTON, WILLIAM. First Lieutenant in Capt. James Mackey's Company on April 10, 1776 (P-319).

FARIS, JAMES. Took Oath of Allegiance in 1778 (A-14). James "Farias" md Elizabeth Moody by lic. Feb. 14, 1794 (O-14).

FARMER, JOSEPH. 1st Lieutenant in Capt. John Oglevie's Company of Militia in the Elk Battalion, 1778 (E-54).

FARREL, FRANCIS. Private in Capt. W. Alexander's Company, 30th Battalion, enrolled July 27, 1776 (C-86, G-62).

FEDERY, RICHARD. Oath of Allegiance in 1778 (A-8).

FEE, JOHN. Oath of Allegiance in 1778 (A-16).

FERGUSON (FORGESON), BENJAMIN. Private in Capt. Stephen Hyland's Co. of Militia on September 8, 1775 (T-MS.1814). Took Oath of Allegiance in 1778 (A-5). Benjamin Ferguson married Mary Rutter by license April 1, 1761 (R-61).

FERGUSON, SAMUEL. Oath of Allegiance in 1778 (A-4).

FERGUSON, WILLIAM. Oath of Allegiance in 1778 (A-5).

FERVOTT, PETER. Sergeant in Capt. Henry Dobson's Co., 6th Maryland Line. On Guard in N.C. in October, 1780 (G-347).

FIELDS, JAMES. Oath of Allegiance in 1778 (A-15).

FINLEY, JOHN. Oath of Allegiance in 1778 (A-10). John Finley married Margaret Rowland by license March 12, 1787 (O-8).

FINLEY, JOHN E. Oath of Allegiance in 1778 (A-16).

FINLEY, ROBERT. Two men with this name took the Oath of Allegiance in 1778 (A-10, A-16).

FINLEY, SAMUEL R. Oath of Allegiance in 1778 (A-16).

FINLEY, WILLIAM. Oath of Allegiance in 1778 (A-16).

FINLEY, WILLIAM JR. Oath of Allegiance in 1778 (A-16).

FITSGARELD, JAMES. Oath of Allegiance in 1778 (A-14).

FITZGERALD, TIMY. Private in Capt. Henry Dobson's Company in 6th MD Line in 1780. Enlisted Dec. 22, 1778 (G-348).

FLACK, JAMES. Sergeant in Capt. Henry Dobson's Company in the 6th MD Line in 1780. Enlisted April 28, 1779 (G-347).

FLINTHAM, BENJAMIN. Oath of Allegiance in 1778 (A-4).

FLINTHAM, R. Oath of Allegiance in 1778 (A-3).

FOARD: See "Ford."

FOARD, JOHN. Of Elk Neck. Captain, Maryland Line (C-82). (See information under "John Ford.")

FOARD, RICHARD BOULDING (c1759-1806). "Richard Bolden Ford" took the Oath of Allegiance in 1778 (A-18). He married Ann----- and had three children: Levi George (born 1779, married Ann Bayard); James (married (1) Jamima Logue, (2) Margaret Davis, (3) Temperance Myers); and, Mary (married Nathan Boulding). He died August 9, 1806 (U-312, V-100).

FOARD, WILLIAM. Of Elk Neck. Born 1758. Served as a Matross in the Artillery, Maryland Line (C-82). Appears on rolls of matross volunteers, January 24 - February 3, 1776, at which time he states he was born in Cecil County, is now age 18, and his occupation is a Labourer (T-MS.1814).

FORD, EDWARD. Oath of Allegiance in 1778 (A-18).

FORD, HEZEKIAH. Sergeant in Capt. James Mackey's Company circa 1776. (C-85). "Hezekiah Foard" was an Ensign and Adjutant in the 2nd Maryland Line on September 18, 1779 (L-47) and subsequently became Lieutenant (C-82). Order to "Treasurer, Western Shore, February 9, 1822, to pay to Hezekiah Ford, of Cecil County, an old Rev. officer, half pay of a Lieutenant during the remainder of his life, as remuneration for his meritorious services." (N-342). He married Sarah Lawrenson by license Dec. 14, 1786 (O-8).

FORD, JOHN (1752-1824). Married (1) in 1770-71, Millicent Hyland, sister of Col. Stephen Hyland; (2) in 1808, Catherine Hedrick; (3) in 1812, Mary Wilson. Children: Charles Tilden (born 1774, married Mary Mauldin); Martha (born 1776, married (1) John Cazier, (2) Isaac Foster); Cornelia (married Thomas Cazier); Rebecca (married a Jones); Araminta (married John Hugh Brown); John H. (born 1784); Stephen H. (born 1791); Lambert (married Nancy Hamm); George W. (born 1795, married Elizabeth Ann Dorsey); and, William W. (U-315, V-101). John Ford was a Private, a Corporal and then commissioned Captain in the 18th Battalion under Col. John D. Thompson in 1778 and later served in Maryland Line (S-MdHR6636-9-93, E-56). He fought in the Battles of Long Island, Brandywine, King's Mountain, Germantown, Monmouth, Guilford Court House, and Camden. Taken prisoner at Camden, August 16, 1780. His home was taken over by Hessian Gen. Knyphausen on August 25, 1777, and subsequently burned (C-28). He was among those who received a military clothing allowance on March 6, 1779 (L-38). Two men by this name took the Oath of Allegiance in 1778 (A-2, A-4).

FORD, NATHANIEL. Oath of Allegiance in 1778 (A-11).

FORD, RICHARD. Oath of Allegiance in 1778 (A-2). Richard Ford md Priscilla Punteley by lic. Dec. 9, 1788 (O-10).

FORD, RICHARD JR. Oath of Allegiance in 1778 (A-2).

FORD, RICHARD SR. Oath of Allegiance in 1778 (A-3).

FORD, THOMAS. Oath of Allegiance in 1778 (A-2).

FORD, WILLIAM. Took the Oath of Allegiance in 1778 (A-4). Private in Capt. Joshua George's Company, 18th Battalion, August 18, 1776 (C-84, G-61).

FORDIN, THOMAS. Oath of Allegiance in 1778 (A-4).

FOREACRES, JOSEPH. Oath of Allegiance in 1778 (A-8).

FOREMAN, THOMAS MARSH. Major in the Maryland Line (C-82).

FORGESON: See "Ferguson."

FORSTER (FORRESTER), ALEX. His name appeared on a list of Matross volunteers in the Maryland Line, January 24 to February 3, 1776, at which time he states he was born in Maryland, is now age 30, and is a Labourer (T-MS.1814).

FORSTER (FORRESTER), CORNELIUS. Name appeared on a list of Matross volunteers in the Maryland Line, January 24 to February 3, 1776, at which time he states he was born in Maryland, is now age 21, and is a Labourer (T-MS.1814).

FORSTER, JESSE. Oath of Allegiance in 1778 (A-8).

FORSTER (FORRESTER), JOHN. His name appeared on a list of Matross volunteers in the Maryland Line, January 24 to February 3, 1776, at which time he states he was born in Maryland, is now age 28, and is a Labourer (T-MS.1814).

FORSTER, JOHN SR. Oath of Allegiance in 1778 (A-8).

FORSTER, JOHN JR. Oath of Allegiance in 1778 (A-8).

FORSTER, THOMAS. Oath of Allegiance in 1778 (A-4). Thomas Forster married Mary Hunter, daughter of Willam Hunter, by license dated March 30, 1738 (R-63).

FORSTER, WILLIAM. Oath of Allegiance in 1778 (A-15). William Forster md Rachel Stalcup by lic. April 15, 1790 (O-11).

FOSTER, ARCHIBALD. Two men with this name took the Oath of Allegiance in 1778 (A-6).

FOSTER, BENJAMIN. Oath of Allegiance in 1778 (A-5).

FOSTER, FRANCIS. Took Oath of Allegiance in 1780 (B-110). Francis Foster md Rebecca McConnell, March 4, 1780 (O-3).

FOSTER, JAMES. Born in 1762 in Ireland, he came to America when six years old and lived in Cecil County. He enlisted in April, 1777, and served under Captains Moffit, Miller and Brevard. He was in Battles of Gray's Hill, Couch's Bridge, Germantown, and Monmouth, and discharged in Fall of 1780. After the war he lived in Cecil County, MD and Chester County, PA. In 1796 he moved to Frederick County, VA where he died November 24, 1841. He applied for and received pension S8501 for services in the 3rd Maryland Line from May 28, 1778 to November 1, 1780 (NGS Qtrly., Vol. 35, No. 2, p. 59 (1947). He also took the Oath of Allegiance in Cecil County in 1778 (A-2). James Foster married Catherine Boyce by lic. October 30, 1780 (O-4).

FOSTER, JESSE. Oath of Allegiance in 1778 (A-7). He appears to have served because he is among those who were due a military clothing allowance on Mar. 6, 1779 (L-38). Jesse Foster md Sarah Lewis by lic. dated July 24, 1792 (O-14).

FRAMPTON, MOSES. Oath of Allegiance in 1778 (A-14).

FRANKLIN, BENJAMIN. Oath of Allegiance in 1778 (A-4).

FREEMAN, EPHRAIM. Oath of Allegiance in 1778 (A-18).

FRENCH, THOMAS. Oath of Allegiance in 1778 (A-7).

FRENCH, WILLIAM. Bugler in Colonel Harry Lee's Partisan Cavalry, April 7, 1778 to June 28, 1783 (G-587, G-588). Trumpeter in Major Henry (Col. Harry) Lee's Partizan Corps as of February 17, 1780 (K-156).

FREW, DAVID. Private in Capt. Stephen Hyland's Company of Militia on September 8, 1775 (T-MS.1814). Took the Oath of Allegiance in 1778 (A-8).

FREW, JAMES. Oath of Allegiance in 1778 (A-8). James Frew (or Trew?) married Grace McKnight, Jan, 14, 1778 (O-1).

FRIER, WILLIAM. Oath of Allegiance in 1778 (A-16).

FULLAM, JAMES. Oath of Allegiance in 1778 (A-6).

FULLER, WILLIAM. Private in Capt. Henry Dobson's Co., 6th Maryland Line. Waggoner in N.C. in October, 1780 (G-349).

FULTON, ALEXANDER. Oath of Allegiance in 1778 (A-10).

FULTON, WILLIAM. Born in Ayrshire, Scotland and migrated to Lancaster, Pennsylvania with his father. Moved to Cecil County, Maryland before the Revolution. Took the Oath of Allegiance in 1778 (A-16). Was Second Lieutenant in Capt. James Mackey's Company in 1777 (S-MdHR6636-9-93) and then First Lieutenant, April 21, 1778 (C-85, E-55). His musket and flag were donated to the Masonic Museum of Washington Lodge No. 59, F and M, of Philadelphia, Pennsylvania. He died in 1816 (C-68, C-69). William Fulton married Ester (Esher?) Alexander by license dated Feb. 4, 1792 (O-12).

FURNER, EDWARD. Private in Capt. Joshua George's Company, 18th Battalion, August 18, 1776 (C-84, G-61).

FYFE, JAMES. Oath of Allegiance in 1778 (A-6).

GALE, GEORGE. Soldier in the Maryland Line (C-82).

GALLIHER, JOHN. Oath of Allegiance in 1778 (A-5).

GALLIHER, JOHN JR. Oath of Allegiance in 1778 (A-6).

GALLINOUGH, EDWARD. Private in Capt. W. Alexander's Co., 30th Battalion, enrolled July 27, 1776 (C-86, G-62).

GALLOWAY, JAMES. Oath of Allegiance in 1778 (A-7). James "Gallaway" md Mary Beck, widow, Feb. 22, 1718 (R-66).

GANTT (GAULT?), JAMES. Oath of Allegiance in 1778 (A-9).

GARDINER, GEORGE. Oath of Allegiance in 1778 (A-1).

GARDINER, WILLIAM.  Oath of Allegiance in 1778 (A-1).

GARMON, THOMAS.  Oath of Allegiance in 1778 (A-7).

GARNER, DAVID.  Oath of Allegiance in 1778 (A-8). Recruited on October 16, 1780, and "sent to Chester Town" (CG-345).

GARNER, JAMES.  Oath of Allegiance in 1778 (A-5).

GARRISH (GERISH), EDWARD.  Private in Capt. Stephen Hyland's Company of Militia on September 8, 1775 (T-MS.1814). Took the Oath of Allegiance in 1778 (A-8).

GARRISH, WILLIAM.  Oath of Allegiance in 1778 (A-5).

GARROTT, WILLIAM.  Private in Capt. Joshua George's Company, 18th Battalion, August 18, 1776 (C-84, G-61).

GASTON, JAMES.  Private in Capt. Baker's Company of Militia on August 1, 1775 and Capt. Williams' Company on March 3, 1776 in the 30th Battalion (F-157).

GATCHELL, ELISHA (QUAKER).  Born circa 1708 in Pennsylvania, a son of Elisha Gatchell (d. 1754) and Rachel Willcox of Essex County, Massachusetts. He married Mary Worley on October 8, 1733 at Nottingham Meeting in Cecil County, Maryland. His second wife was Anne------. Elisha died in 1789. (Data from Jon H. Livezey, Esq., a descendant, in 1988). Elisha took the Oath of Allegiance in 1778 (A-6).

GATCHELL, ELISHA JR. (QUAKER).  Oath of Allegiance in 1778 (A-6). One "Elisha Gatchel" was a Private in Capt. John Oglevie's Company, July 25, 1776 (C-85, G-647).

GATCHELL, JEREMIAH (QUAKER).  Born on November 2, 1734 in Chester County, Pennsylvania, a son of Elisha Gatchell and Mary Worley. He married Hannah Brown (1734/5-1774). Died on March 8, 1802 in Cecil County. (Data from Jon H. Livezey, Esq., a descendant, in 1988). Jeremiah took the Oath of Allegiance in 1778 (A-6).

GATCHELL, SAMUEL (QUAKER).  Oath of Allegiance, 1778 (A-6).

GEAR (GEARS), PEREGRINE.  Oath of Allegiance in 1778 (A-12).

GEORGE, JOHN (Nov. 30, 1753 - 1819).  Son of Sampson George (1729-1761) and Sara Currier. John married Elizabeth----- and their son Stephen (1787-1854) married Mary Simpers (1790-1854). John George took the Oath of Allegiance in 1778 (A-6, and Maryland Society, Sons of the American Revolution, application of descendant Calvin S. George, National No. 133727, State No. 3044, approved October 23, 1989). Source O-3 states that one John George married Frances Clark by license March 8, 1779 in Cecil County.

GEORGE, JOSHUA.  Captain in the 4th Battalion, Flying Camp, July

23, 1776 (D-84, I-18, W-157). Captain in the 18th Battalion under Col. Charles Rumsey on August 18, 1776 (C-84, G-61, W-226) and Major, 18th Battalion, under Col. John D. Thompson, 1777 through 1778 (K-116, E-55, H-245, E-55, S-MdHR6636-9-93, S-MdHR4570-72). Two men by this name took the Oath of Allegiance in 1778 (A-11, A-17). One married Elizabeth Thompson, December 20, 1786 (O-8).

GEORGE, NICHOLAS. Private in Capt. Stephen Hyland's Company of Militia on September 8, 1775 (T-MS.1814). Took the Oath of Allegiance in 1778 (A-8).

GEORGE, WILLIAM. Private in Capt. Henry Dobson's Company in the 6th Maryland Line in 1780 (G-348).

GETTRICK (?), WILLIAM. Private in Capt. Baker's Company of Militia on August 1, 1775 and in Capt. Williams' Company on March 3, 1776 in the 30th Battalion (F-157).

GIBNEY, SIMON. Private in Capt. W. Alexander's Company, 30th Battalion, enrolled July 15, 1776 (C-86, G-63).

GIBSON (GIPSON), ANDREW. Oath of Allegiance in 1778 (A-8).

GIBSON, ROBERT. Private in Capt. Stephen Hyland's Company of Militia on September 8, 1775 (T-MS.1814).

GIBSON, WILLIAM. Two men with this name took the Oath of Allegiance in 1778 (A-6, A-13). One William Gibson married Mary Mitchell by lic. dated Nov. 15, 1778 (O-2).

GILES, THOMAS. Paid for riding express at the Head of Elk on July 5, 1780 (I-300).

GILLASPY, FRANCIS. Oath of Allegiance in 1778 (A-5).

GILLEN, JAMES. Oath of Allegiance in 1778 (A-15).

GILLESPIE, JAMES. Oath of Allegiance in 1778 (A-10).

GILLESPIE, RICHARD. Recruited, October 16, 1780 and reported "sick in Cecil County" (G-345).

GILLILAND, THOMAS. Oath of Allegiance in 1778 (A-6).

GILLIS, JAMES. Private in Major Henry Lee's Partizan Corps on February 17, 1780 (K-156).

GILLIS (GILLES), JOHN. Oath of Allegiance in 1778 (A-6).

GILMORE, JAMES. Oath of Allegiance in 1778 (A-10).

GILPIN, JOSEPH (1725-1790). Son of Samuel. Resided north of Elkton. One of the Justices who administered the Oath of Allegiance in March, 1778 (A-7). He worked with Henry Hollingsworth in providing food and quarters for troops passing through Cecil County (C-21).

He was elected a delegate to the Maryland Provincial Convention on May 16, 1775 and also a delegate on July 26, 1775, June 21, 1776, and August 14, 1776 (C-31, I-2, J-321, J-322, J-513, K-2, K-28, P-3). Appointed by the Maryland Council as one of the Collectors of all the gold and silver coin that could be procured in Cecil County, January 27, 1776 (P-132). He was paid for "Waggonage" on September 4, 1776 (W-256). He was also Clothing Collector on March 6, 1779 (L-38), and received a certificate for wheat on Jan. 9, 1780 (I-259). He married Sarah Elizabeth Reed (1742-1802) on Nov. 8, 1764 and their children were: John (born 1765, married Mary Hollingsworth); Samuel (born 1767); Hannah (born 1770); Sarah (born 1772); Jane (born 1774); Elizabeth (born 1776, married Mark Alexander); Joseph (born 1778); Mary (born 1780, married James Partridge in 1800); and, Rachel, born 1783 (J-513, U-332).

GILPIN, JOSIAH. Along with Henry Hollingsworth and Robert Alexander, he was involved in finding a location for the erection of barracks at Elk Point in 1777 (I-77).

GILPIN, SAMUEL. Captain in 2nd Battalion under Col. Henry Hollingsworth, 1777 (S-MdHR6636-9-93). He was involved in purchase of cattle for MD troops, April 25, 1778 (I-162). Received a certificate for flour, Jan. 26, 1780 (I-265).

GILPIN, SAMUEL JR. Oath of Allegiance in 1778 (A-6). Was a Militia Captain in the Elk Battalion on April 21, 1778 (C-87, E-15, E-54). His father Samuel was a Quaker, but Samuel Jr. did not share his beliefs (C-21). His brother George was a Colonel in the Virginia Militia. His brother Joseph was also a patriot and a Justice in Cecil County. Samuel was among those who were due a military clothing allowance on March 6, 1779 (L-38).

GLASGOW, ADAM. Oath of Allegiance in 1778 (A-13). "Adam Glascow" was an Ensign in a company of militia raised at Charles Town on October 1, 1776 (W-312). "Adam Glasgow" was commissioned Ensign on Oct. 3, 1776 (G-74). He was a Captain in the 30th Battalion in 1777 (S-MdHR6636-9-93).

GLASGOW, JAMES. Oath of Allegiance in 1778 (A-13).

GLASGOW, ROBERT. Oath of Allegiance in 1778 (A-13). Robert Glasgow md Elizabeth Kilpatrick, Dec. 7, 1783 lic. (O-6).

GLASGOW, WILLIAM SR. Oath of Allegiance in 1778 (A-10).

GLASGOW, WILLIAM 3RD. Oath of Allegiance in 1778 (A-10).

GLASS, GEORGE. Private in Capt. John Oglevie's Company, July 25, 1776 (C-85, G-647).

GLASS, JOHN. Oath of Allegiance in 1778 (A-6).

GLASSFORD, HENRY. Oath of Allegiance in 1778 (A-11). "Harry Glasford" married Ann Reed by lic. Feb. 20, 1783 (O-5).

GLENN, JOHN. Oath of Allegiance in 1778 (A-1).

GLENN, SAMUEL. Justice who administered the Oath of Allegiance in Cecil County in March, 1778. (A-18)

GOFTON, JOHN. Oath of Allegiance in 1778 (A-14).

GOLD, JOHN. Oath of Allegiance in 1778 (A-14).

GOOD, JOHN. Oath of Allegiance in 1778 (A-5).

GOODING, ISAAC. Oath of Allegiance in 1778 (A-14).

GOODING, WILLIAM. Oath of Allegiance in 1778 (A-11).

GORDON, ARCHIBALD. Private in Capt. Henderson's Company in Col. Hollingsworth's 2nd MD Regiment on Feb. 14, 1777 for three months. He re-enlisted under Captains Miller and Dennis after serving in New Jersey, and was assigned to the 11th PA Regiment. He transferred to Capt. Michael Rudulph's Company in Col. Harry Lee's Partisan Cavalry, and served from 1780 to May 26, 1783 (G-587, G-589). He subsequently applied for and received pension S34904 in 1818, and was still living in 1820 in Cecil County, MD. (NGS Qtrly., Vol. 36, No. 1, p. 34 (1948). Order passed Nov. session, 1807 to "Treasurer, West. Shore, to pay to Archibald Gordon, of Cecil County, late a meritorious soldier in the Rev. War, in qtrly. payments, half pay of a Private as a provision to him in his indigent situation when advanced in life, and for those services by which his country has been so essentially benefited." (N-347). Archibald Gordon md Lydia McMin, Mar 7, 1795 lic. (O-15).

GORDON, DAVID. Oath of Allegiance in 1778 (A-7).

GORDON, JOHN. Oath of Allegiance in 1778 (A-10).

GORTRILL, GEORGE. Oath of Allegiance in 1778 (A-9).

GOTTIER, FRANCIS. Oath of Allegiance in 1778 (A-7).

GRACE, WILLIAM. Of Elk Neck. Oath of Allegiance in 1778 (A-8). Private in Capt. Walter Alexander's Company, 30th Battalion, enrolled August 3, 1776 (C-86, G-63). William Grace md Elizabeth Moore by license June 30, 1789 (O-10).

GRAHAM, JAMES. Oath of Allegiance in 1778 (A-10).

GRAHAM, MOSES. Private in Capt. Henry Dobson's Company in the 6th Maryland Line, in N. C. in October, 1780 (G-348).

GRANT, GEORGE. Private in Capt. Stephen Hyland's Company of Militia on September 8, 1775 (T-MS.1814). Took the Oath of Allegiance in 1778 (A-8).

GRANTLY, JAMES. Private in Capt. Baker's Company of Militia on August 1, 1775 and in Capt. Williams' Company on March 3, 1776 in the 30th Battalion (F-157).

GRAY, JOHN. Oath of Allegiance in 1778 (A-4).

GRAY, STARRET. Oath of Allegiance in 1778 (A-16). He appears to have served because he is among those who were due a military clothing allowance on March 6, 1779 (L-38).

GREAR (GREAS?), WILLIAM. Private in Capt. Stephen Hyland's Company of Militia on September 8, 1775 (T-MS.1814).

GREAVES, ISAAC. Private in Capt. Henry Dobson's Company in the 6th MD Line. Aide to Capt. Somerville, 1780 (G-349).

GREEN, JOHN. Two men with this name took the Oath of Allegiance in 1778 (A-6, A-17).

GREEN, WILLIAM. Private in Capt. Baker's Company of Militia on August 1, 1775 and in Capt. Williams' Company on March 3, 1776 in the 30th Battalion (F-157). Took the Oath of Allegiance in 1778 (A-6).

GREENTREE, ISAAC. On May 7, 1776, he was paid for riding express for John D. Thompson on April 24, 1776 (P-414).

GREENWOOD, ALEX. Drum and Fifer in Capt. Henry Dobson's Co. in 6th Maryland Line, in N. C. in October, 1780 (G-347).

GREHAMS, WILLIAM. Oath of Allegiance in 1778 (A-6).

GRIFFE, WILLIAM. Oath of Allegiance in 1778 (A-13).

GRIFFITH, JOHN. Oath of Allegiance in 1778 (A-6).

GRIFFITH, THOMAS. Oath of Allegiance in 1778 (A-6).

GRIMES, RICHARD. Oath of Allegiance in 1778 (A-7).

GROUCER, ADAM. Oath of Allegiance in 1778 (A-16).

GRUBB, ANDREW. Oath of Allegiance in 1778 (A-5).

GUFFEY, JAMES. Oath of Allegiance in 1778 (A-5).

GUFFEY, JOHN. Oath of Allegiance in 1778 (A-6).

GUFFEY, JOSEPH. Oath of Allegiance in 1778 (A-6).

GUTHRIE, WILLIAM. Oath of Allegiance in 1778 (A-16).

GUY, RICHARD. Oath of Allegiance in 1778 (A-12).

GUY, SAMUEL. Oath of Allegiance in 1778 (A-13).

GUYE, ROBERT. Oath of Allegiance in 1778 (A-6).

HADABUCK, JOHN. Took the Oath of Allegiance in 1778 (A-5). John

"Huddabuck" married Mary Ferguson, December 27, 1790 (O-11).

HAGUE, JOSEPH.  Oath of Allegiance in 1778 (A-11).

HAINES, JOB.  When French troops camped near Rising Sun on April 11, 1781, Gen. Lafayette spent the night in a house on the plantation of the late Marshall J. Hunt, occupied at the time by Job Haines. In appreciation of their hospitality, the General gave each of Haines' sons a piece of money before he left the next morning (J-344).

HALL, ELIHU (1723/24-1790/91), son of Elisha. He married Catherine Orrick on June 16, 1757 and they had these children: Elihu, Jr. (born 1758, married Gertrude Covenhoven); John (born 1760); James (born 1762); Elisha John (born 1764); Susan (born 1766, married Major Robert Lyon); Charles (born 1767); Samuel Chew (born 1769); George Whitefield (born 1770); Elizabeth Harrison (born 1772, married first an Ogle and second a Gordon); Henry (born 1773); Catherine Orrick (born 1775, married a Churchman); Washington (born 1776, married Ann Ginn); and, Julia Reed (born 1778). (U-357). Elihu was a Justice who administered the Oath of Allegiance in Cecil County in March, 1778 (A-1). He became a 1st Lieutenant in the Maryland Line and a Major in the Militia in 1776 (J-323). He reviewed and passed recruits enrolled by Lt. Andrew Porter on July 27, 1776 (G-62, C-82, C-87). "Elihu Hall, Sr." was a Judge of Elections on July 3, 1776 (K-35). On September 9, 1778, "Elihu Hall of Elisha" was promoted to Lieutenant Colonel and he was still in the service as of November 17, 1779, in the 30th Battalion (S-MdHR4570-72, E-18, E-57, H-267, K-116). He received a certificate for wheat, March 7, 1780 (I-274). Elihu died in January, 1790 but his will was not probated until 1791 (J-482, U-357).

HALL, ELIHU JR.  Born August 9, 1758, a son of Elihu Hall and Catherine Orrick, he married Gertrude von Covenhoven in 1779 and had these children: Nicholas (married Mary Gillespie); Susan (married a Morgan); Sarah (born 1782, married George Gillespie); Eleanor (married James Wells); Elihu III (married Ann Porter); and, Catherine (married William Richardson). He was a Second Lieutenant in the 1st Maryland Regiment under Col. John H. Stone (U-357).

HALL, ISAAC.  Oath of Allegiance in 1778 (A-6). Ensign in Capt. Cazier's Company of Militia, June 7, 1781 (E-20). Isaac Hall married Mary Bowman, July 16, 1795 (O-15).

HALL, JAMES.  Oath of Allegiance in 1778 (A-7).

HALL, JOHN.  Private in Capt. Baker's Company of Militia on August 1, 1775 and in Capt. Williams' Company on March 3, 1776 in the 30th Battalion (F-157). Three men with this name took the Oath of Allegiance in 1778 (A-7, 11, 13). One John Hall married Jean Guffy, March 28, 1788 (O-9).

HALL, JOHN JR.  Private in Capt. Baker's Company of Militia on August 1, 1775 and in Capt. Williams' Company on March 3, 1776 in the 30th Battalion (F-157). Took the Oath of Allegiance in 1778 (A-6).

HALL, JOSEPH. On October 2, 1777 he made a request to the state for money for military hospital supplies (I-123).

HALL, WILLIAM. Private in Capt. Joshua George's Company, 18th Battalion, August 18, 1776 (C-84, G-61). William Hall married Catherine Walmsley, July 11, 1780 (O-4).

HALLURAN, THOMAS. Private in Capt. Walter Alexander's Co., 30th Battalion, enrolled July 22, 1776 (C-86, G-63).

HALTHAM. See "Holtham."

HAMBLETON, JOHN. Quartermaster in the Susquehanna Battalion under Col. George Johnson on January 6, 1776 (J-323).

HAMILTON, GEORGE. Ensign in Capt. W. Alexander's Company, 30th Battalion, by July 1, 1776 (C-86, G-63). Ensign in a "company belonging to the Eastern Shore Battn." (W-174). He later became a Captain in the Maryland Line (C-87).

HAMILTON, JOHN. Lieutenant, October 16, 1780 (G-345). One John Hamilton married Catherine Margaretta Forester, a daughter of Rev. George William Forester of Kent County, Maryland, on July 2, 1772 (R-78).

HAMILTON, JOHN JR. Private in Capt. Walter Alexander's Company, 30th Battalion, enrolled July 1, 1776 by Ensign George Hamilton (C-86, G-63). John Hamilton, Jr. married Frances Davis (Hughes) by lic. dated Nov. 20, 1782 (O-5).

HAMILTON, PATRICK. Oath of Allegiance in 1778 (A-5).

HAMILTON, SAMUEL. Recruit, October 16, 1780 (G-345).

HANDY, GEORGE. Lieutenant in Major Henry (Col. Harry) Lee's Partizan Corps (Lee's Legion), February 17, 1780 (K-156).

HARGAN, JOHN. Private in Capt. Baker's Company of Militia on August 1, 1775 and in Capt. Williams' Company on March 3, 1776 in the 30th Battalion (F-157).

HARLEY (HORLEY), WILLIAM. Oath of Allegiance in 1778 (A-7).

HARRIES, JOHN. Oath of Allegiance in 1778 (A-15).

HARRIS, WILLIAM. Private in Capt. Henry Dobson's Company in the 6th Maryland Line, in N. C. in October, 1780 (G-348).

HARRIS, WILLIAM JR. Oath of Allegiance in 1778 (A-10).

HARRIS, WILLIAM SR. Oath of Allegiance in 1778 (A-10).

HARRISON, RICHARD. Private in Capt. Joshua George's Company, 18th Battalion, August 18, 1776 (C-84, G-61).

HARRISON, WILLIAM. Lieutenant in Capt. Veazey's Company. Paid 200 pounds by the Maryland Council for provisions for his company on July 10, 1776 (W-19, C-82).

HART, ROBERT. Oath of Allegiance in 1778 (A-4). Second Lieutenant in Capt. William Veazey's Co., 30th Battn., 1777 (C-87, K-116, S-MdHR6636-9-93, S-MdHR4570-72).

HART, ROBERT JR. Private in Capt. Stephen Hyland's Company of Militia on September 8, 1775 (T-MS.1814). Took the Oath of Allegiance in 1778 (A-8). Became Ensign in Capt. Hyland's Company in the Susquehanna (or 30th) Battalion and subsequently a 2nd Lieutenant in 1778 (E-58). Robert Hart md Ann Hyland by license dated July 10, 1779 (O-3).

HART, THOMAS. Private in Capt. Stephen Hyland's Company of Militia on September 8, 1775 (T-MS.1814). Took the Oath of Allegiance in 1778 (A-8).

HARTHORN (HATHORN), JOHN. Oath of Allegiance, 1778 (A-13).

HARTHORN (HATHORN), JOSHUA. Oath of Allegiance, 1778 (A-13).

HARTSHORN (HARTSHORNE), JOHN. Son of Jonathan Hartshorne and Ann Glasgow (J-535). He took the Oath of Allegiance in 1778 (A-13) and he served as Quartermaster in the Elk Battalion of Militia on January 6, 1776. Commissioned a First Lieutenant on October 3, 1776, he was ordered to Philadelphia on Oct. 15, 1776 under Capt. James Maxwell (C-87, G-74, J-323, W-312, W-316). He was Adjutant of the Fourth Maryland Line on January 25, 1778, Lieutenant on May 21, 1779 and subsequently a Major, 30th Battalion and Recruiting Officer at Head of Elk in 1782 (J-535, L-48, L-112, C-87, S-MdHR6636-9-93). An order was passed on February 13, 1836, to the "Treasurer, Western Shore to pay to Nancy Williams, widow of John Hartshorn, who was a Lieutenant in the Revolutionary War, during widowhood, half pay of a Lieutenant for the services of her late husband" (N-352). However, Source J-535 states he married Miss Agnes Miller and died leaving no children. John's brothers were Joshua, Jonathan, Benjamin and Samuel. His sisters were Elizabeth Patterson, Rebecca McCullough and Mary Cresswell (J-535). Source Q-115 states John married Agnes Miller on April 17, 1788 in Cecil County, Maryland. Source O-9 states John Hartshorne married Agnes Miller by license dated April 15, 1788 and Agnes Hartshorn married Thomas Williams by license dated August 21, 1800 (O-20).

HARTSHORN, JONATHAN. Oath of Allegiance in 1778 (A-13).

HARTSHORN, JONATHAN JR. Oath of Allegiance in 1778 (A-13).

HARTSHORN, THOMAS. Oath of Allegiance in 1778 (A-13).

HARVEY, JOSHUA. Private in Col. Harry Lee's Partizan Cavalry,

January 1, 1779 through December, 1780 (G-587).

HARVEY, MATHEW. Private in Major Henry (Col. Harry) Lee's Partizan Corps on February 17, 1780 (K-156).

HARVEY, PHINEAS. Private in Capt. W. Alexander's Company, 30th Battalion, enrolled July 24, 1776 (C-86, G-62).

HARVEY, WILLIAM. Oath of Allegiance in 1778 (A-6).

HARVIE (HERVIE), ROBERT. Oath of Allegiance in 1778 (A-6).

HARVIE, THOMAS. Oath of Allegiance in 1778 (A-6).

HARWARD, HENRY. Oath of Allegiance in 1778 (A-6).

HASSON (HARSON), BENJAMIN. Oath of Allegiance in 1778 (A-6). Private in Capt. John Oglevie's Company, July 25, 1776. (C-85, G-647).

HASSON (HUSSON), JAMES. Oath of Allegiance in 1778 (A-6). Private in Capt. John Oglevie's Company, July 25, 1776. (C-85, G-647).

HAYES, HENRY. Oath of Allegiance in 1778 (A-14).

HAYES, JAMES. Oath of Allegiance in 1778 (A-11). "James Hays" was a Private in Capt. Joshua George's Company, 18th Battalion, August 18, 1776 (C-84, G-61). "James Hayes" was also recruited on October 16, 1780 (G-345).

HAYES, RICHARD. Oath of Allegiance in 1778 (A-14). "Richard Hays" was a Private in Capt. Joshua George's Company, 18th Battalion, August 18, 1776 (C-84, G-61). Richard Hayes married Susannah Vansant, March 17, 1778 (O-1).

HEATH, CHARLES. Oath of Allegiance in 1778 (A-17). Captain of Militia in 18th Battalion under Col. John D. Thompson, 1777-1778 (E-56, S-MdHR6636-9-93).

HEDRICK, GEORGE. Oath of Allegiance in 1778 (A-5).

HEDRICK, MICHAEL. Oath of Allegiance in 1778 (A-4).

HEGARTY, ANDREW. Fifer in the Maryland Line under Capt. Henry Dobson (C-82, J-322).

HEGON, JAMES. Oath of Allegiance in 1778 (A-10).

HELM, MICHAEL. Oath of Allegiance in 1778 (A-1).

HEMPHILL, JAMES. Oath of Allegiance in 1778 (A-15).

HEMPHILL, JOSEPH. "Joseph Hemphill" was a Private in Col. Harry Lee's Partisan Cavalry, April 7, 1778 t December, 1780 (C-83, G-586, 587). "Joseph Kemphill" was a Private in Major Henry (Col.

Harry) Lee's Partizan Corps on February 17, 1780 (K-156). Joseph Hemphill married Jane Moody by license dated September 23, 1789 (O-10).

HEMPHILL, ROBERT. Took the Oath of Allegiance in 1778 (A-6). Private in Capt. Walter Alexander's Company, in the 30th Battalion, enrolled August 3, 1776 (C-86, G-63).

HENDERSON, DAVID. Private in Col. Harry Lee's Partisan Cavalry, January 1, 1779. Promoted to Sergeant April 1, 1780 and served through December, 1780 (G-587, K-156). David Henderson married Sarah Kimble by license dated December 13, 1791 (O-12).

HENDRICKSON, AUGUSTINE. Oath of Allegiance in 1778 (A-11).

HENDRICKSON, EPHRAIM. Recruited, October 16, 1780 (G-345).

HENDRICKSON, HENRY. Oath of Allegiance in 1780 (B-112).

HENDRICKSON, JOHN. Oath of Allegiance in 1778 (A-11).

HENECY, PETER. Private in Capt. Henry Dobson's Company in the 6th Maryland Line, in N. C. in October, 1780 (G-349).

HENERSON, JAMES. Oath of Allegiance in 1778 (A-15).

HENERSON, WILLIAM. Oath of Allegiance in 1778 (A-15).

HENNIE, JOHN. He appears to have served because he was due a military clothing allowance on March 6, 1779 (L-38).

HENRY (HENREY), DAVID. Private in Capt. Baker's Company of Militia on August 1, 1775 and in Capt. Williams' Company on March 3, 1776 in the 30th Battalion (F-157). Took the Oath of Allegiance in 1778 (A-4).

HENRY, SAMUEL. Private in Capt. Baker's Company of Militia on August 1, 1775 and in Capt. Williams' Company on March 3, 1776 in the 30th Battalion (F-157).

HERON, J. G. Captain in the Maryland Line (C-87).

HESSEY (HERSEY), ISAAC. Oath of Allegiance in 1778 (A-4).

HESSEY, JAMES. Oath of Allegiance in 1778 (A-12).

HEWIT, JAMES. Oath of Allegiance in 1778 (A-5).

HIBBETS, ISAAC. Oath of Allegiance in 1778 (A-16).

HIBBETS, JAMES. Oath of Allegiance in 1778 (A-6).

HICKMAN, WILLIAM. Oath of Allegiance in 1778 (A-11).

HIGGINS, THOMAS. Quartermaster in the Militia (C-87).

HILL, CHARLES. Corporal in Capt. Henry Dobson's Company in the 6th Maryland Line, in N. C. in October, 1780 (G-347).

HILL, DAVID. Oath of Allegiance in 1778 (A-6). David Hill married Rebecca Manly by license Feb. 25, 1789 (O-10).

HILL, GEORGE. Oath of Allegiance in 1778 (A-8). Private in Col. Harry Lee's Second Troop of the Partisan Cavalry, April 7, 1778 to June 19, 1783 (C-83, G-586-588, K-156). George Hill married Elizabeth Manly, May 23, 1789 (O-10).

HILL, JAMES. Oath of Allegiance in 1778 (A-4). James Hill married Ann Cavender by license Sept. 27, 1791 (O-12).

HILL, JOHN. Oath of Allegiance in 1778 (A-6). Ensign in Capt. James Mackey's Company of Militia, 2nd Battalion, on April 10, 1776, and became a First Lieutenant on April 21, 1778 (C-85, E-55, P-319, S-MdHR6636-9-93). John Hill married Sarah Naley on November 20, 1777 (O-1, R-86).

HILL, JONATHAN. Oath of Allegiance in 1778 (A-8).

HILL, SAMUEL. Oath of Allegiance in 1778 (A-6).

HILLONS, ABRAHAM. Oath of Allegiance in 1778 (A-10).

HINMAN (HINDMAN), JAMES. Oath of Allegiance in 1778 (A-6). "James Hindman" was a Private in Capt. John Oglevie's Company, July 25, 1776 (C-85, G-647).

HINMAN, ROBERT. Oath of Allegiance in 1778 (A-10).

HINMAN, SAMUEL. Oath of Allegiance in 1778 (A-10).

HITCHCOCK, THOMAS. Oath of Allegiance in 1778 (A-8).

HITCHCOCK, WILLIAM. Private in Capt. Stephen Hyland's Company of Militia on September 8, 1775 (T-MS.1814). Took the Oath of Allegiance in 1778 (A-8).

HITCHMAN, WILLIAM. Oath of Allegiance in 1778 (A-10).

HODGSON, JONATHAN. Oath of Allegiance in 1778 (A-4).

HODGSON, JONATHAN JR. Oath of Allegiance in 1778 (A-4).

HODGSON, RICHARD. Oath of Allegiance in 1778 (A-4). Private in Capt. Walter Alexander's Company, in 30th Battalion, enrolled August 3, 1776 (C-86, G-63). Richard Hodgson married Sarah Ellis by license January 9, 1786 (O-7).

HODGSON, ROBERT. Oath of Allegiance in 1778 (A-4). Second Lieutenant in Capt. John Ford's Company, 18th Battalion, under Col. John D. Thompson, in 1777 (S-MdHR6636-9-93). Was promoted to First

Lieutenant on June 22, 1778 (E-56).

HOGANS, WILLIAM. Oath of Allegiance in 1778 (A-4).

HOLLAND (HALLON), JACOB. Oath of Allegiance in 1778 (A-11).

HOLLAND (HOLLAN), JOHN. Oath of Allegiance in 1778 (A-2).

HOLLAND, JNO. Oath of Allegiance in 1778 (A-17).

HOLLIDAY, JOHN JR. Private in Capt. Henry Dobson's Company in the 6th Maryland Line, 1780 (G-348). John "Holladay" married Rebecca Simpers by license January 3, 1788 (O-9).

HOLLINGS, JONATHAN. Oath of Allegiance in 1778 (A-14).

HOLLINGSWORTH, GEORGE. Oath of Allegiance in 1778 (A-15).

HOLLINGSWORTH, HENRY. (September 17, 1737 - September 29, 1803), a son of Zebulon Hollingsworth and Ann Maulden. He married first to Sarah Husband and had two children: Polly (born 1771, married first John Gilpin and second Fresby Henderson), and William (born 1773, married Ann Black). He married second to Jane Evans by license dated February 12, 1778 and had four children: Hannah (married James Partridge), Betsy; Nancy (married John Tally); and, Henry (V-138, O-1). He began his military career in 1775 with the first company raised in Cecil County. On Feb. 6, 1776 he made an agreement with the Council of Safety to carry on a saltpetre works and to manufacture gun barrels and bayonets for the Maryland troops at his forge on Big Elk River (I-24, K-38, P-138). He was Lieutenant Colonel and Adjutant in the Elk (2nd) Battalion on Jan. 6, 1776 (I-36, J-323), and a Colonel (S-MdHR6636-9-93), when severely wounded in the throat prior to the Battle of Brandywine in 1777 (I-60, I-64, K-78). Retired from active service, he became Quartermaster or Commissioner (Supply Agent) for the Eastern Shore and part of Harford Co. (K-18) and subsequently Deputy Quartermaster General (I-174, I-211). He also shipped supplies to Valley Forge, on Feb. 19, 1778 (L-23) and served on several committees in Cecil County including one that issued Bills of Credit and paper money for the State in 1781 (C-12, C-13, C-14, C-87). He took the Oath of Allegiance in 1778 (A-15). He died September 29, 1803. Reinterred in Elkton Cemetery.

HOLLINGSWORTH, JACOB. Oath of Allegiance in 1778 (A-7). 2nd Lieutenant in Capt. Jonathan Booth's Company, in the Elk Battalion, 1777-1778 (E-55, S-MdHR6636-9-93). Jacob's brother was Col. Henry Hollingsworth (C-14).

HOLLINGSWORTH, JAMES. Oath of Allegiance in 1778 (A-15).

HOLLINGSWORTH, SAMUEL. Acting Commissary of Issues (Head of Elk) in 1778 (I-182). Oath of Allegiance in 1778 (A-7).

HOLLINGSWORTH, STEPHEN. Oath of Allegiance in 1778 (A-7).

HOLLINGSWORTH, THOMAS.  Oath of Allegiance in 1778 (A-7).

HOLLINGSWORTH, ZEBULON (May 17, 1735 - March 24, 1812). He married Mary Evans on June 22, 1764 and they had these children: Levi (born 1765, married Ann Dorsey); Peggy (born 1766, married William Cooch); Robert (born 1768, married Jeanne Talandier); William (died young); James (died young); John (born 1774); William (born 1780, married Mary Eliza); and, Evans. (U-395). Zebulon took Oath of Allegiance in 1778 (A-15), and in 1780 he gave 285 barrels of flour to be delivered at the Head of Elk (U-395). His brother was Col. Henry Hollingsworth (C-14).

HOLMS, ABRAHAM.  Private in Capt. W. Alexander's Company, 30th Battalion, enrolled July 24, 1776 (C-86, G-62).

HOLT, GEORGE. Oath of Allegiance in 1778 (A-14). George Holt married Catherine Price, daughter of William Price, on June 6, 1763 (R-89).

HOLT, ISAAC.  Oath of Allegiance in 1778 (A-8).

HOLTHAM, JOSEPH.  Oath of Allegiance in 1778 (A-4). "Joseph Haltham" was a Private in Capt. Joshua George's Company, 18th Battalion, August 18, 1776 (C-84, G-61).

HOLTHAM, SPENCER.  Oath of Allegiance in 1778 (A-4). Spencer "Hottham" married Elizabeth Morrison on November 13, 1788 (O-10).

HOMES, GEORGE.  Oath of Allegiance in 1778 (A-7).

HONEYMAN, ROBERT.  Oath of Allegiance in 1778 (A-16).

HOOPER, ABRAHAM.  Oath of Allegiance in 1778 (A-4).

HOOPER, ISAAC.  Oath of Allegiance in 1778 (A-17).

HOPKINS, JOHN.  Oath of Allegiance in 1778 (A-15).

HOUSLY, JOHN.  Private in Capt. Henry Dobson's Company in the 6th Maryland Line, in N. C. in October, 1780 (G-348).

HOWARD, JOHN.  Private in Col. Harry Lee's Partisan Cavalry, April 1, 1778 through December, 1780 (G-587).

HOWELL (HOWEL), JAMES.  Oath of Allegiance in 1778 (A-5).

HOWELL (HOWEL), WILLIAM. Oath of Allegiance in 1778 (A-5). William "Howell," son of George and Mary Howell, both from County Cork, Ireland, married Ruth Smith, daughter of William and Sarah Smith, on November 9, 1755 (R-92).

HOWLAND (NOWLAND), ALIAS.  Oath of Allegiance, 1778 (A-17).

HOWLAND (NOWLAND), RICHARD.  Oath of Allegiance, 1778 (A-17).

HUCANS: See "Hukill."

HUDDABUCK: See "Hadabuck."

HUDSON, JACOB. Oath of Allegiance in 1778 (A-18).

HUDSON, JOHN. Oath of Allegiance in 1778 (A-18).

HUGGINS, CHARLES. Oath of Allegiance in 1778 (A-7).

HUGGINS, THOMAS. Quartermaster in the Elk Battalion of Colonel Charles Rumsey on January 6, 1776 (J-323).

HUGHES, ANDREW. Oath of Allegiance in 1778 (A-4). Andrew Hughes married Rebecca Price on April 23, 1788 (O-9).

HUGHES, EVIN. Private in Capt. Joshua George's Company, 18th Battalion, August 18, 1776 (C-84, G-61).

HUGHES, ROLAND. Oath of Allegiance in 1778 (A-4).

HUGHES, SAMUEL. Oath of Allegiance in 1778 (A-2).

HUGHES (HUGHS), THOMAS. Lt. Colonel in Susquehanna Battalion under Col. George Johnson, January 6, 1776 (J-323, I-18), and formed a company at Charles Town on October 1, 1776 (W-316). Reviewed and passed recruits on July 25, 1776 (C-63). Thomas Hughes married Frances Forrester, of Georgetown, Kent County, by license May 16, 1774. Thomas Hughes and Frances Dorcas Forester were actually married in Kent County on August 25, 1774 (R-92).

HUKILL, ABIAH. "Abiah Hukill" was a Private in Col. Harry Lee's Partisan Cavalry, April 7, 1778 to December, 1780 (C-83, G-586, 587). "Abiah Hucans" was a Private in Major Henry Lee's Partizan Corps on February 17, 1780 (K-156).

HUKILL, DANIEL. Oath of Allegiance in 1778 (A-2).

HUKILL, JAMES. Oath of Allegiance in 1778 (A-4). James Hukill married Milicent Manly, February 12, 1780 (O-4).

HUKILL, JEREMIAH. Oath of Allegiance in 1778 (A-2).

HUKILL, JESSE. Two men with this name took the Oath of Allegiance in 1778 (A-2, A-12). One Jesse Hukill married Sarah Miller by license August 6, 1780 (O-4).

HUKILL, JOSEPH. Oath of Allegiance in 1778 (A-11). "Joseph Hukins" was a Private in Capt. Joshua George's Company, 18th Battalion, August 18, 1776 (C-84, G-61).

HUKILL, PETER. Oath of Allegiance, 1778 (A-4). Peter Hukill married Mary Eliason by license February 2, 1778 (O-1).

HUKILL, RICHARD. Oath of Allegiance in 1778 (A-2).

HUKILL, SPENCER. Oath of Allegiance in 1778 (A-2).

HUKINS: See "Hukill."

HULET, JAMES. Oath of Allegiance in 1778 (A-8).

HULL, JOHN. Oath of Allegiance in 1778 (A-16).

HULL, WILLIAM. Oath of Allegiance in 1778 (A-15).

HUNT, JOSEPH. Oath of Allegiance in 1778 (A-18).

HUNTER, JAMES. Oath of Allegiance in 1778 (A-5).

HURLY, JOHN. Oath of Allegiance in 1778 (A-14). "John Hurley" was a Private in Capt. Joshua George's Company, 18th Battalion, August 18, 1776 (C-84, G-61). One John Hurley was also recruited on October 16, 1780 (G-345).

HUSLER, WILLIAM. Private in Capt. Joshua George's Company, 18th Battalion, August 18, 1776 (C-84, G-61).

HUSSA, JAMES. Private in Capt. Joshua George's Company, 18th Battalion, August 18, 1776 (C-84, G-61).

HUSTON, WILLIAM. Oath of Allegiance in 1778 (A-6). William "Hewston" married Isabel Crookshanks by license dated July 23, 1777 (O-1, R-85). William "Huston" married Susannah Boyd by license August 24, 1791 (O-12).

HUTCHESON, JESSE. Oath of Allegiance in 1778 (A-16).

HUTCHESON, JOSEPH. Oath of Allegiance in 1778 (A-17).

HUTCHESON, SAMUEL. "Samuel Hutcheson" was Ensign in Capt. Brevard's Company of Militia in the 18th Battalion and was promoted to 2nd Lieutenant on June 22, 1778 (E-56, S-MdHR6636-9-93). "Samuel Hutchinson" was a Captain in the Militia (C-87). Took Oath of Allegiance, 1778 (A-2).

HYLAND, EDWARD (January 10, 1755 - May 30, 1799). Son of John Hyland, Jr. (1730-1765) and Mary Juliustra (1725 - 1777). Edward Hyland married Juliana Arrants (1756-1800) in 1776 and had children: Nicholas (born 1779, married first Jane Hart and second Ruth McCraken); William (married Catherine Ann Foster); Johnson (married Margaret Loran); Joshua (married first Margaret Crouch and second Elizabeth Crouch); Stephen (married Maria Kankey?); Mary (1777-1847, married first Alexander Wilson of Scotland, and second Capt. John Hyland Ford); Rebecca (born 1780, md Rev. Fredus Aldridge); Amelia (md William Pennington); and, Araminta (married Benjamin Mauldin). (U-417). He furnished food for the Army and took Oath of Allegiance in 1778 (A-15, U-417, and Maryland Society, Sons of the American Revolution application of descendant Robert Clark Wilson, National No. 123270, State No. 2731, approved January 24, 1984).

HYLAND, ISAAC. Oath of Allegiance, 1778 (A-8). Isaac Hyland married Mary Johnson by license March 7, 1779 (O-3).

HYLAND, JACOB. Oath of Allegiance in 1778 (A-8).

HYLAND, JOHN. Ensign in Capt. William Veazey's Company in the 30th Battalion in 1777 (S-MdHR6636-9-93). Took the Oath of Allegiance in 1778 (A-8). One John Hyland married Martha Tilden on April 29, 1739 (R-94).

HYLAND, NICHOLAS. Private in Capt. Stephen Hyland's Company of Militia on September 8, 1775 (T-MS.1814). Took the Oath of Allegiance in 1778 (A-8). Nicholas Hyland, son of Col. Nicholas Hyland, married Margery Kankey, daughter of John and Ann Kankey, on August 2, 1764 (R-94).

HYLAND, STEPHEN (1743-1806). Son of Capt. John Hyland and Martha Tilden. Stephen married first to Rebecca Tilden in December, 1774, and had a son John (born 1775), and then to Araminta Hamm on March 20, 1777, a granddaughter of Augustine Herman of Bohemia Manor, and had Stephen, Jr. (married first Marie Kankey and second Marjorie Maulden), Nicholas (born 1779), Jacob (born 1781, married Elizabeth Thackery), Mary (married William Craig), Martha (married William A. Schaeffer) and Lambert (R-94, U-417). Stephen was a Justice who administered the Oath of Allegiance in March, 1778 (A-8). He served as a delegate to the State Provincial Convention on May 16, 1775 (I-2, K-2). He was commissioned a Captain by September 8, 1775, a Lieutenant Colonel in the 18th Battalion in 1777-1778 and a Colonel, in the 30th Battalion, on September 9, 1778, and served at least to 1781 (C-31, C-87, E-57, J-522, J-523, K-116, K-2, S-MdHR6636-9-93, S-MdHR4570-72, P-438, T-MS.1814).

HYNSON, NATHANIEL. Oath of Allegiance in 1778 (A-12).

IGANS (EGANS), JAMES. Oath of Allegiance in 1778 (A-1).

IRELAND, NATHAN. Private in Capt. Stephen Hyland's Militia Company on September 8, 1775 (T-MS.1814). Nathan Ireland married Sarah Price(?) by license August 26, 1787 (O-8).

IRON, ALEXANDER. Oath of Allegiance in 1778 (A-8).

IRVAN (?), BAZEL. Oath of Allegiance in 1778 (A-5).

IRWIN, JOHN. Oath of Allegiance in 1778 (A-7).

IVORY, PATRICK. Drummer in the Maryland Line (C-82), having initially enlisted on May 23, 1776 and then discharged on February 12, 1779, he re-enlisted on May 20, 1779 and was reported as deserted on December 19, 1779 (G-11, G-125).

JACK, JOHN. Oath of Allegiance in 1778 (A-5).

JACKSON, DANIEL. Oath of Allegiance in 1778 (A-8).

JACKSON, EDWARD (1740-1804). He married Margaret McMullen on January 26, 1768 and had seven children: James (born 1769, married Mary McCarrahan); John (born 1770, married Grissell Craig); Edward (born 1773, married Mary Fox); Samuel (born 1778, married Margaret Ann Fox); Robert (married Sarah Williams); Margaret (married first John Boyd and second Hugh Boyd); and Hugh (married Elizabeth Whitelock). Edward Jackson served as a Private in Capt. George Richard Bird's Co., 4th Maryland Battalion (U-419, V-150, R-95). Two men with this name took the Oath of Allegiance in 1778 (A-5, A-8). Another Edward Jackson married Sarah Greenland on January 12, 1773 (R-95).

JACKSON, HENRY. Oath of Allegiance in 1778 (A-8).

JACKSON, JOHN. Drummer in 1776 and then Private in Capt. Henry Dobson's Co., 6th MD Line, in 1780 (J-322, G-348). John Jackson md Mary Ewing by license May 26, 1784 (O-6).

JACKSON (JACSON), WALTER. Oath of Allegiance in 1778 (A-2).

JACKSON, WILLIAM. Two men with this name took the Oath of Allegiance in 1778 (A-4, A-8).

JACOBS, JESSE. Sergeant in Capt. Henry Dobson's Company in the 6th Maryland Line, in N. C. in October, 1780 (G-347).

JAMES, MORGAN. Oath of Allegiance in 1778 (A-3).

JAMES, SETH. A school teacher who lived near Chestnut Hill, he and his wife had the honor of lodging Gen. Washington and his servant for one night in August, 1777 (J-331).

JAMISON, GEORGE. Oath of Allegiance in 1778 (A-16).

JAMISON, ADAM. Lieutenant and Recruiting Officer at Head of Elk on April 2, 1782 (L-111, L-112).

JAMISON (JAMESON), JOHN. Private in Capt. John Oglevie's Company, July 25, 1776 (C-85, G-647). Took the Oath of Allegiance in 1778 (A-6).

JAMISON (JAMESON), WILLIAM. Private in Capt. John Oglevie's Company, July 25, 1776 (C-85, G-647). Took the Oath of Allegiance in 1778 (A-6).

JANVIER, PHILIP. Oath of Allegiance in 1778 (A-7). Philip "Javyr" married Lidia----- in New Castle, Delaware on September 31 (sic), 1768 (R-96).

JARALIMAN, JOHN. Private in Capt. Joshua George's Company in the 18th Battalion, August 18, 1776 (C-84, G-61).

JARVIS, JOHN. Oath of Allegiance in 1778 (A-11).

JARVIS, WILLIAM. Oath of Allegiance in 1778 (A-15).

JAVINS, DANIEL. Private in Capt. Henry Dobson's Company in 6th MD Line. On Furlough in Maryland, Oct., 1780 (G-349).

JEFFERSON, WILLIAM. Recruited, October 16, 1780 (G-345).

JEFFRIS, WILLIAM. Oath of Allegiance in 1778 (A-10).

JENKINS, SAMUEL. Private in Major Henry (Col. Harry) Lee's Partizan Corps (Lee's Legion), February 17, 1780 (K-156).

JEWELL, CORNELIUS. Oath of Allegiance in 1778 (A-8).

JOB, ARCHIBALD (QUAKER) (1726-1805). He married Margaret Rees and had 7 children: Morris (born 1753, married Lydia Bond); Daniel (married Mary Megredy); Sarah (married James Trimble); Elizabeth (born 1765, married John Megredy); Margaret (married John Reynolds); Thomas (married Charity Rees); and, Enoch (V-152). He took the Oath of Allegiance in 1778 (A-6). Source V-152 states that Archibald Job served as a Scout for Gen. George Washington, and was a Manufacturer of Arms in Maryland.

JOB, DANIEL (QUAKER). Oath of Allegiance in 1778 (A-6).

JOB, MORRIS (QUAKER). Oath of Allegiance in 1778 (A-6). "Morrico Jobe" married Lidya Bond, Feb. 1, 1779 (O-2).

JOB, THOMAS JR. (QUAKER). Oath of Allegiance in 1778 (A-6).

JOBSON, JOHN. Oath of Allegiance in 1778 (A-12). One John Jobson md Hester Holyday (widow), July 23, 1711 (R-97).

JOHNSON, DAVID. Oath of Allegiance in 1778 (A-6).

JOHNSON, ELISHA. Took the Oath of Allegiance in 1778 (A-8). Elisha Johnson married Ann Baker, March 21, 1778 (O-1).

JOHNSON, GEORGE. Colonel in the Susquehanna Battalion, January 6, 1776 (C-87). (Source J-323 states he is believed to have been an aid to Gen. Washington during the New Jersey campaign in 1777-1778.) George Johnson married Ann Shepard on January 23, 1755 (R-98).

JOHNSON, ISAAC. Oath of Allegiance in 1778 (A-5). Isaac Johnson married Sarah Dickson on November 2, 1770 (R-98).

JOHNSON, JACOB. Two men with this name took the Oath of Allegiance in 1778 (A-4, A-15). One Jacob Johnson married Elizabeth Drake on April 5, 1730 (R-98).

JOHNSON, JAMES. Second Lieutenant in the Militia (C-87).

JOHNSON, JOHN. Private in Capt. John Oglevie's Company, July 25, 1776 (C-85, G-647). Took the Oath of Allegiance in 1778 (A-6). Private in Major Henry (Col. Harry) Lee's Partizan Corps (Lee's

Legion) on February 17, 1780 (G-587 K-156). Drummer in Maryland Line (C-82). (Ed.: It appears that this data may pertain to more than one John Johnson)

JOHNSON, JOSIAH. Oath of Allegiance in 1778 (A-7). Josiah "Jonson" married Hanah Merrall on March 26, 1777 (R-101).

JOHNSON, LEVI. Oath of Allegiance in 1778 (A-15).

JOHNSON, MATHIAS. Oath of Allegiance in 1778 (A-7).

JOHNSON, ROBERT (DR.) Oath of Allegiance in 1778 (A-9).

JOHNSON, SIMON. Oath of Allegiance in 1778 (A-7). One Simon Johnson married Catherine Vandeveare on November 4, 1738 (R-98), and one Simon Johnson married Sarah Short on December 10, 1795 (O-15).

JOHNSON, THOMAS. Ensign in Capt. Robert Porter's Company. (S-MdHR6636-9-93). Resigned September 9, 1778 (E-57). Took the Oath of Allegiance in 1778 (A-4). One Thomas Johnson married Milliscent Hyland on July 1, 1722 (R-98).

JOHNSON, WILLIAM. Private in Capt. John Oglevie's Company, July 25, 1776 (C-85, G-647). Took Oath of Allegiance in 1778 (A-6). (Ed.: Also see "William Johnston/Johnstone")

JOHNSTON, ISAAC. Oath of Allegiance in 1778 (A-16).

JOHNSTON, JAMES. Private in the Militia by October 1, 1778. (S-MdHR6636-12-37A).

JOHNSTON, JOHN. Private in Capt. Jeremiah Baker's Company, August 1, 1775 and Capt. Baruch Williams' Company, March 3, 1776 (F-157, I-27). Oath of Allegiance in 1778 (A-16).

JOHNSTON, THOMAS. Oath of Allegiance in 1778 (A-16).

JOHNSTON, WILLIAM. He appears to have served because he was due a military clothing allowance, March 6, 1779 (L-38). (Ed.: Also see "William Johnson" and "William Johnstone")

JOHNSTON (JOHNSTONE), WILLIAM. William Johnston or Johnstone was commissioned a Second Lieutenant in the Militia in Capt. James Maxwell's Company, raised at Charles Town on Oct. 1, 1776 (W-312, W-316) and ordered to Philadelphia on October 15, 1776 (C-87, G-74). "William Johnson" was a First Lieutenant in Capt. James Maxwell's Company in 1778 (E-57, S-MdHR6636-9-93).

JONES, CHARLES. Oath of Allegiance in 1778 (A-8).

JONES, JOHN. Second Lieutenant in Capt. Samuel Gilpin's Company in the Elk Battalion on April 21, 1778 (E-54, S-MdHR6636-9-93). Oath of Allegiance in 1778 (A-6).

JONES, MOSES. Private in Capt. Stephen Hyland's Militia Company on September 8, 1775 (T-MS.1814). He took the Oath of Allegiance in 1778 (A-8). Moses Jones married Rebecca Ruten on January 14, 1766 (R-100).

JONES, NATHANIEL. Recruited, October 16, 1780 (G-345).

JONES, ROBERT. Oath of Allegiance in 1778 (A-15).

JONES, SAMUEL. Oath of Allegiance in 1778 (A-6).

JONES, THOMAS. Four men with this name took the Oath of Allegiance in 1778 (A-4, A-6, A-7, A-11). One married Elizabeth Knight by license November 30, 1785 (O-7). Another Thomas Jones married Elizabeth Baxter, daughter of Col. James and Elizabeth, December 14, 1761 (R-100).

JONES, WILLIAM. Two men with this name took the Oath of Allegiance in 1778 (A-4, A-15). One William Jones md Sarah Lynch by license November 10, 1778 (O-2). Another William Jones married Sarah Moore, May 15, 1784 (O-6).

JONSON: See "Johnson."

JONSON, JOHN. Oath of Allegiance in 1778 (A-10).

JONSON, WILLIAM. Private in Capt. Walter Alexander's Company, enrolled August 3, 1776 (C-86, G-63). Took the Oath of Allegiance in 1778 (A-10).

JORDAN, HUGH. Oath of Allegiance in 1778 (A-16).

JORDAN, THOMAS. Oath of Allegiance in 1778 (A-16).

JUSTICE, EDWARD. Private in Capt. Jeremiah Baker's Co. on August 1, 1775 and Capt. Baruch Williams' Co. on March 3, 1776 (F-157, I-27). Oath of Allegiance in 1778 (A-5).

JUSTICE, WILLIAM. Oath of Allegiance in 1778 (A-5).

KANKEY, JOHN. Private in Capt. Stephen Hyland's Militia Company on September 8, 1775 (T-MS.1814). He took the Oath of Allegiance in 1778 (A-8). John Kankey married Rebecca Hyland on June 6, 1738 (R-101).

KANKEY, JOHN JR. Private in Capt. Stephen Hyland's Militia Company on September 8, 1775 (T-MS.1814). He took the Oath of Allegiance in 1778 (A-8).

KEARNES, THOMAS. Private in Capt. Henry Dobson's Co., 6th MD Line. Waiter to General Gates in Oct., 1780 (G-349).

KEITH, ROBERT. Oath of Allegiance in 1778 (A-1).

KEITLY, HENRY. Oath of Allegiance in 1778 (A-15).

KEITLY, JOHN. Oath of Allegiance in 1778 (A-15).

KEITLY (KITELY, CITELY, CEITLY), THOMAS. (Of Elk Neck). Private in Capt. Walter Alexander's Company, enrolled August 3, 1776 (C-86, G-63). Thomas "Keatly" married Catharine Moody by license dated July 19, 1794 (O-14).

KELLER, GEORGE. Recruit, October 16, 1780, "delivered by James Creswell, a recruiting officer of Cecil County, to Lieutenant John Hamilton." (G-345).

KELLY, EBENEZER. Oath of Allegiance in 1778 (A-7). Ebenezer Kelly married Rachel Foster, October 18, 1790 (O-11).

KELLY, JAMES. It appears he may have served as he is listed in the "deserters taken up in Harford County for two of the classes of this county and delivered to Col. Dallam" and among the "deserters sent to Chester Town." (G-346)

KELLY (KELLEY), JOHN. Private in Capt. Jeremiah Baker's Company on August 1, 1775 and in Capt. Baruch Williams' Company on March 3, 1776 (F-157, I-27). Took the Oath of Allegiance in 1778 (A-5). Second Lieutenant in Capt. Jeremiah Baker's Company in the 30th (or Susquehanna) Battalion in 1778 (E-58, S-MdHR6636-9-93).

KELLY (KELLEY), NICHOLAS. Private in Capt. Jeremiah Baker's Company, August 1, 1775 and in Capt. Baruch Williams' Company, March 3, 1776 (F-157, I-27).

KELLY, SAMUEL. His pension S38112, which he applied for in Morgan County, Kentucky in 1834, states he was born in Cecil County, Maryland in 1756 and enlisted there in September, 1777. After the war he moved to Prince Edward County, Virginia, and also Pennsylvania, Tennessee and then Kentucky. Thomas Hamilton, a fellow soldier, made affidavit to this in Kentucky on Apr. 8, 1834. (See Annie W. Burns' "Maryland Soldiers: Revolutionary War," p. 61).

KELLY (KELLEY), THOMAS. Ensign in Capt. Edward Daugherty's Company in 1777 and in Capt. Philip Cole's Company, 30th (or Susquehanna) Battalion on September 9, 1778 (E-57, S-MdHR6636-9-93). Took the Oath of Allegiance in 1778 (A-5). Thomas Kelly married Mary Connelly by license dated April 12, 1790 (O-11).

KEMPTON, THOMAS. He was reported "supposed to be gone to the British Army" prior to October 20, 1778 (K-121).

KENT, JAMES. Oath of Allegiance in 1778 (A-10).

KENT, THOMAS. Oath of Allegiance in 1778 (A-10).

KENT, WILLIAM. Oath of Allegiance in 1778 (A-13).

KERR, GEORGE. Oath of Allegiance in 1778 (A-10).

KERR, NATHANIEL. Oath of Allegiance in 1778 (A-10).

KERR, SAMUEL. Oath of Allegiance in 1778 (A-10).

KEY, JAMES. Oath of Allegiance in 1778 (A-4).

KEY, JOHN ROSS (September 19, 1754 - October 13, 1821). Of Charlestown, Cecil County; died in Frederick County, MD. Married Ann Phoebe Penn Dagworthy Charloton and their son was Francis Scott Key, author of "The Star Spangled Banner," who married Mary Tayloe Lloyd (C-82, U-438). John served in the militia in 1775 and was commissioned Second Lieutenant in Frederick County on June 21, 1775 in the 2nd Rifle Company, Maryland Line (C-82, G-28, U-438).

KIDD, ANDREW. Oath of Allegiance in 1778 (A-10).

KIGHT (RIGHT?), JOHN. Oath of Allegiance in 1778 (A-6).

KILLGORE (KILGOUR), JAMES. Took the Oath of Allegiance in 1778 (A-16). "James Kilgour" served in Militia (C-87).

KILLGORE, WILLIAM. Private in the Militia by October 1, 1778 (S-MdHR6636-12-37A). Took the Oath of Allegiance in 1778 (A-7). He was due a military clothing allowance on March 6, 1779 (L-38).

KILLPATRICK, WILLIAM. Oath of Allegiance in 1778 (A-5).

KILPATRICK, SAMUEL. Oath of Allegiance in 1778 (A-5). Samuel "Killpatrick" married Jannet Good on November 16, 1761 (R-103). Samuel "Kilpatrick" married "the late Elenor Foster, elias Kilpatrick," on March 8, 1775 (R-103).

KINCADE (KINKEAD, KINCAID), JOHN. Private in Major Henry (Col. Harry) Lee's Partizan Corps circa February 17, 1780 to August 20, 1783 (G-588, G-590, I-611, K-156). (Ed.: John Kincaid served in Cecil Co., but was from Delaware.)

KING, ABNA. Second Lieutenant in Capt. James Dougherty's Company, 30th Battalion, September 9, 1778 (E-58).

KING, JOHN. Private in Capt. Jeremiah Baker's Company on August 1, 1775 and Capt. Baruch Williams' Co. on March 3, 1776 (F-157, I-27). Oath of Allegiance in 1778 (A-6).

KING, THOMAS. Private in Capt. John Oglevie's Company, July 25, 1776 (C-85, G-647). Oath of Allegiance in 1778 (A-6).

KING (RING?), WILLIAM. Oath of Allegiance in 1778 (A-18).

KINNARD (KINARD), JOHN. Private in Major Henry (Col. Harry) Lee's Partizan Corps on April 7, 1778 through at least 1780 (G-587, K-156).

KIRK, ABNER. Oath of Allegiance in 1778 (A-9). Abner Kirk married

Sarah Chambers, December 21, 1786 (O-8).

KIRK, ALEXANDER. Oath of Allegiance in 1778 (A-4).

KIRK, GARRET. Oath of Allegiance in 1778 (A-11). "Garratt Kirk" married Sarah Wingate, December 28, 1778 (O-1). (Source R-104 states they married December 28, 1777.)

KIRK, JACOB. Oath of Allegiance in 1778 (B-114).

KIRK, JOHN. Oath of Allegiance in 1778 (A-14). John Kirk married Ann Parsley by license dated Dec. 7, 1778 (O-2). And a John Kirk married Sarah Roberts by license dated December 25, 1789 (O-11).

KIRK, JOSEPH. Private in Capt. Joshua George's Company in the 18th Battalion, August 18, 1776 (C-84, G-61). Took the Oath of Allegiance in 1778 (A-11).

KIRK, TIMOTHY. One of the Justices who administered the Oath of Allegiance in Cecil County in March, 1778 (A-9).

KIRK, ZACHARIAH. Oath of Allegiance in 1778 (A-12).

KIRKPATRICK, JOHN. Oath of Allegiance in 1778 (A-5).

KITE, WILLIAM. Private in Capt. Walter Alexander's Company, enrolled July 24, 1776 (C-86, G-62). Took the Oath of Allegiance in 1778 (A-7).

KLEINHOFF, WILLIAM. Oath of Allegiance in 1778 (A-4).

KLEINHOFF, WILLIAM JR. Oath of Allegiance in 1778 (A-3).

KNIGHT, GEORGE. Private in Capt. Stephen Hyland's Militia Company on September 8, 1775 (T-MS.1814).

KNIGHT, JOHN LEACH. Captain in the 18th Battalion under Col. John D. Thompson, April 21, 1778 (S-MdHR6636-9-93, E-55). One of the Court Justices who administered the Oath of Allegiance in March, 1778 (A-3). One John Knight married Prudence Reynolds, February 17, 1778 (O-1).

KNOX, ROBERT. Oath of Allegiance in 1778 (A-5). Robert Knox married Lidia Williams, March 29, 1779 (O-3).

LACKLAND, JAMES. Oath of Allegiance in 1778 (A-6).

LACKLAND, MATHEW. Oath of Allegiance in 1778 (A-9).

LACKLAND, NATHAN. Oath of Allegiance in 1778 (A-6).

LAFFERTY, WILLIAM. Oath of Allegiance in 1778 (A-10).

LAING, JOHN. Oath of Allegiance in 1778 (A-11).

LANCASTER, JEREMIAH. Private in Capt. Joshua George's Company, 18th Battalion, August 18, 1776 (C-84, G-61). Took the Oath of Allegiance in 1778 (A-11).

LANCASTER, SINCLAIR (ST. CLAIR). Born circa 1760. Married Rebecca Ford and their daughter Elizabeth married Jacob Hugg. Sinclair was a First Lieutenant, 18th Battalion, and promoted to Captain on June 22, 1778 (U-448, E-56, S-MdHR6636-9-93). Took Oath of Allegiance in 1778 (A-4). Source U-448 gives name as "Samuel Sinclair Lancaster."

LANGLEY, JOHN. Oath of Allegiance in 1778 (A-16).

LANGWELL (LANGVILL, LONGWELL), HUGH. He took the Oath of Allegiance in 1778 (A-16).

LANGWELL (LANGVILL, LONGWELL), ROBERT. Private in Capt. Walter Alexander's Company, enrolled July 24, 1776 (C-86, G-62). Took the Oath of Allegiance in 1778 (A-16).

LANGWELL (LANGVILL, LONGWELL), WILLIAM. He took Oath of Allegiance in 1778 (A-16).

LASHLEY (LASHLY), GEORGE. Order passed March 12, 1827 for the "Treasurer to pay to George Lashley, of Cecil County, during life, half yearly, half pay of a Private, for his services during Rev. War." Order passed May 27, 1836, for the "Treasurer, Western Shore, to pay to Granville S. Townsend $20.44, for benefit of Mary Sproul and Nancy Lashly, heirs and legal representatives of George Lashly, a Revolutionary War pensioner, deceased, which balance was due said Lashly at his death" (N-364). George "Lasly" married Amelia Johnson by license Dec. 30, 1778 (O-2).

LASSLIE, JOHN. Oath of Allegiance in 1778 (A-6). John "Lasley" married Kazia Price, April 15, 1783 (O-5).

LASSLIE, ROBERT. Oath of Allegiance in 1778 (A-6).

LASSLIE, THOMAS. Oath of Allegiance in 1778 (A-4).

LATHAM, AARON. Private in Capt. Joshua George's Company, 18th Battalion, August 18, 1776 (C-84, G-61). Took the Oath of Allegiance in 1778 (A-4). Aaron Latham married Sarah Bryson by license dated December 5, 1782 (O-5).

LATHAM, SYLVESTER. Private in Capt. Joshua George's Company, 18th Battalion, August 18, 1776 (C-84, G-61). Took the Oath of Allegiance in 1778 (A-4).

LAUGHLIN, ROBERT. Oath of Allegiance in 1778 (A-11).

LAWIS (LEWIS), JOHN. Oath of Allegiance in 1778 (A-15).

LAWRENSON, JAMES. Private in Capt. Joshua George's Company, 18th Battalion, August 18, 1776 (C-84, G-61). Took the Oath of

Allegiance in 1778 (A-4).

LAWREMORE, JAMES. Oath of Allegiance in 1778 (A-5).

LAWSON, GEORGE. Oath of Allegiance in 1778 (A-15).

LAWSON, JOHN. Oath of Allegiance in 1778 (A-16).

LAWSON, PETER. Was elected to be a representative to the Maryland Convention on May 16, 1775 (I-2, K-2) and was a Delegate on July 26, 1775 (P-3). He was a signer of the Declaration of Freemen in Maryland in 1775 (J-322).

LEE, EPHRAIM. Private in Capt. Joshua George's Company, 18th Battalion, August 18, 1776 (C-84, G-61). Took the Oath of Allegiance in 1778 (A-12). Ephraim Lee married Susannah Walmsley by license September 20, 1779 (O-3).

LEE, HARRY (1756-1818). "Lightfoot" Harry (or Henry) Lee was a Major, later Lieutenant Colonel and then Colonel, from Virginia, who enrolled Maryland troops into his Partisan Cavalry (or Partizan Corps, or Lee's Legion). Men from Cecil County served with him from 1778 to 1783 (C-83, G-586, G-587, K-156, U-454).

LEE, JAMES. Oath of Allegiance in 1778 (A-8).

LEE, RICHARD. Oath of Allegiance in 1778 (A-17).

LEE, WILLIAM. Oath of Allegiance in 1778 (A-10).

LEECH, JOHN. Oath of Allegiance in 1778 (A-15).

LEHU, JOHN. Oath of Allegiance in 1778 (A-5). John "Layhua" married Hannah Walker by license March 10, 1778 (O-1). John "Lashu" md Hannah Maud Cayhan, June 5, 1790 (O-11).

LEMON, ARCHIBALD. Private in Capt. Joshua George's Company, 18th Battalion, August 18, 1776 (C-84, G-61).

LEONARD, JAMES. Order passed in December session, 1817, for the "Treasurer, Western Shore, to pay to James Leonard of Cecil County, an old soldier, quarterly, the half pay of a Private, as a further remuneration for his services during the Revolutionary War." On March 9, 1826, the "Register of Land Office (did) issue to James Leonard, a warrant for 50 acres of land, belonging to this state in Allegany County, unpatented, "as a donation granted by this state, to the Revolutionary War soldiers who served in the Maryland line, during the Revolutionary War, and to which he is considered entitled." (N-365)

LEONARD, WILLIAM. Oath of Allegiance in 1778 (A-11).

LESLOW, PETER. Oath of Allegiance in 1778 (A-17).

LESSLIE, DANIEL. Oath of Allegiance in 1778 (A-10).

LESSLIE, WILLIAM.  Oath of Allegiance in 1778 (A-11).

LEWIS, DAVID.  Oath of Allegiance in 1778 (A-3).

LEWIS, JOHN.  Two men with this name took the Oath of Allegiance in 1778 (A-4, A-8). One John Lewis married Hesten Phillips on November 10, 1727 (R-110).

LEWIS, RICHARD.  Oath of Allegiance in 1778 (A-7). Richard Lewis married Ann Arrants by license July 28, 1778 (O-2).

LEWIS, SAMUEL.  Private in Capt. Walter Alexander's Company, enrolled August 3, 1776 (C-86, G-63). Took the Oath of Allegiance in 1778 (A-4).

LIGGET, GEORGE.  Oath of Allegiance in 1778 (A-9).

LIN, MATHEW.  Oath of Allegiance in 1778 (A-7).

LINCH, WILLIAM.  Oath of Allegiance in 1778 (A-8).

LINCOLN, JOHN.  Private in Capt. Henry Dobson's Co., in the 6th Maryland Line, in N. C. in October, 1780 (G-348).

LINSEY, DANIEL.  Private in Capt. Walter Alexander's Company, enrolled July 27, 1776 (C-86, G-62).

LINTON, GEORGE.  Oath of Allegiance in 1778 (A-15).

LITTLE, JAMES.  Private in Capt. Stephen Hyland's Militia Company on September 8, 1775 (T-MS.1814). He took the Oath of Allegiance in 1778 (A-8). James Little married Mary Reynolds by license dated May 6, 1783 (O-5).

LITTLE, NATHANIEL.  Took Oath of Allegiance in 1778 (A-8). Nathaniel "Litell" married Mary Jackson, November 1, 1744 (R-110).

LITTLE, ROBB.  Oath of Allegiance in 1778 (A-5).

LITTLE, WILLIAM.  Oath of Allegiance in 1778 (A-5).

LOCK, WILLIAM.  It appears that he served as he is listed among "deserters taken up in Harford County for two of the classes of this county and delivered to Col. Dallam" and among the "deserters sent to Chester Town." (G-346)

LOGAN, HUGH.  Oath of Allegiance in 1778 (A-6).

LOGAN, MATTHEW.  Oath of Allegiance in 1778 (A-5).

LOGAN, SAMUEL.  Oath of Allegiance in 1778 (A-6).

LOGAN, WILLIAM.  Oath of Allegiance in 1778 (A-13).

LOGUE, EPHRAIM. Oath of Allegiance in 1778 (A-4). Ephraim "Longe" married Elizabeth Cusex, Dec. 27, 1790 (O-12).

LOGUE, ISAAC. Oath of Allegiance in 1778 (A-4).

LOGUE, JAMES. Oath of Allegiance in 1778 (A-17).

LOGUE, MANASSA. Oath of Allegiance in 1778 (A-4). "Manasseh Loge" married Sarah Derrel, February 27, 1734/35 (R-111).

LONG, ALEXANDER. Oath of Allegiance in 1778 (A-10).

LONG, ANDREW. Oath of Allegiance in 1778 (A-12).

LONG, JOHN. Oath of Allegiance in 1778 (A-10).

LONG, JOSEPH. Private in Capt. Henry Dobson's Company, 6th MD Line. On Command with Gen. Smallwood in 1780 (G-349).

LONGWELL: See "Langwell."

LOUTTIT, JAMES. Oath of Allegiance in 1778 (A-11).

LOUTTIT, JOSHUA. Oath of Allegiance in 1778 (A-14).

LOVE, JAMES. Oath of Allegiance in 1778 (A-1).

LOVE, JOHN. Oath of Allegiance in 1778 (A-6). Private in Capt. Henry Dobson's Company in the 6th Maryland Line. He enlisted on December 22, 1778, and was on Guard Duty at Camp Hillsborough, North Carolina in 1780 (G-349).

LOVE, ROBERT. First Lieutenant in Capt. William Ewing's Company in the 30th (or Susquehanna) Battalion on September 9, 1778 (E-58, S-MdHR6636-9-93).

LOVE, SAMUEL (1728, Scotland - April 23, 1779, Cecil County) He married Rosanna Graham (1738-1814) in 1758 and they had nine children: Jane (born 1759, married George Kidd); Mary (born 1761, married John Burlin); Margaret (born 1763, married Hugh McCoy); Elizabeth (born 1765, married Alec Nesbit); Robert (born 1767, married Ann McCoy); Anna (born 1770); Rosanna (born 1772); Samuel (born 1774, married Catherine McCoy); and, James (born 1777, married Rachel Henderson). Samuel was a "member of the Home Guard of Cecil County" and a Private in the 2nd Company of the Upper Battalion of Col. Zadok Magruder (G-474, V-176). He took the Oath of Allegiance in 1778, Cecil County (A-10).

LOW, ISAAC. Oath of Allegiance in 1778 (A-10).

LOW, WILLIAM. Oath of Allegiance in 1778 (A-1).

LOWRY, JAMES. Oath of Allegiance, 1778 (A-15). One James Lowry married Mary Veazey, April 27, 1748 (R-112), and one married Catharine Elliott, March 10, 1792 (O-12).

LOWRY, JOHN. Two men with this name took the Oath of Allegiance in 1778 (A-8, A-16).

LOWRY, WILLIAM. Oath of Allegiance in 1778 (A-7). William Lowry married Sarah Aldridge, March 24, 1785 (O-7).

LUCKEY, ROBERT. Oath of Allegiance in 1778 (A-1).

LUM, JACOB (August, 1748 - April 3, 1829). He married Rachel Hyland (1751-1816) and had 11 children: John (born 1771, married first Hester Adams and second Sophia McIntire Bouldin); Isaac (born 1773); Michael (born 1775); Jacob (born 1777, married Rebecca Alexander); Michael (born 1778); Ann (born 1780); Edward (born 1782); Millicent (born 1786, md John Cochran); Julia (born 1787, married William Richardson); Hyland (born 1790); and, Elizabeth (born 1793) (V-178). He took Oath of Allegiance in 1778 (A-8). Was Ensign in Capt. Thomas Savin's Company, 2nd Battalion, in 1777 and promoted to Second Lieutenant in Capt. Abraham Cazier's Co., Elk Battn. on September 9, 1778 (E-55, K-116, S-MdHR6636-9-93, S-MdHR4570-72).

LUM, MICHAEL. Took the Oath of Allegiance in 1778 (A-8). Michael Lum married Mary Makenne, July 9, 1739 (R-112).

LUSBY, EDWARD. Oath of Allegiance in 1778 (A-11).

LUSBY, JOSEPH. Oath of Allegiance in 1778 (A-12).

LUSBY, ROBERT. Oath of Allegiance in 1778 (A-14).

LUTTON, JAMES. Oath of Allegiance in 1778 (A-15).

LUTTON, ROBERT. Oath of Allegiance in 1778 (A-6).

LYNCH, GEORGE. Oath of Allegiance in 1778 (A-1).

LYNCH, JAMES. Oath of Allegiance in 1778 (A-8).

LYNCH, JOHN. Oath of Allegiance in 1778 (A-1). One John Lynch married Margaret McClane, April 4, 1784 (O-6) and one John married Mary Wilson February 2, 1787 (O-8).

LYNN, JOHN. Lieutenant in Capt. Henry Dobson's Company in the 6th Maryland Line, in N. C. in Oct., 1780 (G-346).

LYON, HEETOR. Oath of Allegiance in 1778 (A-10).

LYON, HUGH. Oath of Allegiance in 1778 (A-10).

LYON, JAMES. Oath of Allegiance in 1778 (A-10).

LYON, JAMES JR. Oath of Allegiance in 1778 (A-10).

LYON, JOHN. Oath of Allegiance in 1778 (A-10).

LYON, JOSEPH. Oath of Allegiance in 1778 (A-10).

LYON, ROBERT. Oath of Allegiance in 1778 (A-10). Robert Lyon married Susannah Hall by license December 2, 1783 (O-6).

MACKELWEE, JOHN. Oath of Allegiance in 1778 (A-6).

MACKEY (MACKY), DAVID. (Of New Munster). This David Mackey was a resident of North Milford Hundred in Cecil County, Maryland, and became Lieutenant Colonel, 6th Battalion, in Chester County, Pennsylvania in 1776 (C-69, C-83). Another David "Macky" was a Private in the Cecil County Militia by October 1, 1778 (S-MdHR6636-12-37A). He took the Oath of Allegiance in 1778 in Cecil County (A-16).

MACKEY (MACKY), JAMES JR. Sergeant in 34th Battalion of Militia under Capt. James Mackey, Sr., and Colonel B. Johnson, January 23, 1777 (C-67, C-69, C-85). Took the Oath of Allegiance in 1778 (A-6). In 1794 he established the Cecil Manufacturing Company on Little Elk Creek and presented a sample of their cloth to President Jefferson who supposedly wore it for his inauguration (C-67). One James Mackey married Catherine Mackey by license June 3, 1784 (O-6) and one James Mackey married Sarah Wallace by license October 9, 1784 (O-6).

MACKEY (MACKY), JAMES SR. (Son of Robert Mackey, d. 1772 at "Hopewell" on Little Elk Farm). "James Macky, Esq." was commissioned a Captain of Militia in the 30th Battalion on April 10, 1776, and the Elk Battalion of Col. Henry Hollingsworth and then served under Col. Edward Parker on Apr. 9, 1778 (C-67, C-68, C-85, E-25, E-55, N-371, P-319, S-MdHR6636-9-93). He took the Oath of Allegiance in 1778 (A-16). Resigned his commission on April 3, 1779 (I-213).

MACKEY (MACKY), JOHN. Private in the Militia by October 1, 1778 (S-MdHR6636-12-37A). Two men with this name took the Oath of Allegiance in 1778 (A-6, A-16). One John Mackey married Jane Mackey, March 8, 1780 (O-3).

MACKEY (MACKY), ROBERT. Oath of Allegiance in 1778 (A-16).

MACKEY, THOMAS (Of New Munster). Served in the 3rd Battalion of the Maryland Line under Col. Nathaniel Ramsay (C-82).

MACKEY, WILLIAM. Enrolled as a Private in Capt. Alexander's Company, 30th Battalion, on July 27, 1776, and became a First Lieutenant in Capt. James Mackey's Company (C-85, C-85, G-62). Took the Oath of Allegiance, 1778 (A-16). By 1782 he was a Captain in the Cecil County Militia (C-69). William Mackey married Mary Mackey, Dec. 30, 1779 (O-3).

MADDOX, ALEXANDER. Oath of Allegiance in 1778 (A-7).

MAFFITT, JAMES. Recruited, October 16, 1780 (G-345).

MAFFITT (MOFFITT), SAMUEL. Captain in the Elk Battalion under Col. Henry Hollingsworth and then under Col. Edward Parker, April 9, 1778 (E-25, E-54, S-MdHR6636-9-93) and was recommended to be a Major on October 1, 1778 (I-190, S-MdHR6636-12-37A). Took Oath of Allegiance, 1778 (A-6). On July 18, 1781 he requested a relief from duty (I-412).

MAHAFEY, JOSEPH. Oath of Allegiance in 1778 (A-6).

MAHANNY, THOMAS. Private in Capt. Henry Dobson's Company in the 6th Maryland Line, in N. C. in October, 1780 (G-349).

MAHONEY, STEPHEN. Private in Capt. Walter Alexander's Company, 30th Battalion, enrolled July 27, 1776 (C-86, G-62).

MAHONEY, WILLIAM. Recruited, October 16, 1780 (G-345).

MAJORS, ROWLAND. Oath of Allegiance in 1778 (A-9).

MALOAN, JOHN. Oath of Allegiance in 1778 (A-2).

MALONE (MELONE, MELOANE), ANDREW. Private in Capt. Veazey's Company in the 2nd Maryland Regiment of State Troops from 1775 to 1777 and then re-enlisted in 1777 for 3 years by Ensign under Colonel Smallwood. He was in the Battles of Long Island, Staten Island, Brandywine, Germantown, White Plains, Princeton, Stoney Point and Monmouth. Andrew was discharged January 10, 1780 (G-138). He applied for and received pension S1828 in Calloway Co., Kentucky where he died in August, 1834. His widow, Rachael, also applied and received pension W27972. She died July 29, 1839. Her maiden name was Ozier (Orzier) and she had been married to a Yelefrau before marrying Andrew Malone (Meloan) in Maryland in 1781 or 1782. Family record included with the pension application: Andrew Meloan (born February 18, 1754); Rachael Ozier (born May 23, 1753); Sarah Yelefrau (born March 3, 1775); Mary Yelefrau (born Jan. 7, 1777); John Yelefrau born (Dec. 20, 1778); Thomas Meloan (born November 24, 1784); Elizabeth Meloan (born Oct. 1, 1786); Andrew Meloan, Jr. (born October 22, 1788); Isabel Meloan (born July 13, 1790); Obadiah Meloan (born Oct. 2, 1792); Alex Meloan (born Dec 1794); Adam R. Feris (born Sept 13, 1798; John Price (born Dec. 3, 1801); Sally Meloan (born April 20, 1839? (1804?); Rachael Caldwell (born Feb. 3, 1805); John Caldwell (born November 10, 1807); Betsey Ann Caldwell (born February 14, 1809); Mary H. Caldwell (born May 2, 1815); Polly Trimble (died August 14, 1831); P. O. Meloan (died November 2, 1833); James Price married Sarah Yelefrau November 3, 1800; David Trimbell married Polly Yelefrau October 19, 1812; and, Robert Caldwell married Permile Meloan March 22, 1804. In 1854 Thomas Malone was aged 70, Elizabeth Lockridge was aged 68, and Obediah A. Melone was aged 60; children of Andrew Malone (Meloan). (Most of this data was taken from abstracts by Annie W. Burns in "Maryland Soldiers: Revolutionary War," p. 24).

MANLEY (MANLY), JACOB. Oath of Allegiance in 1778 (A-15). Jacob

Manley married Rebecca Lum, Dec. 15, 1768 (R-116).

MANLEY, JESSE. Oath of Allegiance in 1778 (A-8). "Tesey Manley" married Rachel George by lic. Jan. 2, 1779 (O-2).

MANLEY (MANLY), JOHN. Oath of Allegiance in 1778 (A-15). Private in Major Henry (Col. Harry) Lee's Partizan Corps on April 7, 1778, and was a Sergeant by December, 1780 (G-587, K-156). Granted leave "till called for" on June 17, 1783 (G-588). John "Manly" married Mary Connolly on March 26, 1788 (O-9), and John "Manley" married Susannah Cox, April 15, 1790 (Q-118). (Lic. April 13, 1790, O-11).

MANLY, THOMAS. Private in Major Henry (Col. Harry) Lee's Partizan Corps as early as April 7, 1778 and serving to at least December, 1780 (C-83, G-586, G-587).

MANSFIELD, JAMES. Private in Capt. Joshua George's Company, 18th Battalion, August 18, 1776 (C-84, G-61). Took the Oath of Allegiance in 1778 (A-17).

MANSFIELD, ROBERT. Oath of Allegiance in 1778 (A-4).

MANSFIELD, WILLIAM. Oath of Allegiance in 1778 (A-3).

MANTLE (MONTLE), GEORGE. Private in Capt. Henry Dobson's Co., 6th Maryland Line, in N.C. in October, 1780 (G-348).

MANTLE, JOHN. Sergeant in Capt. Henry Dobson's Co., in the 6th Maryland Line, in N. C. in October, 1780 (G-347).

MANUEL, THOMAS. Oath of Allegiance in 1778 (A-7).

MARCHANT, JAMES. Oath of Allegiance in 1778 (A-10).

MARQUES, JOHN. Oath of Allegiance in 1778 (A-13).

MARQUES, JOHN JR. Oath of Allegiance in 1778 (A-13). John "Marquis, Jr." married Eleanor Meak, Sept 8, 1779 (O-3).

MARQUES, ROBERT. Oath of Allegiance in 1778 (A-13).

MARQUES, ROBERT JR. Oath of Allegiance in 1778 (A-13).

MARQUES, SAMUEL. Oath of Allegiance in 1778 (A-13). Samuel "Marquiss" married Rachel Touchstone, Oct 30, 1784 (O-6).

MARR, DAVID. Private in Capt. Joshua George's Company, 18th Battalion, August 18, 1776 (C-84, G-61).

MARSHALL, JOHN. Private in Capt. Henry Dobson's Company in the 6th Maryland Line in 1780, having enlisted Dec. 20, 1778 for 3 years, and was serving at Hillsborough, N. C. in October, 1780 (G-348). Order was passed on March 22, 1833 for the "Treasurer of the Western Shore to pay to John Marshall, of Cecil County, during life, quarterly, half pay of a Private, in consideration of services rendered by him during the Revolutionary War" (N-373).

MARSHALL, WILLIAM. Oath of Allegiance in 1778 (A-13).

MARTIN (MARTAIN), EDWARD. Private in Capt. W. Alexander's Co., 30th Battn., enrolled July 24, 1776 (C-86, G-62).

MARTIN, HUGH. Oath of Allegiance in 1778 (A-16).

MARTIN, JAMES. Oath of Allegiance in 1778 (A-17).

MARTIN, JOHN. Oath of Allegiance in 1778 (A-12). Private in Capt. Henry Dobson's Company in the 6th Maryland Line, having enlisted February 10, 1780 for 3 years. On Guard in Hillsborough, North Carolina in October, 1780 (G-349). John Martin married Elizabeth Can, May 11, 1782 (O-5).

MARTIN, WILLIAM. Oath of Allegiance in 1778 (A-12). Sergeant in Capt. Henry Dobson's Company in the 6th Maryland Line. On Furlough from North Carolina to Maryland in October, 1780 (G-347).

MATHEWS, WILLIAM. Took the Oath of Allegiance in Court on February 20, 1779 (M-37).

MATTHEWS, CHARLES. Oath of Allegiance in 1778 (A-8).

MATTHEWS (MATHEWS), JAMES. Oath of Allegiance in 1778 (A-9).

MATTHEWS, ROBERT. Private in Capt. Henry Dobson's Company in the 6th Maryland Line, having enlisted May 15, 1778 for 3 years. On Guard in N. C. in October, 1780 (G-349).

MATTHEWS, WILLIAM. Oath of Allegiance in 1778 (A-17).

MAULDIN (MAULDEN), BENJAMIN (Dec. 3, 1754? - March 3, 1804). Son of Francis. Married Mary Morrey and had 8 children: Francis (born 1774); Rebecca (born 1776, married first to Capt. Jeremiah Baker and second to Samuel Hogg); Benjamin (born 1778); Mary (born 1781, married to Charles Tilden Ford); Thomas (born 1784); James (born 1786); John (born 1788); Benjamin (born 1791, married first to Sarah Thomas and second to Araminta Hyland) (U-507). Private in Capt. Stephen Hyland's Company of Militia on September 8, 1775 (T-MS.1814). Took Oath of Allegiance, 1778 (A-8, J-511).

MAULDIN (MAULDEN), HENRY. Son of Francis. Private in Capt. Joshua George's Company, 18th Battalion, August 18, 1776 (C-84, G-61). Took the Oath of Allegiance in 1778 (A-8). After the war he settled in South Carolina (J-511).

MAULDIN (MOULDEN), WILLIAM. Son of Francis. 2nd Lieutenant in Capt. Stephen Hyland's Company on September 8, 1775 (T-MS.1814) and May 23, 1776 (P-438). He took the Oath of Allegiance in 1778 (A-8), and was a First Lieutenant under Capt. William Veazey in the

30th Battalion, Sept. 9, 1778 (S-MdHR4570-72, S-MdHR6636-9-93, E-58, J-511, K-116). He resigned his commission at Turkey Point on July 24, 1779 (I-207). William Mauldin married Margery Hyland by license dated January 24, 1786 (O-8).

MAUNTETH, WILLIAM. Oath of Allegiance in 1778 (A-8).

MAXWELL, JAMES. Raised a militia company at Charles Town on October 1, 1776 and was Commissioned a Captain on October 3, 1776. His Flying Camp Co. was ordered to Philadelphia on October 15, 1776. He was also a Captain in the 30th or Susquehanna Battalion, April 21, 1778 and later a Major (C-87, E-57, G-74, S-MdHR6636-9-93). He was one of the Justices who administered the Oath of Allegiance (A-10) and he also took the Oath of Allegiance in 1778 (A-17).

MAXWELL, JAMES JR. Took Oath of Allegiance in 1778 (A-11). Corporal in Capt. Henry Dobson's Company in 6th Maryland Line in 1780 (G-347). Order passed in November session, 1811, for the "Treasurer Western Shore to pay to James Maxwell, of Cecil County, late a meritorious soldier in the Rev., half pay of a Corporal, as a provision to him in his indigent situation, now advanced in life, and as a further remuneration to him for those services by which his country has been so essentially benefitted." (N-373)

MAXWELL, JOHN. Oath of Allegiance in 1778 (A-7).

MAXWELL, WILLIAM JR. Oath of Allegiance in 1778 (A-10).

MAXWELL, WILLIAM SR. Oath of Allegiance in 1778 (A-10).

MAY, HUGH. Private in Capt. Walter Alexander's Company, 30th Battalion, enrolled July 22, 1776 (C-86, G-63).

MAY, JOHN. Private in Capt. Henry Dobson's Co., 6th Maryland Line. Hospitalized at Fish Kills, October, 1780 (G-349).

MAY, THOMAS. Was Judge of Elections on November 8, 1776 to elect representatives to the Maryland Convention (K-55). He took the Oath of Allegiance in 1778 (A-7).

MAYBEN (MAYBON), EDWARD. Oath of Allegiance in 1778 (A-16).

MAYBERRY, BENJAMIN. Recruited, October 16, 1780 (G-345).

McALESTER, DANIEL. Oath of Allegiance in 1778 (A-7).

McBRIDE, HANNAH. She was among those who received a military clothing allowance on March 6, 1779 (L-38).

McBRIDE, JAMES. Oath of Allegiance in 1778 (A-15). One James McBride married Mary Pew, June 9, 1778 (O-2), and a James McBride married Deborah Thompson on Sept. 5, 1792 (O-13).

McCALL, JOHN. Private in Capt. Jeremiah Baker's Company on August

1, 1775 and Capt. Baruch Williams' Company, March 3, 1776 (F-157, I-27). Oath of Allegiance in 1778 (A-5).

McCANN (McCONN), HUGH. Oath of Allegiance in 1778 (A-5).

McCANN, MICHAEL. Private in Capt. Henry Dobson's Company in the 6th Maryland Line, in N. C. in October, 1780 (G-347).

McCANN (McCANE), PATRICK. Oath of Allegiance in 1778 (A-5).

McCARTNEY, JOHN. Oath of Allegiance in 1778 (A-3).

McCASHLIN, WILLIAM. Oath of Allegiance in 1778 (A-16).

McCASKER, MICHAEL. Private in Capt. Walter Alexander's Co., 30th Battalion, enrolled July 27, 1776 (C-86, G-62).

McCAULEY, DANIEL. Oath of Allegiance in 1778 (A-7).

McCAULEY (McCULLEY), HENRY. Oath of Allegiance, 1778 (A-6).

McCAULEY, JAMES. Oath of Allegiance in 1778 (A-7). Private in the Militia by October 1, 1778 (S-MdHR6636-12-37A).

McCAULEY, JOHN. Oath of Allegiance in 1778 (A-6).

McCAY, ALEXANDER. Oath of Allegiance in 1778 (A-6).

McCAY, HUGH. Oath of Allegiance in 1778 (A-10).

McCAY (McKAY), JOHN (c1728, Scotland - March 17, 1794, Cecil County, MD). Married Frances----- and had 12 children: John, Jr. (married Elizabeth Arbuckle in 1785---Ed. Note: Source U-479 mistakenly gives her name as "Arguckle," and Source O-7 mistakenly gives his names as "McCoy."); Hugh; William; James; Ester (married a Rowland); Ann (married a Love); Jean; Agnes; Elizabeth; Frances; Catherine; and Margaret (U-479, V-181). Two men with this name took the Oath of Allegiance in 1778 (A-10, A-16). "John McCoy" (or MaCay) was a Private in Capt. Joshua George's Company, in 18th Battalion, on August 18, 1776 (C-84, G-61). "John McKay" (or McCay) was a Private in the Maryland Line and was placed on the pension rolls in January, 1820, under the Act of March 18, 1818 (N-370).

McCAY, JOSEPH. Oath of Allegiance in 1778 (A-3).

McCAY (McKAY), WILLIAM. Oath of Allegiance in 1778 (A-3).

McCELVEY (McCOLVEY), OWEN. Oath of Allegiance, 1778 (A-12).

McCIBBINS, JAMES. Oath of Allegiance in 1778 (A-6).

McCLAREY, BASSETT. Private in Capt. Joshua George's Company, in the 18th Battalion on August 18, 1776 (C-84, G-61).

McCLEAN, JAMES. Oath of Allegiance in 1778 (A-10).

McCLEAN, JOHN. Oath of Allegiance in 1778 (A-10).

McCLEAN, ROBERT. Oath of Allegiance in 1778 (A-10).

McCLEARY, THOMAS. Oath of Allegiance in 1778 (A-13).

McCLELLAND, GEORGE. Private in Capt. John Oglevie's Company of Militia, July 25, 1776 (C-85, G-647).

McCLELLAND, NATHANIEL. Oath of Allegiance in 1778 (A-11). Nathaniel "McCleland" married Elizabeth Wheatley by license dated January 13, 1784 (O-6).

McCLELON, JAMES. Oath of Allegiance in 1778 (A-7).

McCLELON, ROBERT. Oath of Allegiance in 1778 (A-7).

McCLINTOCK, JOHN. Private in Capt. Walter Alexander's Company, 30th Battalion, enrolled July 24, 1776 (C-86, G-62). He took the Oath of Allegiance in 1778 (A-16).

McCLOUD, ALEXANDER. Oath of Allegiance in 1778 (A-14).

McCLOUD, JOHN. Oath of Allegiance in 1778 (A-15). John McCloud married Ann Vanlear, March 28, 1778 (O-1).

McCLUER, WILLIAM. Oath of Allegiance in 1778 (A-8).

McCLURE, CHARLES. Oath of Allegiance in 1778 (A-10).

McCLURE, WILLIAM. Oath of Allegiance in 1778 (A-9).

McCLUREY, JOHN. Oath of Allegiance in 1778 (A-4).

McCLUREY, SAMUEL. Oath of Allegiance in 1778 (A-4).

McCOLLA, JOHN. Private in the 4th Regiment, Light Dragoons under Captain Moylan in Col. Harry Lee's Legion, for a three year term that began April 10, 1777 (G-588, G-599).

McCOLLACH, JOHN. "John McCulloch" was an Ensign in Capt. Jeremiah Baker's Company in 1777, and "John McCollock" was a 2nd Lieutenant in that same company in the 30th Battalion on September 9, 1778 (E-58, S-MdHR6636-9-93). "John McCollach" took Oath of Allegiance in 1778 (A-6).

McCOLLACH, SAMUEL. Oath of Allegiance in 1778 (A-6).

McCOLLAGH (McCOLLACH), SAMUEL JR. Private in Capt. Jeremiah Baker's Company, 30th Battalion, August 1, 1775, and in Capt. Baruch Williams' Co., March 3, 1776 (F-157, I-27).

McCOLLOM, JAMES. Oath of Allegiance in 1778 (A-17). John McCollom md Margaret Reed by license Jan. 8, 1782 (O-5).

McCONKEY, JOHN. Oath of Allegiance in 1778 (A-6).

McCONKEY, WILLIAM. Oath of Allegiance in 1778 (A-6).

McCONNELL, JOHN. Oath of Allegiance in 1778 (A-6).

McCONNELL, SAMUEL. Sergeant in Capt. Henry Dobson's Co., 6th Maryland Line in 1780, having enlisted June 10, 1778 for 3 years (G-347). An Order passed in November session, 1812, for the "Treasurer of the Western Shore to pay to Samuel McConnell, of Cecil County, a sum of money equal to half pay of a Sergeant, as a remuneration for his services during the Revolutionary War." (N-369)

McCONNELL, STEPHEN. Private in Capt. Walter Alexander's Co., 30th Battalion, enrolled July 24, 1776 (C-86, G-62).

McCOOLE, JOHN. Private in Capt. Joshua George's Company, 18th Battalion, August 18, 1776 (C-84, G-61).

McCOULOUGH, ALEXANDER. Oath of Allegiance in 1778 (A-5).

McCOULOUGH, JAMES. Oath of Allegiance in 1778 (A-5). James "McCullough" married Jane Green, May 16, 1779 (O-3).

McCOLLOUGH, JOHN. Private in Capt. Jeremiah Baker's Company in the 30th Battalion, August 1, 1775 and in Capt. Baruch Williams' Company, March 3, 1776 (F-157, I-27). He took the Oath of Allegiance in 1778 (A-10).

McCOULOUGH, WILLIAM. Oath of Allegiance in 1778 (A-5).

McCRACKEN (McCRAKEN), JAMES. Private (Dragoon) in Major Henry (Col. Harry) Lee's Partizan Corps, April 7, 1778. Discharged August 20, 1783 (G-587, G-588, I-611, K-156).

McCREA, HUGH. Oath of Allegiance in 1778 (A-15). Private in the Militia by October 1, 1778 (S-MdHR6636-12-37A).

McCRERY, JOHN. Oath of Allegiance in 1778 (A-6).

McCRERY, THOMAS SR. Oath of Allegiance in 1778 (A-6). He appears to have served because he was due a military clothing allowance on March 6, 1779 (L-38).

McCULLOCH, WILLIAM. Private in Capt. Jeremiah Baker's Co., in the 30th Battalion, August 1, 1775, and Capt. Baruch Williams' Company, March 3, 1776 (F-157, I-27).

McCULLOUGH: See "McCollach" and "McCoulough."

McCULOGH, WILLIAM. Oath of Allegiance in 1778 (A-13).

McCURDEY, DANIEL. Private in Capt. Joshua George's Company, in the 18th Battalion, August 18, 1776 (C-84, G-61).

McCURDEY, DAVID. Private in Capt. Joshua George's Company, in the 18th Battalion, August 18, 1776 (C-84, G-61).

McCURDEY, JOHN. Private in Capt. Joshua George's Company, in the 18th Battalion, August 18, 1776 (C-84, G-61).

McCUTCHEN, FRANCIS. Oath of Allegiance in 1778 (A-16). "Francis McCutcheon" appears to have served since he was due a military clothing allowance, March 6, 1779 (L-38).

McCUTCHEN, JOHN. Oath of Allegiance in 1778 (A-16).

McDEAD, JOHN. Oath of Allegiance in 1778 (A-9).

McDONALD, PATRICK. Recruited, October 16, 1780 (G-345).

McDOWELL, BENJAMIN. Private in Capt. Stephen Hyland's Company of Militia on September 8, 1775 (T-MS.1814). He took the Oath of Allegiance in 1778 (A-8).

McDOWELL, HUGH. Private in Capt. John Oglevie's Company of Militia, July 25, 1776 (C-85, G-647). Also served as a Matross in the Artillery of the Maryland Line (C-82).

McDOWELL, JOHN. Two men with this name took the Oath of Allegiance in 1778 (A-6, A-8).

McDOWELL, JOSEPH. Oath of Allegiance in 1778 (A-4).

McDOWELL, MATTHEW. Private in Capt. John Oglevie's Company of Militia, July 25, 1776 (C-85, G-647). He took the Oath of Allegiance in 1778 (A-6).

McDUGAL, JOSEPH. Oath of Allegiance in 1778 (A-2). Private in the Militia by October 1, 1778 (S-MdHR6636-12-37A).

McELPIN, THOMAS. Oath of Allegiance in 1778 (A-16).

McFADEN, PATRICK. Private in Capt. Walter Alexander's Co., 30th Battalion, enrolled July 27, 1776 (C-86, G-62).

McFALL, DANIEL. Oath of Allegiance in 1778 (A-6).

McGAHAN, HENRY. Private in Capt. Joshua George's Company, in the 18th Battalion, August 18, 1776 (C-84, G-61).

McGARRETY, JAMES. Oath of Allegiance in 1778 (A-5).

McGARRETY, RICHARD. Oath of Allegiance in 1778 (A-5).

McGAUGHEY, ALEXANDER. Oath of Allegiance in 1778 (A-4).

McGIFFIN, NATHANIEL. Oath of Allegiance in 1778 (A-6).

McGILLAN, MICHAEL. Oath of Allegiance in 1778 (A-2).

McGILLAN, MICHAEL JR. Oath of Allegiance in 1778 (A-2).

McGLOCHLIN, OWEN. Oath of Allegiance in 1778 (A-16).

McGOWEN, HEKET. Oath of Allegiance in 1778 (A-15). One "Hackrey McGowne" md Ann Pettit, Sept. 8, 1778 (O-2).

McGOWEN, JAMES. Oath of Allegiance in 1778 (A-11).

McGOWEN, JOHN. Oath of Allegiance in 1778 (A-11).

McGREAGOR, WILLIAM. He is named among the "deserters sent to Chester Town" on October 16, 1780 (G-346).

McGUFFIN, DANIEL. Private in Capt. John Oglevie's Company of Militia, July 25, 1776 (C-85, G-647).

McGUIRE, HUGH. Oath of Allegiance in 1778 (A-12).

McGUIRE, PATRICK. He had fled the state and "supposed to be gone to the British Army," by September 1, 1777 (K-121).

McHENDRICKS, JAMES. Private in Capt. Edward Veazey's Company in 1776 (C-85).

McHERD, ALEXANDER. Oath of Allegiance in 1778 (A-16).

McHUGH, WILLIAM. Oath of Allegiance in 1778 (A-7).

McINTYRE, JOHN. Oath of Allegiance in 1778 (A-16).

McKEOWN, JOHN. Married Mary Winchester, February 16, 1780 (Cecil County license). A daughter, Elizabeth McKeown (1790-1871), married Joseph Grant (1797-1883). (O-4 and data from Jon H. Livezey, Esq., a descendant, in 1988). John McKeown took the Oath of Allegiance in 1778 (A-5).

McKEOWN, SAMUEL. Two men with this name took the Oath of Allegiance, 1778 (A-5, A-6). "Samuel McKeown, Gentleman" was Second Lieutenant in Capt. Samuel Maffitt's Company in the 2nd or Elk Battalion by April 21, 1778 (E-25, E-54, N-370, S-MdHR6636-12-37A, S-MdHR6636-9-93).

McKEOWN, WILLIAM. Private in Capt. Jeremiah Baker's Company in the 30th Battalion, August 1, 1775, and Capt. Baruch Williams' Company, March 3, 1776 (F-157, I-27). He took the Oath of Allegiance in 1778 (A-6).

McKEY, JOHN ALEX. Sergeant in Capt. Henry Dobson's Company in the 6th Maryland Line. He was On Command in the Light Infantry in North Carolina in October, 1780 (G-347).

McKIBBIN, JAMES. Private in Capt. John Oglevie's Company of Militia, July 25, 1776 (C-85, G-647). (See "McCibbins".)

McKINLEY, ALEXANDER. Oath of Allegiance in 1778 (A-16).

McKINSEY, JOHN. Oath of Allegiance in 1778 (A-3).

McLAUGHLIN, JAMES. Oath of Allegiance in 1778 (A-5).

McLAUGHLIN (McLOUGHLIN), MATTHEW. He was named among those due a military clothing allowance, March 6, 1779 (L-38).

McLEAN, JAMES. Oath of Allegiance in 1778 (A-5).

McMAHON, BENJAMIN. Private in Capt. John Oglevie's Company of Militia, July 25, 1776 (C-85, G-647).

McMAHON, MORRIS. Recruited, October 16, 1780 (G-345).

McMASTER, ROBERT. Oath of Allegiance in 1778 (A-13).

McMULLAN (McMULLEN), JOHN. Oath of Allegiance, 1778 (A-2).

McMULLIN (McMULLEN), SAMUEL. Oath of Allegiance, 1778 (A-5).

McMULLIN, SAMUEL JR. Oath of Allegiance in 1778 (A-5).

McMULLON, DANIEL. Oath of Allegiance in 1778 (A-10).

McMULLON (McMULLEN), ROBERT. Oath of Allegiance, 1778 (A-10)

McNAMARA (McNAMARR), GEORGE. Private in Capt. Joshua George's Co., 18th Battalion, Aug. 18, 1776 (C-84, G-61).

McNAMARA, PATRICK. Private in Capt. Edward Veazey's Company in 1776 (C-85).

McNAUGHT, HUGH. Oath of Allegiance in 1778 (A-10).

McNEELY, JOSEPH. Oath of Allegiance in 1778 (A-10).

McNEIL, WILLIAM. Sergeant in Capt. Henry Dobson's Co., in the 6th Maryland Line, in N. C. in October, 1780 (G-347).

McNINEK (McNINEH), JAMES. Oath of Allegiance in 1778 (A-6).

McSHEEHY, EUGENE LEWIS. Oath of Allegiance in 1778 (A-6).

McSHEEHY, MARMADUKE. Oath of Allegiance in 1778 (A-7).

McVEY, BENJAMIN. Private in Capt. Jeremiah Baker's Company, in the 30th Battalion, August 1, 1775 and in Capt. Baruch Williams' Company, March 3, 1776 (F-158, I-27).

McVEY (McVEGH), JACOB. (Son of Benjamin McVey). Private in Capt. Jeremiah Baker's Company, 30th Battalion, August 1, 1775 and in Capt. Baruch Williams' Company, March 3, 1776 (F-158, I-27). Took the Oath of Allegiance in 1778 (A-6).

McVEY (McVEGH), JOHN. (Son of Benjamin McVey). Private in Capt. Jeremiah Baker's Company, 30th Battalion, August 1, 1775 and in Capt. Baruch Williams' Company, March 3, 1776 (F-158, I-27). Took the Oath of Allegiance in 1778 (A-6).

McVEY, JOHN. Private in Capt. Jeremiah Baker's Company, in the 30th Battalion, August 1, 1775, and in Capt. Baruch Williams' Company, March 3, 1776 (F-158, I-27). One John McVey married Mary Shields, April 30, 1787 (O-8).

McVEY (McVEGH), JOHN SR. Private in Capt. Jeremiah Baker's Company, in 30th Battalion, August 1, 1775 and in Capt. Baruch Williams' Company, March 3, 1776 (F-158, I-27).

McVINCHY, EDWARD. Oath of Allegiance in 1778 (A-13).

McWHIRTER, JOHN. Oath of Allegiance in 1778 (A-4).

McWILLIAMS, WILLIAM. Private in Capt. Joshua George's Company, 18th Battalion, August 18, 1776 (C-84, G-61).

MEANS, BENJAMIN. Took the Oath of Allegiance in 1778 (A-16). "Benjamin Muns" (Means?) was among those who received a military clothing allowance on March 6, 1779 (L-38).

MEANS, JOHN. Oath of Allegiance in 1778 (A-7).

MEAS, ROBERT. Oath of Allegiance in 1778 (A-5).

MEDLICOTT (MIDDLECUT), JAMES. Private in Capt. Joshua George's Company, 18th Battalion, August 18, 1776 (C-84, G-61). Took the Oath of Allegiance in 1778 (A-17).

MEGLOHLAND, MATHEW. Oath of Allegiance in 1778 (A-6).

MEKINS (MEKENS), JOSHUA. Oath of Allegiance in 1778 (A-2). Joshua "Meekins" md Hannah Price, Sept. 16, 1785 (O-7).

MEKINS (MAKENS), RICHARD. Oath of Allegiance in 1778 (A-2).

MEKINS, RICHARD JR. Oath of Allegiance in 1778 (A-4).

MENE, BENJAMIN. Oath of Allegiance in 1778 (A-6).

MENTEHEN (MENTEKEN), JAMES. Oath of Allegiance, 1778 (A-6).

MERCER (MARCER), JAMES. Oath of Allegiance in 1778 (A-11). One James Mercer married Ann Othoson, Sept. 8, 1779 (O-3) and James Mercer married Ann Groves, May 4, 1795 (O-15).

MERCER, THOMAS SR. Oath of Allegiance, 1778 (A-12). Thomas Mercer married Jane Oliver, December 13, 1732 (R-121).

MERCER, WILLIAM. Oath of Allegiance in 1780 (B-116).

MERIT, WILLIAM. Oath of Allegiance in 1778 (A-15).

MICHELL, WILLIAM. Oath of Allegiance in 1778 (B-116).

MILLBOURN, NICHOLAS. Oath of Allegiance in 1778 (A-7). "Nich. Milburn" was a Private in Capt. Henry Dobson's Company, 6th Maryland Line, in N. C. in 1780 (G-347). "Nicholas Milburn" md Jane Moody, Jan. 25, 1785 (O-7).

MILLER, ANDREW. Captain of Militia in the Elk Battalion under Col. Henry Hollingsworth and then under Col. Edward Parker by April 9, 1778 (C-87, E-26, S-MdHR6636-12-37A, E-54). Took the Oath of Allegiance in 1778 (A-2).

MILLER, BENJAMIN. Oath of Allegiance in 1778 (A-2).

MILLER, HENRY. Oath of Allegiance in 1778 (A-8). Henry Miller, Jr. married Sarah Knox, August 10, 1780 (O-4).

MILLER, JAMES. Oath of Allegiance in 1778 (A-5).

MILLER, JOHN. Oath of Allegiance in 1778 (A-8). John Miller married Margaret McCray, August 3, 1778 (O-2) and a John Miller married Rebecca Davis, October 19, 1794 (O-15).

MILLER, SAMUEL. One of the Justices who administered the Oath of Allegiance in March, 1778 (A-5). Captain in the 30th Battalion under Col. Joseph Baxter in 1777 and under Colonel Stephen Hyland, September 9, 1778 (E-57, K-116, S-MdHR4570-72, S-MdHR6636-9-93).

MILLER, THOMAS. Oath of Allegiance in 1778 (A-6). Thomas Miller married Elizabeth Wilson, April 14, 1795 (O-15).

MILLER, WILLIAM. Two men with this name took the Oath of Allegiance in 1778 (A-7, A-18). One William Miller married Rebecca Bradford, June 13, 1778 (O-2).

MILLIGAN, JAMES. Oath of Allegiance in 1778 (A-5).

MILLS, JOHN. Corporal in Capt. Walter Alexander's Company, enrolled July 24, 1776 (C-86, G-62). Took the Oath of Allegiance in 1778 (A-7).

MILLS, ROBERT. Oath of Allegiance in 1778 (A-7).

MINOR, JOHN. Private in Capt. John Oglevie's Company of Militia, July 25, 1776 (C-85, G-647).

MITCHELL, ABRAHAM (1733-1817). Born in Lancaster County, Pennsylvania, he came to Cecil County at age 25 and settled at Head of Elk (Elkton) where he established his medical practice. He married Mary Thompson, daughter of Dr. Ephraim Thompson, on November 19, 1772. Their sons were George Edward Mitchell, Ephraim Thompson Mitchell, and Abraham David Mitchell (J-496). Dr. Abraham Mitchell took the Oath of Allegiance in 1778 (A-7). During the Revolution, he converted his home into a hospital for the use of wounded soldiers of the Continental line (J-496).

MITCHELL, ANDREW. Private in Capt. Joshua George's Company, 18th Battalion, August 18, 1776 (C-84, G-61). Took the Oath of Allegiance in 1778 (A-6).

MITCHELL, JOHN. Private in Maryland Continental Line (C-82).

MITCHELL, JOHN JR. Oath of Allegiance in 1778 (A-7).

MITCHELL, ROBERT. He served as a Matross in the Artillery of the Maryland Line (C-82). As shown on the muster rolls of January 24 to February 3, 1776, he was age 22, born in Charlestown, and was a sadler by occupation (T-MS.1814).

MITCHELL, WILLIAM. Private in the Maryland Line of the Continental Army (C-82). Oath of Allegiance, 1778 (A-7).

MOFFITT: See "Maffitt."

MONEY, HYLAND. Oath of Allegiance in 1778 (A-8).

MONEY, ISAAC. Private in Capt. Joshua George's Company, 18th Battalion, August 18, 1776 (C-84, G-61). Took the Oath of Allegiance in 1778 (A-11). Isaac Money married Rachel Husley, January 14, 1784 (O-6).

MONEY (MOONEY), JOHN (January 26, 1743 - 1825). He married Mary----- and had 3 children: Aletha (married a Cosden), William, and Susan (U-197). John Money took the Oath of Allegiance in 1778 (A-14).

MONEY, ROBERT. 2nd Lieutenant in Capt. John W. Veazey's Company in the 18th or Sassafrass Battalion, June 22, 1778 (E-56). Took the Oath of Allegiance in 1778 (A-14).

MONEY, SAMUEL. Private in Capt. Joshua George's Company, 18th Battalion, August 18, 1776 (C-84, G-61). Took the Oath of Allegiance in 1778 (A-11).

MONTGOMERY, HUGH DR. (Of Charlestown). Served as a Surgeon in the Maryland Line of the Continental Army (C-82). Hugh Montgomery married Mary Gibson, May 14, 1789 (O-10).

MONTGOMERY, JOHN. Took Oath of Allegiance in 1778 (A-4). "Dr. John H. Montgomery" married Mary Currer, December 14, 1784 (O-7).

MOODY, ALEXANDER. Oath of Allegiance, 1778 (A-7). Alexander Moody married Leah Moody, February 25, 1789 (O-10).

MOODY, BENJAMIN. Private in Capt. John Oglevie's Company of Militia, July 25, 1776 (C-85, G-647).

MOODY, JOHN. Two men with this name took the Oath of Allegiance in 1778 (A-5, A-15).

MOORE (MOOR), ALEXANDER. Private in Capt. Stephen Hyland's Militia Company on September 8, 1775 (T-MS.1814). He took the Oath of Allegiance in 1778 (A-8).

MOORE, FERDINAND. Oath of Allegiance in 1778 (A-10).

MOORE, GEORGE. Oath of Allegiance in 1778 (A-10).

MOORE (MOOR), HUGH. Private in Capt. Jeremiah Baker's Company, in the 30th Battalion, August 1, 1775 and in Capt. Baruch Williams' Company, March 3, 1776 (F-158, I-27). He took the Oath of Allegiance in 1778 (A-5).

MOORE, ROBERT. Oath of Allegiance in 1778 (A-9).

MOORE, ROBERT JR. Oath of Allegiance in 1778 (A-10).

MOORE, ROBERT SR. Oath of Allegiance in 1778 (A-10).

MORAN, BENJAMIN. Private in Capt. Henry Dobson's Company in the 6th Maryland Line. On Detachment with Gen. Smallwood in North Carolina in October, 1780 (G-349).

MORAN, WILLIAM. Private in Capt. Henry Dobson's Company in the 6th Maryland Line, in N. C. in October, 1780 (G-348).

MORGAN, DAVID. Two men with this name took the Oath of Allegiance in 1778 (A-7, A-16).

MORGAN, JAMES (c1748 - September 17, 1823). He married Sarah Bryon and had eight children: William (born 1780 (married Jane Jones); Ann (married a Price); Elizabeth (married a Hyland); Araminta (married a Veazey); Rebecca (married a Nowland); James; Abigail; and, Sarah (U-200). James took the Oath of Allegiance in 1778 (A-14).

MORGAN, JOHN. Oath of Allegiance in 1778 (A-2).

MORGAN, MATTHEW. Private in Capt. John Oglevie's Company of Militia, July 25, 1776 (C-85, G-647).

MORGAN, RULIF. Oath of Allegiance in 1778 (A-5). "Rulof" Morgan was an Ensign in Capt. Samuel Miller's Company, in the 30th Battalion, in 1777 (S-MdHR6636-9-93).

MORGAN, THOMAS. Oath of Allegiance in 1778 (A-5).

MORGAN, WILLIAM. Oath of Allegiance in 1778 (A-12).

MORLEDGE, SAMUEL.  Oath of Allegiance in 1778 (A-8).

MORRISON, DAVID.  Private in Capt. John Oglevie's Company of Militia, July 25, 1776 (C-85, G-647).

MORRISON, MICHAEL.  Private in Capt. Joshua George's Company in the 18th Battalion, August 18, 1776 (C-84, G-61).

MORRISON, SAMUEL.  Oath of Allegiance in 1778 (A-4).

MORRISON, WILLIAM.  Oath of Allegiance in 1778 (A-4).

MORROW, JAMES.  Private in Capt. John Oglevie's Company of Militia, July 25, 1776 (C-85, G-647).  Two men with this name took the Oath of Allegiance in 1778 (A-6, A-7).

MORROW (MORRAU), JOHN.  Oath of Allegiance in 1778 (A-11).

MORYNIN (VOIYNLN?), JACOB.  Oath of Allegiance in 1778 (A-5).

MOSS, JOSEPH.  Private in Capt. Joshua George's Company, 18th Battalion, August 18, 1776 (C-84, G-61).  Took the Oath of Allegiance in 1778 (A-14).  Joseph Moss married Jemima Pennington, June 16, 1778 (O-2).

MOULDIN:  See "Mauldin."

MUIR, JOHN.  Oath of Allegiance in 1778 (A-13).

MULLIN (MULLAN), CHARLES.  Oath of Allegiance in 1778 (A-2).

MULLIN (MULLAN), JOHN.  Oath of Allegiance in 1778 (A-2).

MULLIN (MULLON), THOMAS.  Oath of Allegiance in 1778 (A-10).

MULLIN (MULLEN), WILLIAM.  Private in Capt. John Oglevie's Company of Militia, July 25, 1776 (C-85, G-647).  Took the Oath of Allegiance on February 26, 1778 (A-6).

MULLINS, JONATHAN.  Private in Capt. Walter Alexander's Co., 30th Battalion, enrolled July 24, 1776 (C-86, G-62).

MULLOT, PETER.  Oath of Allegiance in 1778 (A-7).  Peter "Mullet" married Mary Flannagin, Dec. 19, 1791 (O-12).

MUNFORD, PETER.  Recruited, October 16, 1780 (G-345).

MUNKS, JAMES.  He appeared to have served because he is named on a List of Defectives from the Maryland Line on October 2, 1780, as being a resident of "Scicell County" (C-414).

MURPHY (MURPHEY), EDWARD.  Oath of Allegiance in 1778 (A-5).

MURPHY (MURPHEY), FRANCIS.  Oath of Allegiance, 1778 (A-11).

MURPHY (MURPHEY), JOHN. Oath of Allegiance in 1778 (A-10).

MURPHY, JOSEPH. Oath of Allegiance in 1778 (A-15).

MURPHY (MURPHEY), THOMAS. Oath of Allegiance in 1778 (A-8).

MURRAY, ALEXANDER. 2nd Lieutenant in Maryland Line (C-82).

MUSE, WALKER, Ensign in the Maryland Line (C-82).

NASH. GEORGE. Oath of Allegiance in 1778 (A-7).

NASH, JOHN. Oath of Allegiance in 1778 (A-7).

NEAD, JOHN. He appears to have served because he was due a military clothing allowance on March 6, 1779 (L-38).

NEEDS, JAMES. Recruited, October 16, 1780 (G-345).

NEIGHBOURS, JOSEPH. Recruited, October 16, 1780 (G-345).

NEILL, THOMAS. Oath of Allegiance in 1778 (A-7).

NELSON, JOHN. Oath of Allegiance in 1778 (A-3).

NELSON, WILLIAM. First Lieutenant in Capt. Charles Heath's Company, 18th or Bohemia Battalion, June 22, 1778 (E-56, S-MdHR6636-9-93). Took Oath of Allegiance in 1778 (A-4).

NESBIT: See "Nisbett."

NEWEL, RICHARD. Oath of Allegiance in 1778 (A-13).

NEWEL, STEPHEN. Oath of Allegiance in 1778 (A-13).

NEWEL (NEWELL), THOMAS. Private in Capt. John Oglevie's Company, July 25, 1776 (C-85, G-647). Took the Oath of Allegiance in 1778 (A-13).

NICHOLAS, JOHN. Oath of Allegiance in 1778 (A-17).

NICKELSON, JOHN. Private in Capt. Jeremiah Baker's Company, 30th Battalion, August 1, 1775 and Capt. Baruch Williams' Company, March 3, 1776 (F-158, I-27). Took the Oath of Allegiance in 1778 (A-6).

NIGLE, JACOB. Oath of Allegiance in 1778 (A-5). (Ed.: In brackets and over Jacob Nigle's name was the name of one Jacob Voiynln or Morynin. The words "for his name" were written beside that of Jacob Nigle as if to imply a name change or an inference that they were one and the same.)

NISBETT, JAMES. Oath of Allegiance in 1778 (A-10).

NISBETT, JOHN. Oath of Allegiance in 1778 (A-10).

NISBETT, JOSEPH JR.   Oath of ALlegiance in 1778 (A-10).

NISBETT, JOSEPH SR.   Oath of Allegiance in 1778 (A-10).

NISBETT, ROBERT.   Oath of Allegiance in 1778 (A-10). Robert "Nesbit" married Eleanor Lyon, November 9, 1779 (O-3).

NOBLE, PHILEMON.   Oath of Allegiance in 1778 (A-4).

NORTON, EDWARD.   Oath of Allegiance in 1778 (A-8).

NORTON, NATHAN.   (Of Charlestown). Was a soldier in the Delaware Regiment during the Revolutionary War (C-83).

NOWELL, JAMES.   Private in Capt. Henry Dobson's Company in the 6th Maryland Line, in N. C. in October, 1780 (G-348).

NOWLAN (NEWLAN), NATHAN.   Oath of Allegiance in 1778 (A-17).

NOWLAND (NOLAND), ELIAS.   Ensign in Capt. Charles Heath's Company in the 18th Battalion, June 22, 1778 (E-56, S-MdHR6636-9-93). "Alias Nowland" took the Oath of Allegiance in 1778 (A-17).

NOWLAND, GILBERT.   Private in Capt. Joshua George's Company, 18th Battalion on August 18, 1776 (C-84, G-61). Gilbert Nowland married Esther Hollings, January 5, 1778 (O-1).

NOWLAND, JOHN (c1753 - February 15, 1815). He married Lydia Weldon (1769-1857) on August 11, 1788, and had a son, Benoni who married Margaret Miller (U-547). John was a Private in Capt. Joshua George's Company in the 18th Battalion on August 18, 1776 (C-84, G-61). John "Noland" took the Oath of Allegiance in 1778 (A-6).

NOWLAND, RICHARD.   Oath of Allegiance in 1778 (A-17).

NUGENT, SILVESTER.   Oath of Allegiance in 1778 (A-8).

NUTT, WILLIAM.   Oath of Allegiance in 1778 (A-7). He appears to have served because he was due a military clothing allowance on March 6, 1779 (L-38).

OAR, ROBERT.   Oath of Allegiance in 1778 (A-6).

OBOURN (OSBORN), JAMES.   Oath of Allegiance in 1778 (A-7).

O'FLINN, PATRICK.   Oath of Allegiance in 1778 (A-10).

OGLEVIE (OGLEVEE), JOHN.   Captain in the Militia under Col. Henry Hollingsworth on April 10, 1776 and Elk Battalion, April 9, 1778 (C-85, D-117, E-29, E-54, S-MdHR6636-9-93, G-647, S-MdHR6636-12-37A, I-47, W-131, W-132). He took the Oath of Allegiance in 1778 (A-6) and was among those due a military clothing allowance, March 6, 1779 (L-38). (Source P-320 mistakenly gives his name as "Ogelby.")

OLDHAM, EDWARD (December 8, 1756 - November 4, 1798). He married Mary Ensor (1764-1819) on November 21, 1784 and had eight children: Maria (born 1786); Elizabeth (born 1787); Edward (born 1789); Augustine H. (born 1790); George Washington (born 1792, married Susan Ann Biddle); Charles (born 1793); Hamet (born 1795); and, Ann (U-549). Edward was a Lieutenant, Captain and then Major (V-211, C-87). (Ed.: Not to be confused with Edward Oldham of Baltimore County who was also a Captain in the MD Line.)

OLDHAM, JEREMIAH. Oath of Allegiance in 1778 (A-6).

OLDHAM, MOSES. Oath of Allegiance in 1778 (A-6).

OLDHAM, NATHAN. Oath of Allegiance in 1778 (A-6). Nathan Oldham married Elizabeth Giles, Nov. 18, 1766 (R-132).

OLDHAM, RICHARD. Ensign in the Militia (C-87). Took the Oath of Allegiance in 1778 (A-6).

OLDHAM, ROBERT. Oath of Allegiance in 1778 (A-6).

OLDHAM, THOMAS. Oath of Allegiance in 1778 (A-6).

O'NAIL, FELIX. He appeared to have served because he is named as "a recruit, deserted" and is listed among the "deserters sent to Chester Town," Oct. 16, 1780 (G-346).

ORRICK, JAMES. Oath of Allegiance in 1778 (A-15). James "Orick" married Hannah Slycer, August 6, 1783 (O-6).

OTHOSON, GARRETT. Private in Capt. Joshua George's Company, 18th Battalion, August 18, 1776 (C-84, G-61). Took the Oath of Allegiance in 1778 (A-11).

OWENS, DAVID. Oath of Allegiance in 1778 (A-6).

OWENS, ELIAS. Oath of Allegiance in 1778 (A-2).

OWENS, FRANCIS. Oath of Allegiance in 1778 (A-5).

OWENS, JOHN. Oath of Allegiance in 1778 (A-8).

OWENS, JOSEPH. Oath of Allegiance in 1778 (A-8). Private in Major Henry (Col. Harry) Lee's Partizan Corps as early as April 7, 1778 and served through at least December, 1780, and possibly longer (K-156, C-83, G-586, G-587).

OWENS, STEPHAN. Private in Capt. Henry Dobson's Company in the 6th Maryland Line, in North Carolina in October, 1780 (G-348). One "Stephen Owen" married Mary Ann Gaunce, November 1, 1804 (Q-120), and one "Stephen Owens" married Elizabeth Harwood, January 18, 1785 (O-7).

OWENS, THOMAS. Private in Capt. Walter Alexander's Company, 30th Battalion, enrolled July 24, 1776 (C-86, G-62). Two men with this name took the Oath of Allegiance in March, 1778 (A-7, A-15). Another (or the same) Thomas Owens (or Owins) was a Private in Major Henry (Col. Harry) Lee's Partizan Corps in June, 1778 (C-83, G-586, G-587).

OWINGS, BARTHOLOMEW. Oath of Allegiance in 1778 (A-11).

PALMER, THOMAS. Oath of Allegiance in 1778 (A-5).

PARKER, EDMOND. He appears to have served because he is listed among those who were due a military clothing allowance on March 6, 1779 (L-38).

PARKER, EDWARD. First Major in the Elk Battalion under Col. Charles Rumsey on January 6, 1776, Lieutenant Colonel in 1777 under Col. H. Hollingsworth, and Colonel of the Elk Battalion, Apr. 21, 1778 (E-30, E-54, I-60, I-177, J-323. S-MdHR6636-9-93). Took Oath of Allegiance in 1778 (A-6). Military clothing allowance on March 6, 1779 (L-38). One Edward Parker was ordered by the Council of Safety on September 28, 1776, to furnish linen sufficient to make tents for Capt. Evans' Company (W-307).

PARKER, SAMUEL. Oath of Allegiance in 1778 (A-7).

PARKER, SAMUEL JR. Oath of Allegiance in 1778 (A-16).

PARKS, DAVID. Oath of Allegiance in 1778 (A-6).

PARKS, JOHN. He appears to have served because he was due a military clothing allowance on March 6, 1779 (L-38).

PARRY, EDWARD. Oath of Allegiance in 1778 (A-7).

PARSLEY, BENJAMIN. Oath of Allegiance in 1778 (A-11).

PARSLEY, EDWARD. Oath of Allegiance in 1778 (A-14). One Edward married Rebecca Walmsley, January 3, 1779 (O-2), and one married Priscilla Mulsey, Nov. 24, 1789 (O-10).

PARSLEY, THOMAS. Private in Capt. Joshua George's Company, 18th Battalion, August 18, 1776 (C-84, G-61).

PARSLEY, THOMAS JR. Oath of Allegiance in 1778 (A-11).

PASSMORE, WILLIAM. Oath of Allegiance in 1778 (A-6).

PATTEN, THOMAS. Oath of Allegiance in 1778 (A-5).

PATTEN, WILLIAM. Oath of Allegiance in 1778 (A-13).

PATTERSON, DAVID JR. Oath of Allegiance in 1778 (A-10).

PATTERSON, HUGH. Two men with this name took the Oath of

Allegiance in 1778 (A-11, A-15).

PATTERSON, JOHN. Two men with this name took Oath of Allegiance in 1778 (A-13, A-16). One was a Second Lieutenant in 1776 and then First Lieutenant in Capt. Robert Porter's Company, 30th Battalion, under Col. C. Baxter in 1777 and under Col. S. Hyland on September 9, 1778 (C-84, E-57 G-61, S-MdHR6636-9-93, S-MdHR4570-72, K-116). The other John Patterson was a Private in Capt. W. Alexander's Co., enrolled July 24, 1776 (C-86, G-62).

PATTERSON, JOSEPH. Oath of Allegiance in 1778 (A-15).

PATTERSON, ROBERT. Oath of Allegiance in 1778 (A-6).

PATTERSON, SAMUEL. Oath of Allegiance in 1778 (A-10).

PATTERSON, WILLIAM. Private in Capt. Joshua George's Company, 18th Battalion, August 18, 1776 (C-84, G-61). William Patterson md Jane Callendar, May 31, 1780 (O-4).

PATTON, DAVID. Oath of Allegiance in 1778 (A-10). David Patton married Eleanor Guy, November 3, 1788 (O-9).

PATTON, JAMES. Oath of Allegiance in 1778 (A-10).

PATTON, MICHAEL. Oath of Allegiance in 1778 (A-10).

PATTON, THOMAS. Oath of Allegiance in 1778 (A-10). Thomas Patton married Millicent Rice, August 7, 1790 (O-11).

PAUL, JOHN. Oath of Allegiance in 1778 (A-18).

PAYENTER, SAMUEL. Private in Capt. Walter Alexander's Co., 30th Battn., enrolled July 22, 1776 (C-86, G-62).

PEALE, JAMES. (Of Charlestown). Lieutenant in the Maryland Line (C-82).

PEARCE, BENJAMIN. Oath of Allegiance in 1778 (A-4). Benjamin Pearce married Margarett Ward, daughter of Henry Ward, July 31, 1734 (R-136).

PEARCE, BENJAMIN JR. Oath of Allegiance in 1778 (A-4). Benjamin Pearce married Ann Ruley, Feb. 8, 1790 (O-11).

PEARCE, GREGRY. "Gregry" was a Private in Capt. Walter Alexander's Company, 30th Battalion, enrolled July 24, 1776 (C-86, G-62).

PEARCE, HENRY WARD. Took the Oath of Allegiance in 1778 (A-14). He was appointed by the Maryland Council to be one of the Collectors of all gold and silver coins that could be be procured in Cecil County (P-132). Henry Ward Pearce, son of Benjamin, married Anna Statia Carroll, daughter of Dominick Carroll, January 16, 1759 (R-136).

PEARCE, JAMES (Free Mulatto). He fled the state and was "supposed to be gone to the British Army" on September 1, 1777 (K-121, S-MdHR4570-88).

PEARCE, NATHANIEL. Oath of Allegiance in 1778 (A-4).

PEARCE, THOMAS. Oath of Allegiance in 1778 (A-17). Thomas Pearce married Sarah Bayard, May 17, 1785 (O-7).

PEARCE, WILLIAM. Oath of Allegiance in 1778 (A-17). Private in Capt. Stephen Hyland's Co., Sept. 8, 1775 (T-MS.1814). William Pearce married Sarah Lynch, May 30, 1779 (O-3), and William Pearce md Amelia Taler, Dec. 2, 1780 (O-4).

PEARCE, WILLIAM JR. Oath of Allegiance in 1778 (A-4).

PEMBERTON, JOHN. Private in Capt. Joshua George's Company, 18th Battalion, August 18, 1776 (C-84, G-61).

PENNINGTON, BARTHOLOMEW. Oath of Allegiance in 1778 (A-3).

PENNINGTON, HYLAND. Oath of Allegiance in 1778 (A-17).

PENNINGTON, JAMES. Took Oath of Allegiance in 1778 (A-11). James Pennington married Elizabeth Beastin, daughter of William Beastin, December 11, 1742 (R-137).

PENNINGTON, JOHN. Two men with this name took the Oath of Allegiance in 1778 (A-14, A-17). There were several men named John Pennington who married in Cecil County: one married Catherine Money by license March 17, 1780 (O-3), one married Rebecca Price by license June 5, 1784 (O-6), one married Elizabeth Severson by license Nov. 28, 1788 (O-10), one married Alice Ward on Oct. 19, 1735 (R-137), one married Margaret Pennington on June 7, 1733 (R-137), one married Elizabeth Umberson on Nov. 25, 1733 (R-137), and John "Peninton" md Sarah Beadle, Apr 3, 1716 (R-137).

PENNINGTON, JOHN SR. Oath of Allegiance in 1778 (A-12). John Pennington, Sr. married Mary Othoson, daughter of Garriot Othoson, in October, 1740 (R-137).

PENNINGTON, ROBERT. Oath of Allegiance in 1778 (A-18). One Robert married Rebecca Price, April 26, 1788 (O-9), and one Robert married Elizabeth Moody, Mar. 14, 1795 (O-15).

PENNINGTON, SAMUEL. Took Oath of Allegiance in 1778 (A-11). Samuel Pennington married Sarah Etherington, November 4, 1789 (O-10).

PENNINGTON, THO. Oath of Allegiance in 1778 (A-17).

PENNINGTON, WILLIAM DRAKE. Took Oath of Allegiance in 1780. (B-117). William Drake Pennington married Mary Hutchison on December 22, 1777 (R-137).

PERRY, DAVID. Oath of Allegiance in 1778 (A-9).

PERRY, JAMES. Private in Capt. John Oglevie's Company, July 25, 1776 (C-85, G-647). Oath of Allegiance in 1778 (A-9). James Perry married Martha Gladen, Feb. 18, 1778 (O-1).

PERRY, LEWELLEN. Oath of Allegiance in 1778 (A-9). "Lewin" Perry married Debrah Barnett, October 27, 1778 (O-2).

PHELPS, JOSEPH. Oath of Allegiance in 1778 (A-8). A Joseph "Philips" married Elizabeth Scott, July 31, 1792 (O-13).

PHILBERT, JOSEPH. Sergeant in Capt. Henry Dobson's Company in the 6th Maryland Line. Enlisted May 30, 1778 for three years. On Guard at Hillsborough, N.C. in 1780 (G-347).

PHILLIPS, JOHN. Private in Capt. John Oglevie's Company, July 25, 1776 (C-85, G-647). John Phillips married Margaret McCallor, June 30, 1780 (O-4).

PHILLIPS, JOHN. Born in Cecil County on May 7, 1734 and moved to Frederick County and then to Rowan County, North Carolina where he was drafted into the Revolutionary War under Capt. John Lopp. Afterwards he moved to Christian County, Kentucky and applied for a pension on September 3, 1832 (age 98) and received it (S31905). (See Annie W. Burns' "Maryland Soldiers: Revolutionary War," page 31.)

PHILLIPS, NATHAN. Private in Capt. Walter Alexander's Co., 30th Battalion, enrolled August 3, 1776 (C-86, G-63). Took Oath of Allegiance in 1778 (A-15). Nathan Phillips married Elizabeth Kankey, July 30, 1777 (O-1, R-139).

PHILLIPS, SAMUEL. Oath of Allegiance in 1778 (A-6). He appears to have served in the military because he is among the List of Defectives from the Maryland Line on Sept. 21, 1780 shown as a resident of Cecil Co. (G-414).

PHILLIPS, WILLIAM. Corporal in Capt. Henry Dobson's Co. in 1777 (C-82, J-322). He is listed among those who received a military clothing allowance on March 6, 1779 (L-38).

PHILLIPS, ZEBULON. Oath of Allegiance in 1778 (A-15).

PLEXCO, GEORGE. Oath of Allegiance in 1778 (A-5).

PLEXCO, HENRY. Oath of Allegiance in 1778 (A-5).

PLUMLEY, GEORGE. Recruited, October 16, 1780 (G-345).

POALK, BARKLEY WILLIAM. Oath of Allegiance in 1778 (A-10).

POALK, DAVID. Took the Oath of Allegiance in 1778 (A-5). David "Pollock" married Anne Rowland in 1786 (Q-121).

POALK, DAVID SR. Oath of Allegiance in 1778 (A-10).

POALK (POACK), SAMUEL. Oath of Allegiance in 1778 (A-16).

POALK, THOMAS. Oath of Allegiance in 1778 (A-10).

POGUE, GEORGE. Oath of Allegiance in 1778 (A-8). Private in Capt. Stephen Hyland's Company, Sept 8, 1775 (T-MS.1814). (Ed.: This name appears twice on this 1775 enrollment.)

POLLOCK: See "Poalk."

POLSON, JOHN. Oath of Allegiance in 1778 (A-15).

POLSON, JOSEPH. Private in Capt. Stephen Hyland's Militia Company on September 8, 1775 (T-MS.1814).

PORTER, ANDREW JR. 2nd Lieutenant and then 1st Lieutenant, Captain Walter Alexander's Company, 4th Battalion, Flying Camp, July, 1776 to December 1, 1776 (an "officer of a company belonging to the Eastern Shore Battalion" as noted in Source W-174), and 2nd Lieutenant in Capt. William Ewing's Company in the 30th Battalion during 1777-1778 (D-119, C-86, G-62, E-58, S-MdHR6636-9-93).

PORTER, ANDREW SR. Oath of Allegiance in 1778 (A-10).

PORTER, BENJAMIN. Ensign in Capt. John W. Veazey's Company, 18th Battalion, and 2nd Lieutenant, June 22, 1778 (E-56, S-MdHR6636-9-93). Took Oath of Allegiance in 1778 (A-12). Benjamin, son of Robert and Elizabeth, married Anne Money, daughter of John and Rachel, Dec 31, 1775 (R-141).

PORTER, EDWARD. Major in the Militia (C-87).

PORTER, JAMES. Captain in the 18th Battalion under Col. John D. Thompson (E-56, S-MdHR6636-9-93). James was involved in a court-martial that was requested by Lieut. Colonel John Thompson of the 18th Battalion, on June 14, 1777 (I-110). The record indicated that Lt. Col. Thompson was dissatisfied that Capt. Porter was not disciplining his men for being absent from muster and he read the April, 1775 Resolves as his authority for court-martial for those who did not comply. It seems that Porter was not impressed, stating that others were more fond of his commission then he was and he cared nothing about it if he should give it up. Col. Thompson confronted Porter's men with the Resolves and all but two (unnamed) agreed to abide by it, and the matter was settled (S-MdHR4581-18).

PORTER, JESSE. Oath of Allegiance in 1778 (A-17). Jesse Porter married Rachel Cann, January 26, 1778 (O-1).

PORTER, JOSEPH. Oath of Allegiance in 1778 (A-10).

PORTER, PATRICK. Oath of Allegiance in 1778 (A-5).

PORTER, ROBERT. Two men with this name took the Oath of Allegiance in 1778 (A-13, A-17). One was a Captain in the 18th Battalion under Col. Rumsey in 1776 and then a Captain in the 30th (or Susquehanna) Battalion under Col. Baxter in 1777 and under Col. Hyland on September 9, 1778 (C-84, E-57, G-61, K-116, S-MdHR6636-9-93, S-MdHR4570-72)

PORTER, ROBERT JR. Oath of Allegiance in 1778 (A-17).

PORTER, WILLIAM. Oath of Allegiance in 1778 (A-18).

PORTERFIELD, JOSIAH. Private in Capt. John Oglevie's Company, July 25, 1776 (C-85, G-647).

PRICE, ANDREW. Oath of Allegiance in 1778 (A-11). Andrew Price married ELizabeth Perry in June, 1725 (R-143).

PRICE, BENJAMIN. Took Oath of Allegiance in 1778 (A-12). Benjamin Price married Sarah Matilda Coppen, March 28, 1793 (O-13).

PRICE, ELIAKIM. Oath of Allegiance in 1778 (A-11).

PRICE, EPHRAIM. Private in Capt. Joshua George's Company, 18th Battalion, August 18, 1776 (C-84, G-61). Took the Oath of Allegiance in 1778 (A-14). Ephraim Price married Amey Simpers, March 21, 1787 (O-8) and one Ephraim Price married Sarah Simpers, December 13, 1794 (O-15).

PRICE, HYLAND. Ensign in Capt. John Ford's Company in the 18th Battalion, and promoted to 2nd Lieutenant on June 22, 1778 (E-56, S-MdHR6636-9-93). He took the Oath of Allegiance in 1778 (A-14). He was also Sub-Sheriff of Cecil County on July 23, 1778 (I-182).

PRICE, HYLANT. Oath of Allegiance in 1778 (A-4).

PRICE, JAMES. Oath of Allegiance in 1778 (A-8). James Price married Sarah Ricketts, daughter of John Thomas Ricketts, December 18, 1740 (R-143).

PRICE, JAMES KIMBLE. Private in Capt. Joshua George's Company, 18th Battalion, August 18, 1776 (C-84, G-61).

PRICE, JESSE. Private in Capt. Walter Alexander's Co., 30th Battalion, enrolled August 3, 1776 (C-86, G-63). Jesse Price (or Pierce?) md Eleanor Ryan, June 11, 1780 (O-4).

PRICE, JOHN. Two men with this name took the Oath of Allegiance in 1778 (A-8, A-14).

PRICE, JOHN HYLAND. Oath of Allegiance in 1778 (A-12).

PRICE, JOSEPH. Oath of Allegiance in 1778 (A-12). Joseph Price married Jane Barrett, widow of Philip Barrett, November 19, 1734 (R-143).

PRICE, LEWIS. Oath of Allegiance in 1778 (A-14).

PRICE, NICHOLAS HYLAND. Oath of Allegiance in 1778 (A-14).

PRICE, NOBLE. Private in Capt. Joshua George's Company, 18th Battalion, August 18, 1776 (C-84, G-61). Took the Oath of Allegiance in 1778 (A-14). Noble Price married Catherine Walmsley, April 16, 1782 (O-5).

PRICE, THOMAS. Oath of Allegiance in 1778 (A-18). Second Lieutenant in Capt. Thomas Savin's Company in 1777, and First Lieutenant in Capt. Abraham Cazier's Company in the Elk Battalion on September 9, 1778 (E-55, S-MdHR4570-72, S-MdHR6636-9-93, K-116). Thomas Price married Margaret Smith, September 2, 1786 (O-8).

PRICE, WILLIAM. Ensign in the Militia (C-87). Two men with this name took the Oath of Allegiance, 1778 (A-14, A-18). "Rev." William Price married Mary Ryland, June 12, 1795 (O-15).

PRICE, WILLIAM JR. Took Oath of Allegiance in 1778 (A-2). William Price, Jr. married Mary Roberts, daughter of John Roberts, February 12, 1737/8 (R-144).

PRITCHARD, JAMES. Captain under Col. Joseph Baxter in the 30th Battalion, 1777-1778 (C-87, E-58, S-MdHR6636-9-93).

PUGH, JOHN. Oath of Allegiance in 1778 (A-15).

PULLIN, JOHN. Oath of Allegiance in 1778 (A-15).

PURDY, EDWARD. Drum and Fifer in Capt. Henry Dobson's Co., 6th Maryland Line, in North Carolina in 1780 (G-347).

PURDY, HENERY. Private in Capt. Henry Dobson's Company in the 6th Maryland Line. Enlisted February 5, 1780 for the duration of the war, or three years. On Guard duty at Hillsborough, North Carolina in 1780 (G-349).

PURDY, JOHN. Private in Capt. Henry Dobson's Company in the 6th Maryland Line, in North Carolina in 1780 (G-348).

PYCKLIN, WILLIAM. Oath of Allegiance in 1778 (A-4).

QUAIL, THOMAS. Private in Capt. Walter Alexander's Company, 30th Battalion, enrolled July 24, 1776 (C-86, G-62).

QUIGLEY (QUIDLEY), CHARLES. Oath of Allegiance, 1778 (A-7).

QUIGLEY, JAMES. Private in Capt. Walter Alexander's Co., in the 30th Battalion, enrolled July 27, 1776 (C-86, G-62). Took the Oath of Allegiance in 1778 (A-3).

RAIN, ISAAC. Oath of Allegiance in 1778 (A-12).

RALSTON, HUGH. Oath of Allegiance in 1778 (A-2).

RALSTON, JOSEPH. Private in Capt. Henry Dobson's Company in the 6th Maryland Line. Enlisted December 23, 1778. On Command in Hillsborough, North Carolina, in 1780 (G-349).

RAMSAY, NATHANIEL. (Of Charlestown). Born May 1, 1741 in Lancaster Co., PA, second son of James Ramsay and Jane Montgomery. Went to Charlestown, MD in 1767 to practice law (C-39). He married Margaret Jane Peale in 1771 and had a son William White Ramsay who married Eleanor Brooke Hall (J-538, U-595). He attended the Maryland Convention from April 24 to May 3, 1775 (K-1) and was also a Deputy to the Convention on May 16, 1775 (I-2, K-2, P-5). He signed the Declaration of the Freemen of Maryland in 1775 (J-322). He was elected Captain in accordance with the Maryland Resolves of January 1, 1776, serving under Col. William Smallwood at the Battle of Long Island on August 27, 1776 (J-538, H-457). On March 27, 1777 he became Lieutenant Colonel in the MD Line under Gen. William Smallwood (J-542). He was with the army at Valley Forge during the winter of 1777-1778 (J-543). He was wounded and taken prisoner at the Battle of Monmouth on June 28, 1778 and was paroled the next day (J-544). He continued to serve in the military and became a supernumerary on January 1, 1781 (and was a Lieutenant Colonel in the 3rd Battalion of Militia). He experimented with explosives and furnished gunpowder to the state (C-39, C-82). In 1783 he moved to Baltimore and upon the organizing of the Maryland Society of the Cincinnati in Annapolis on Nov. 21, 1783, he was elected its Treasurer (J-546). In 1785 he was chosen to represent Maryland in Congress for one year, and in 1790 he was appointed United States Marshal for Maryland by President George Washington (J-547). He died October 24, 1817 (Source U-595 mistakenly states he died in 1812) and was buried in Westminster Cemetery in Baltimore.

RAMSAY, THOMAS. Commissioned 2nd Lieutenant in Capt. Samuel Evans Flying Camp, 4th Battalion, Sept. 28, 1776. Marched to Philadelphia in Oct., 1776 (D-121, G-73, G-74, W-306).

RAMSEY, CHARLES. Oath of Allegiance in 1778 (A-6).

RAMSEY, THOMAS. Private in Capt. John Oglevie's Co., July 25, 1776 (C-85, G-647). Oath of Allegiance in 1778 (A-6). Thos. Ramsey married Elizabeth Aiken, Nov 17, 1779 (O-3).

RANDALL, JOHN. He appears to have served as he was due a military clothing allowance on March 6, 1779 (L-38).

RANKIN, ALEXANDER. Oath of Allegiance in 1778 (A-16).

RANKIN, GEORGE. Oath of Allegiance in 1778 (A-16).

RANKIN, JOHN. Two men with this name took the Oath of Allegiance in 1778 (A-5, A-16).

RATLIFF, JAMES. Oath of Allegiance in 1778 (A-4).

RATLIFF, ROBERT. Oath of Allegiance in 1778 (A-4). Robert Ratliff married Mary Kirk, October 13, 1787 (O-8).

RAWLINGS, JOSEPH. Oath of Allegiance in 1778 (A-17).

RAWLINGS, SEALY. Oath of Allegiance in 1778 (A-12).

RAWLINGS, THOMAS. Oath of Allegiance in 1778 (A-12).

RAY, ROBERT. Private in Capt. Walter Alexander's Company, 30th Battalion, enrolled July 24, 1776 (C-86, G-62).

REA (REAGH), ANDREW. Oath of Allegiance in 1778 (A-10).

REA (RHEA), GEORGE. "George Rea" took Oath of Allegiance in 1778 (A-5). "George Rhea" was an Ensign in Capt. Samuel Miller's Company in the 30th Battalion under Col. Stephen Hyland on September 9, 1778 (E-57, K-116, S-MdHR4570-72). George "Rhea" married Margaret Hill, Oct. 31, 1786 (O-8).

REA (RAE), JAMES. Oath of Allegiance in 1778 (A-14).

REA (REAH), JAMES. Oath of Allegiance in 1778 (A-10).

READ, ALEXANDER. Oath of Allegiance in 1778 (A-16).

READ, ANDREW. Ensign in Capt. Samuel Maffitt's Company in the Elk Battalion of Militia, 1777-1778 (S-MdHR6636-9-93, S-MdHR6636-12-37A, E-32, E-54). Took Oath of Allegiance in 1778 (A-6).

READ (READE), CHARLES. Oath of Allegiance in 1778 (A-12).

READ, GEORGE (September 18, 1733 - September 2, 1798). Born in Cecil County, Maryland, he moved with his family to New Castle County, Delaware when quite young. He married widow Gertrude Ross Till in 1763 and had four children: George (born 1765, married Mary Thompson); William (born 1767, married Ann McCall); John (born 1769, married Martha Merdith); and, Mary (born 1770, married Matthew Pearce) (U-600). He became active in political affairs and was a Signer of the Declaration of Independence on August 2, 1776 (refusing to sign it first on July 2, 1776 because he felt that reconciliation with Great Britain was still possible). He was elected to the legislature in 1776, becoming Vice President of Delaware. When President John McKinly was captured, Read took charge and involved himself untiringly in raising troops and provisions for Washington's Army. He also signed the Constitution on September 17, 1787. He died on September 21, 1798 and is buried in Immanuel Church cemetery in New Castle (C-73).

READ, JOHN. Oath of Allegiance in 1778 (A-16). He appears to have served because he is listed among those who were due a military clothing allowance on Mar. 6, 1779 (L-38).

READ (REED), JOHN JR. Oath of Allegiance in 1778 (A-16). John Reed married Ann Pearce, September 6, 1788 (O-10).

READ, MARY. She is listed among those entitled to receive a military clothing allowance on March 6, 1779 (L-38).

READGRAVE, SAMUEL. Oath of Allegiance, 1778 (A-8). Private in Capt. Stephen Hyland's Co., Sept. 8, 1775 (T-MS.1814).

REDMAN, JAMES. Oath of Allegiance in 1778 (A-4).

REILEY, JOHN (1751-1845). Son of Michael Reiley of County Galway, Ireland who settled in Cecil County, Maryland where John was born December 9, 1751. Family moved to Washington Co., Pennsylvania. John Reiley enlisted as a Private in August, 1776 from Westmoreland County and served in regiments under Col. Macy, Daniel Morgan, and Bayard. He was shot through the body at the Battle of Bonhampton, New Jersey in April, 1777. He became a First Lieutenant on May 20, 1777 in the 12th Pennsylvania and then a Captain in the 3rd Pennsylvania. He wintered at Valley Forge in 1777-1778 with General Washington. After the war ended, he married Elizabeth McCullough on March 25, 1784 in Washington, PA. Their children were Robert Reiley (born January 21, 1785), William Reiley (born October 21, 1786) and Mary Reiley (born January 5, 1789). In 1790 John Reiley went down the Ohio River, landed at Cabin Creek, Kentucky and settled in Campbell County. He had the following children in Kentucky: John Reiley (born December 13, 1791), Margaret Reiley (born Mar. 24, 1794), Smith Reiley (born December 20, 1797), Rebecca Reiley (born September 15, 1800), Davis Reiley (born January 17, 1803), Nancy Reiley (born January 12, 1806), and Jonathan Reiley (born January 15, 1809). In 1818 he received a war pension and in 1820 moved to Rush County, Indiana. His wife died in 1826 and he died in 1845. Both are buried in Hopewell Cemetery near Rushville, Indiana. (Information by Sally Black in "Bluegrass Roots," VII-2, p. 42, 1980).

RENNOLDS, GEORGE. Oath of Allegiance in 1778 (A-8). Private in Capt. Stephen Hyland's Co., Sept. 8, 1775 (T-MS.1814).

REY (KEY?), JAMES. Oath of Allegiance in 1778 (A-4).

REYNOLDS, HENRY (OF WILLIAM). He reportedly fled the state, "supposed to be gone to the British Army," on September 1, 1777 (K-121, S-MdHR4570-88).

REYLEY, MATHEW. Oath of Allegiance in 1778 (A-5).

RHEA: See "Rea."

RICE, ROBERT. Private in Capt. Henry Dobson's Company in the 6th Maryland Line, in North Carolina in 1780 (G-349).

RICE, WILLIAM. Private in Capt. Henry Dobson's Company in the 6th Maryland Line in North Carolina in 1780 (G-349).

RICHARDSON, JAMES. Oath of Allegiance in 1778 (A-6).

RICHARDSON, JONATHAN. Private in Capt. Walter Alexander's Company,

30th Battalion, enrolled August 3, 1776 (C-86, G-63). Took the Oath of Allegiance in 1778 (A-8). He married Mary-----, in Bohemia, Maryland prior to the war. Their daughter Rebecca married a Mason. Jonathan's widow received pension W8772 (or W9772) according to Annie W. Burns in "Maryland Soldiers: Revolutionary War," p. 47.

RICHARDSON, JOSIAH. Oath of Allegiance, 1778 (A-8). Private in Capt. Stephen Hyland's Co., Sept. 8, 1775 (T-MS.1814).

RICHARDSON, ROBERT. Oath of Allegiance in 1778 (A-7).

RICHARDSON, THOMAS (QUAKER). Took the Oath of Allegiance in 1778 (A-2). One Thomas Richardson married Mary Keithley, June 17, 1789 (O-10).

RICHARDSON, WILLIAM. Private in Capt. Joshua George's Company, 18th Battalion, August 18, 1776 (C-84, G-61). Took the Oath of Allegiance in March, 1778 (A-5). Private in Major Henry (Col. Harry) Lee's Partizan Corps in the Continental Army, June, 1778 (C-83, G-586).

RICHARDSON, WILLIAM (MILLER). Private in Major Henry (Col. Harry) Lee's Partizan Corps in the Continental Army, June, 1778 (C-83, G-586). One William Richardson married Ann Cooper(?), February 14, 1784 (O-6).

RICKETTS, BENJAMIN. 2nd Lieutenant in the Militia (C-87). Took the Oath of Allegiance in 1778 (A-7).

RICKETTS (RICKITTS), DAVID. 1st Lieutenant in Capt. Jonathan Booth's Company in 1777 and later Captain in the Militia (C-87, S-MdHR6636-9-93). Took the Oath of Allegiance in 1778 (A-7). He received a military clothing allowance on March 6, 1779 (L-38).

RICKETTS, JOHN. Private in Capt. Walter Alexander's Company, 30th Battalion, enrolled August 3, 1776 (C-86, G-63). Took the Oath of Allegiance in 1778 (A-7). John Ricketts married Sarah Pennington, June 2, 1760 (R-151).

RICKETTS, JOHN JR. Oath of Allegiance in 1778 (A-7). John Ricketts married Mary Rutter, January 9, 1793 (O-14).

RICKETTS, JOHN THOMAS. Oath of Allegiance in 1778 (A-7). John Thomas Ricketts md Mary Barr, Jan. 20, 1783 (O-5).

RICKETTS, REUBIN. Oath of Allegiance in 1778 (A-7). Reuben Ricketts married Gamore Barron, August 7, 1788 (O-10).

RICKETTS, RULIF. Oath of Allegiance in 1778 (A-7).

RIDDELL, JOHN. Oath of Allegiance in 1778 (A-5).

RIDDLE, SAMUEL. First Lieutenant in Capt. Samuel Miller's Company. Reported to have left the State and was replaced by Robert Cather on September 9, 1778 (E-57).

RIDER, JOSEPH. Oath of Allegiance in 1778 (A-3).

RIDLE, HUMPHREY. Oath of Allegiance in 1778 (A-9).

RIGHT, JOHN. Oath of Allegiance in 1778 (A-6).

RIGHT, STEPHEN. Private in Capt. Walter Alexander's Co., 30th Battalion, enrolled July 27, 1776 (C-86, G-62).

RING, WILLIAM. Oath of Allegiance in 1778 (A-18).

RITTER, WILLIAM. Oath of Allegiance in 1778 (A-13).

ROACH, JAMES. Oath of Allegiance in 1778 (A-8). Private in Capt. Stephen Hyland's Co., Sept. 8, 1775 (T-MS.1814). There were several James Roach's in Cecil County: One James married widow Mary Barr, August 4, 1784 (O-6), one James married Ann Thackery, Aug. 7, 1789 (O-10), and one James married Elizabeth Sappington, Oct. 5, 1792 (O-13). (Ed.: Additional research may be necessary in order to determine which James Roach rendered patriotic service.)

ROACH, PHILLIP. Oath of Allegiance in 1778 (A-8). Private in Capt. Stephen Hyland's Co., Sept. 8, 1775 (T-MS.1814).

ROBB, JACOB. Oath of Allegiance in 1778 (A-4).

ROBERTS, JOHN. Oath of Allegiance in 1778 (A-14). One John Roberts married Dorety Morgain, daughter of John Morgain, on July 15, 1740 (R-153), one John Roberts married Ann Severson by license February 5, 1778 (O-1), and one John Roberts married Ann Wroth by license May 16, 1778 (O-2). (Ed.: Additional research may be necessary in order to determine which John Roberts rendered patriotic service.)

ROBERTS, MORGAN JOHN. Oath of Allegiance in 1778 (A-12). Morgan John Roberts md Sarah Ryland, June 5, 1782 (O-5).

ROBERTS, ROBERT. Oath of Allegiance in 1778 (A-14). One Robert Roberts married Sarah Morgan on February 16, 1728 (R-153) and one Robert Roberts married Rebecca Aires by license dated September 8, 1783 (O-6).

ROBERTS, SAMUEL. Oath of Allegiance in 1778 (A-4).

ROBERTS, SAMUEL (PLASTERER). Oath of Allegiance, 1778. (A-4)

ROBERTS, THOMAS. Oath of Allegiance in 1778 (A-14).

ROBERTSON, HENRY. Oath of Allegiance in 1778 (A-7).

ROBINSON, DANIEL. Private in Capt. John Oglevie's Company, July 25, 1776 (C-85, G-647).

ROBINSON, GEORGE. Private in Capt. John Oglevie's Company, July 25, 1776 (C-85, G-647).

ROBINSON (ROBISON), JOHN. Oath of Allegiance in 1778 (A-16). Recruited, Oct. 16, 1780; sent to Chester Town (G-345). John Robinson married Ann Cather, Nov. 11, 1781 (O-5).

ROBINSON (ROBISON), PATRICK. Private in Capt. W. Alexander's Co., 30th Battalion, enrolled July 24, 1776 (C-86, G-62).

ROCK, WILLIAM. Oath of Allegiance in 1778 (A-5).

ROCKHOLD, ASEL. Private in Capt. Henry Dobson's Company in the 6th Maryland Line in 1780 (G-348). (Ed.: He probably is the Asael Rockhold who took the Oath of Allegiance in 1778 in Harford County, Maryland. See Henry C. Peden's Revolutionary Patriots of Harford Co., 1775-1783, p. 193)

RODGERS, ELISHA. Ensign in Capt. John Oglevie's Company in the Elk Battalion on April 10, 1776, and then a Second Lieutenant, June 7, 1781 (E-33, E-55, C-85, G-647, P-320, S-MdHR6636-9-93). Oath of Allegiance, 1778 (A-6). Elisha "Rogers" married Rebecca Ferguson on May 19, 1781 (O-4).

RODGERS, JOHN (1726-1793). Married Elizabeth Reynolds in 1760 and had the following children: Alexander Rodgers, Thomas Reynolds Rodgers, Rebecca Rodgers, John Rodgers (1773-1838, Commodore and founder of the American Navy), George Washington Rodgers (Commodore, U.S. Navy), Mary Rodgers (married Howes Goldsborough), Maria Ann Rodgers (married William Pinkney in 1789), and Elizabeth Rodgers (married Andrew Grey). John Rodgers' family was indeed a prominent one in American history and he was a Colonel in the Militia during the Revolutionary War (C-87). In 1780 he purchased a tavern (built before 1745) in Perryville, a natural stopping place on the Susquehanna River between Philadelphia and Baltimore. Rodgers Tavern became famous for its famous guests, including George Washington, and it is on the National Register of Historic Places (C-50, C-51, and data from Filing Case A at the Md. Hist. Soc.).

ROFF, JOHN. Oath of Allegiance in 1778 (A-4).

ROGERS: See "Rodgers."

ROGERS, MICHAEL. Private in Capt. Henry Dobson's Company in the 6th Maryland Line. Hospitalized in Hillsborough, North Carolina in October, 1780 (G-349).

ROGERS, ROWLAND. He appears to have served because he was due a military clothing allowance on Mar. 6, 1779 (L-38).

ROGERS, SAMUEL. Oath of Allegiance in 1778 (B-119).

ROGERS, THOMAS. Oath of Allegiance in 1778 (B-119).

ROGERS, WILLIAM. Oath of Allegiance in 1778 (B-119).

ROSE, HENRY. Oath of Allegiance in 1778 (A-8).

ROSS, DAVID. Oath of Allegiance in 1778 (A-15).

ROSS, JOSEPH. Oath of Allegiance in 1778 (A-6). He appears to have served because he is listed among those who were due a military clothing allowance, March 6, 1779 (L-38).

ROWLAND, JACOB. Private in Capt. Henry Dobson's Company in the 6th Maryland Line. Roster indicates he was a "Waiter on Mr. J. Jacobs, in Maryland" in October, 1780 (G-349).

ROWLAND, JAMES. Oath of Allegiance in 1778 (A-10).

ROWLAND, ROBERT. Oath of Allegiance in 1778 (A-10). He appears to have served because he is listed as being due a military clothing allowance on March 6, 1779 (L-38). Robert Rowland married Esther McCoy, Sept. 2, 1780 (O-4).

ROWLAND, WILLIAM. Oath of Allegiance in 1778 (A-5).

RUDULPH, JACOB. Married Rachael------, and fathered Thomas and Michael Rudulph, soldiers of the Revolution. He took the Oath of Allegiance in 1778 in Cecil County, Maryland (A-15). After the war he moved with his family to Camden Mills, South Carolina where he died July 8, 1800 (C-17).

RUDULPH, JOHN. Son of Tobias Rudulph. "Fighting Jack" was an Ensign in Captain Jonathan Booth's Company in the 2nd Battalion in 1777 and then a Captain in Major Henry (Col. Harry) Lee's Partizan Corps from 1777 through 1783 (C-17, C-83, G-586, G-587, J-517, K-156, S-MdHR6636-9-93). He took the Oath of Allegiance in 1778 (A-15). John Rudulph married Elizabeth Kimble, November 15, 1790 (O-11).

RUDULPH, MICHAEL. Born January 5, 1758 near Elkton, son of Jacob and Rachael Rudulph. He took the Oath of Allegiance in 1778 before his uncle, the Hon. Tobias Rudulph (A-15). Michael served with his cousin, John Rudulph, in Major Henry (Col. Harry) Lee's Partizan Corps from April, 1778 to at least Oct. 4, 1783 (C-83, G-587, K-156). He signed on as a Sergeant Major and soon became Quartermaster and then Lieutenant. He became an expert at guerrilla warfare and became known as the "Lion of Lee's Legion." In May of 1783 he took a furlough and married Sarah Baker, daughter of Colonel John Baker of Georgia. They settled in Camden County, Georgia. He apparently served until August 20, 1783 (Source I-611 erroneously gives his name as Nicholas instead of Michael). After the Revolution he joined and was subsequently commissioned a Major in the U. S. Army in March, 1792, and served until July 17, 1793, when he resigned ("bored with Indian fighting"). Restless again, he soon afterwards went to sea with Capt. Joseph Lort and was never heard from again (J-518). There are some who believe Michael Rudulph was the Michael Ney who was Napoleon's Field Marshall and was executed in France in 1815, but this has not been proven (J-520, C-15 ff.).

RUDULPH, THOMAS. Older brother of Michael Rudulph and son of Jacob Rudulph. Oath of Allegiance in 1778 (A-7). He moved to Camden County, Georgia after the war (M-17).

RUDULPH, TOBIAS. Justice who administered the Oath of Allegiance in Cecil County in March, 1778 (A-15, M-16). He was paid for "Waggonage" on September 9, 1776 (W-256).

RUDULPH, TOBIAS JR. Oath of Allegiance in 1778 (A-15).

RULEY, ANTHONY. Oath of Allegiance in 1778 (A-14). Anthony Ruley married Elizabeth Cadle, February 14, 1722 (R-157).

RULEY, SETH. Oath of Allegiance in 1778 (A-14). Seth Ruley married Eleanor Parsley, March 27, 1786 (O-7).

RUMSEY, BENJAMIN. Took Oath of Allegiance in 1778 (A-15). Benjamin Rumsey married Mary Hall, daughter of Col. John and Hannah of Baltimore County, on May 24, 1768 (R-157).

RUMSEY, CHARLES. He was elected a Deputy to the Maryland Convention on May 16, 1775 (I-2, K-2, P-13) and Colonel of the Elk Battalion on January 6, 1776, and the 18th Battalion in July, 1776 (C-84, G-61, G-62, I-64, I-87, I-124, J-323). He signed the Declaration of Freemen of Maryland in 1775 (J-322), and took the Oath of Allegiance in 1778 (A-15). In 1779 he was County Lieutenant (I-224).

RUMSEY, THOMAS. Second Lieutenant in Capt. Samuel Evans' Company, September 28, 1776 (C-82, J-322).

RUMSEY, WILLIAM. He was elected a Deputy to the Maryland Convention on May 16, 1775 (I-2, K-2, P-13) and First Major in the Bohemia Battalion on January 6, 1776 (C-87, J-323). He was appointed by the Maryland Council on January 27, 1776 to be one of the Collectors of all the gold and silver coins that could be procured in Cecil County (P-132). He also served as an Election Judge for electing Deputies to the Convention, July 3, 1776 (K-35).

RUSSELL, ABRAHAM. Oath of Allegiance in 1778 (A-10).

RUSSELL, THOMAS. Two men with this name took the Oath of Allegiance in 1778 (A-6, A-8). One Thomas Russell married Ann Thomas on February 17, 1774 (R-157).

RUTHERFORD, JOSEPH. Oath of Allegiance in 1778 (A-5).

RUTLEDGE, CHRISTOPHER. Private in Capt. Walter Alexander's Company, 30th Battalion, enrolled July 24, 1776 (C-86, G-62). Oath of Allegiance in 1778 (A-2). Private in Major Henry (Col. Harry) Lee's Partizan Corps from April 7, 1778 to at least Dec., 1780 (C-83, G-586, G-587, K-156).

RUTTER, ISAAC. Oath of Allegiance in 1778 (A-8). Private in Capt. Stephen Hyland's Company, Sept 8, 1775 (T-MS.1814). Isaac Rutter married Rachel Cavender, June 2, 1785 (O-7).

RYAN, JOHN. Oath of Allegiance in 1778 (A-5).

RYLAND, FREDUS. Oath of Allegiance in 1778 (A-4).

RYLAND, JEHU. Oath of Allegiance in 1778 (A-17).

RYLAND, JOHN. Private in Capt. Joshua George's Company, in the 18th Battalion, August 18, 1776 (C-84, G-61).

RYLAND, JOHN JR. Oath of Allegiance in 1778 (A-14).

RYLAND, JOHN SR. Oath of Allegiance in 1778 (A-14).

SAMON, DANIEL. Oath of Allegiance in 1778 (A-15).

SAMPSON, JAMES. Oath of Allegiance in 1778 (A-18).

SANDERS, WILLIAM. Private in Capt. Jeremiah Baker's Company, August 1, 1775 and in Capt. Baruch Williams' Company, March 3, 1776 (F-158, I-27).

SANDS, ALEXANDER. Oath of Allegiance in 1778 (A-10).

SANDS, JAMES. Oath of Allegiance in 1778 (A-6).

SANDS, JOHN. Private in Capt. John Oglevie's Company, July 25, 1776 (C-85, G-647).

SANDS (SANS), WILLIAM. Oath of Allegiance in 1778 (A-4).

SANNER, JOSEPH. 1st Lieutenant, Elk Battalion, 1778 (E-38).

SAPPINGTON, BENJAMIN. Oath of Allegiance, 1778 (A-17). Benj. Sappington married Elizabeth Wroth, Oct. 22, 1785 (O-7).

SAPPINGTON, JAMES. Private in Capt. Walter Alexander's Co., 30th Battalion, enrolled August 3, 1776 (C-86, G-63).

SAVIN, EDWARD. Private in Capt. Joshua George's Company, 18th Battalion, August 18, 1776 (C-84, G-61). Took the Oath of Allegiance in 1778 (A-11). Edward Savin married Elizabeth Sluyter, April 5, 1791 (O-12).

SAVIN, JOSHUA. Oath of Allegiance in 1778. (A-12)

SAVIN, PEREGRINE. Took Oath of Allegiance in 1778 (A-17). Peregrine Savin married Mary Jarvis, Oct. 3, 1792 (O-13).

SAVIN, RICHARD. First Lieutenant in Capt. James Porter's Company in the 18th Battalion under Col. John D. Thompson on June 22, 1778 (E-56, S-MdHR6636-9-93).

SAVIN, THOMAS. Served as an Election Judge to elect the representatives to the Maryland Convention on July 3, 1776 (K-35). Captain in the 2nd Battalion under Colonel Henry Hollingsworth in 1777 (S-MdHR6636-9-93). Took the Oath of Allegiance in 1778 (A-17). Captain in the Elk Battalion on April 9, 1778 and was promoted to Major on September 9, 1778 (E-54, E-55, K-116, S-MdHR4570-72).

SAVIN, WILLIAM. Oath of Allegiance in 1778 (A-12). William Savin married Araminta Hodgson, March 22, 1790 (O-11).

SAYER, GEORGE. Oath of Allegiance in 1778 (A-6).

SCANLAN, JOHN. Oath of Allegiance in 1778 (A-18).

SCOTT, ALEXANDER. Oath of Allegiance in 1778 (A-7).

SCOTT, ISAAC. Two men with this name took the Oath of Allegiance in 1778 (A-7, A-16).

SCOTT, JAMES. Two men with this name took the Oath of Allegiance in 1778 (A-10, A-13).

SCOTT, JOHN. Second Lieutenant in Captain Samuel Evans Co., Elk Battalion, 1777-1778 and subsequently Captain in the Militia (C-87, E-54, S-MdHR6636-9-93). Two men with this name took the Oath of Allegiance in 1778 (A-13, A-16). One John Scott married Mary Bouching, Nov. 25, 1786 (O-8) and one John married Jane Hull, April 19, 1793 (O-14).

SCOTT, JOHN JR. Oath of Allegiance in 1778 (A-16).

SCOTT, MOSES. Oath of Allegiance in 1778 (A-16).

SCOTT, ROBERT. Private in Capt. Joshua George's Company, 18th Battalion, August 18, 1776 (C-84, G-61). Two men by this name took the Oath of Allegiance, 1778 (A-2, A-16).

SCOTT, THOMAS. Two men with this name took the Oath of Allegiance in 1778 (A-4, A-16).

SCOTT, WILLIAM. Oath of Allegiance in 1778 (A-16). Captain in the Elk Battalion of Militia, June 7, 1781 (E-35).

SCOTT, WILLIAM JR. Oath of Allegiance in 1778 (A-16).

SCURY, ROBERT. Oath of Allegiance in 1778 (A-14).

SEARS, JOHN. Ensign by April 18, 1780 (I-285). Recruiting Officer at the Head of Elk and Lieutenant in the Maryland Line by April 18, 1780 and serving to at least April 2, 1782 (C-82, L-65, L-112). Order was passed on January 26, 1828 for the "Treasurer, Western Shore, to pay to Mary Sears, of Harford County, during life, half yearly, half pay of a Lieut., as further remuneration for her (late) husband John Sears' services during Rev. War." (N-389). John

Sears married Mary Dutton, July 13, 1785 (O-7).

SEARS, WILLIAM. Private in Capt. Joshua George's Company, 18th Battalion, August 18, 1776 (C-84, G-61). William Sears married Anna Couden, January 23, 1780 (O-4).

SEGER, JOSEPH. Oath of Allegiance in 1778 (A-7).

SERVICE, WILLIAM. Oath of Allegiance in 1778 (A-7).

SEVERSON, BENJAMIN. Private in Capt. Joshua George's Company, 18th Battalion, August 18, 1776 (C-84, G-61). Took the Oath of Allegiance in 1778 (A-12). One Benjamin Severson married Ann Wroth, July 5, 1778 (O-2) and one Benjamin married Elizabeth Pennington, October 3, 1787 (O-8).

SEVERSON, JOSEPH. Oath of Allegiance in 1778 (A-8).

SEWELL, JAMES. Private in Capt. Henry Dobson's Co., 6th MD Line. Hospitalized in Hillsborough, N.C. in 1780 (G-349).

SEWELL, THOMAS. Private in Capt. Jeremiah Baker's Company, August 1, 1775 and in Capt. Baruch Williams' Company, March 3, 1776 (F-158, I-27).

SHANNON, JOHN. He fled the state, "supposed to be gone to the British Army" in March, 1778 (K-121, S-MdHR4579-88).

SHARP (SHARPE), SAMUEL (May 2, 1736 - December 29, 1804). He married Sophia----- and had 6 children: Araminta (married Samuel McIntyre); Jehu (1767-1826, married Elizabeth Glass); Sinah (married a Tomb); Bathia; Ledia; and Lavinia (married a Caruthers). (U-642, V-253). Samuel took the Oath of Allegiance in 1778 (A-7).

SHARP, THOMAS. Oath of Allegiance in 1778 (A-16).

SHARPLESS, ROBERT. Corporal in Capt. Henry Dobson's Co., 6th Maryland Line. Sick, absent from Camp Hillsborough, North Carolina in October, 1780 (G-347).

SHEHEE, EDWARD. Private in Capt. Henry Dobson's Company in the 6th Maryland Line. Hospitalized in Annapolis as of October, 1780 (G-349).

SHELL, CHARLES PHILLIP. Oath of Allegiance in 1778 (A-7).

SHELLEY, JOHN. Oath of Allegiance in 1778 (A-4).

SHEPHERD, SAMUEL. Oath of Allegiance in 1778 (A-15).

SHEPPERD, NATHANIEL. Oath of Allegiance in 1778 (A-13).

SHERIDINE, DANIEL. Oath of Allegiance in 1778 (A-5).

SHIELDS, ARCHIBALD. First Lieutenant in Capt. John Ward Veazey's

Company, 18th Battalion, June 22, 1778 (E-56, S-MdHR6636-9-93). Oath of Allegiance in 1778 (A-4).

SHIELDS, EDMOND.  Oath of Allegiance in 1778 (A-4).

SHIELDS, FRANCIS.  Oath of Allegiance in 1778 (A-6).

SHIELDS, JOHN.  Oath of Allegiance in 1778 (A-6).

SHIELDS, THOMAS.  Oath of Allegiance in 1778 (A-7).

SHIELS, PATRICK.  Private in Capt. Walter Alexander's Co., 30th Battalion, enrolled July 18, 1776 (C-86, G-63).

SHIRKEY, CHARLES.  Recruited, October 16, 1780 (G-345).

SHIRLEY, JOHN.  Recruited, October 16, 1780 (G-345).

SHOEMAKER, JOHN.  Private in Capt. Henry Dobson's Company in the 6th Maryland Line in North Carolina in 1780 (G-348).

SHORT, ADAM.  Oath of Allegiance in 1778 (A-15).

SHORT, JONATHAN. Oath of Allegiance in March, 1778 (A-7). Private in Major Henry (Col. Harry) Lee's Partizan Corps from June, 1778 to January 1, 1781 (C-83, G-586, K-156). On April 23, 1787 the Auditor General's Office certified that 15 lbs., 12 sh., and 6 p. was due the Administrator of Jonathan Short's estate for his pay as a Trooper in Col. Lee's Legion, Aug. 1, 1780 to Jan 1, 1781 (G-590). "John" Short married Mary Johnson, July 14, 1791 (O-12).

SHORT, THOMAS.  Oath of Allegiance in 1778 (A-15).

SHORT, WILLIAM.  Oath of Allegiance in 1778 (A-7).

SILVER (?), SAMUEL.  Oath of Allegiance in 1778 (A-13).

SIMCO, WILLIAM.  Oath of Allegiance in 1778 (A-5).

SIMISTER, THOMAS.  Private in Capt. Henry Dobson's Company in 6th Maryland Line, in N. C. in October, 1780 (G-347).

SIMMONS, LAWRENCE.  Oath of Allegiance in 1778 (A-2).

SIMPERS, GEORGE.  Oath of Allegiance in 1778 (A-8).

SIMPERS, JACOB.  Oath of Allegiance in 1778 (A-7). Jacob Simpers married Milicent Mills, April 23, 1782 (O-5).

SIMPERS, JESSE.  Oath of Allegiance in 1778 (A-7).

SIMPERS, JOHN.  Oath of Allegiance in 1778 (A-7). John Simpers married Peggy Crouch, December 26, 1787 (O-9).

SIMPERS, THOMAS.  Oath of Allegiance in 1778 (A-7).

SIMPSON, ALEXANDER. Private in Capt. John Oglevie's Co., July 25, 1776 (C-85, G-647). Alexander Simpson married Margaret Wilson by license dated October 13, 1784 (O-6).

SINGLETON, THOMAS. Oath of Allegiance in 1778 (A-16).

SIRE, JOHN. Oath of Allegiance in 1778 (A-7).

SLEATOR, RICHARD. Oath of Allegiance in 1778 (A-5).

SLOOP, JOSEPH. Private in Capt. Henry Dobson's Company in the 6th Maryland Line. Enlisted in May, 1778 for three years and was serving in North Carolina in 1780 (G-348).

SMART, STEPHEN. Oath of Allegiance in 1778 (A-6).

SMITH, DAVID. He represented the county at the Maryland Convention that met August 14, 1776 (J-322), and was one of the Justices who administered the Oath of Allegiance in Cecil County in March, 1778 (A-13).

SMITH, DINISH. Private in Capt. Walter Alexander's Co., 30th Battalion, enrolled July 27, 1776 (C-86, G-62).

SMITH, FERGUS. 2nd Lieutenant in the 2nd Battalion under Capt. Walter Alexander in 1777 (S-MdHR6636-9-93). Took Oath of Allegiance in 1778 (A-16). First Lieutenant in Capt. Hezekiah South's Company in the Elk Battalion on April 9, 1778 (E-36, E-54, S-MdHR6636-12-37A).

SMITH, HENRY. Two men with this name took the Oath of Allegiance in 1778 (A-7, A-15).

SMITH, HUGH. He appears to have served because he was due a military clothing allowance on March 6, 1779 (L-38).

SMITH, JAMES. Private in Capt. Joshua George's Company, 18th Battalion, August 18, 1776 (C-84, G-61). Took the Oath of Allegiance in 1778 (A-6). Another James Smith (or perhaps the same one) was a Private in Capt. Walter Alexander's Company, 30th Battalion, enrolled July 24, 1776 (C-86, G-62).

SMITH, JOHN. Private in Capt. Walter Alexander's Company, 30th Battalion, enrolled July 27, 1776 (C-86, G-62). Took the Oath of Allegiance in 1778 (A-16). John Smith married Rebecca Connelly, by license dated June 19, 1784 (O-6).

SMITH, JOSEPH. Oath of Allegiance in 1778 (A-6).

SMITH, JOSHUA. Oath of Allegiance in 1778 (A-15).

SMITH, MICHAEL. Private in Capt. Stephen Hyland's Company, September 8, 1775 (T-MS.1814). Private in Capt. Walter Alexander's Company, 30th Battalion, enrolled August 3, 1776 (C-86, G-63).

Oath of Allegiance in 1778 (A-8). Michael Smith married Rebecca Brooks, Aug 11, 1778 (O-2).

SMITH, NATHAN. He served as a Private in Harford County, Maryland (enlisting July 25, 1776) and married Anne Chew on July 3, 1784 in Cecil County (G-60, Q-123, O-6).

SMITH, ROBERT. Oath of Allegiance in 1778 (A-6). One Robert Smith married Ann McCrea, March 21, 1786 (O-7) and one Robert Smith married Polly Savin, Feb. 5, 1793 (O-13).

SMITH, SAMUEL. Oath of Allegiance in 1778 (A-5).

SMITH, THOMAS. Private in Capt. Jeremiah Baker's Company, August 1, 1775 and in Capt. Baruch Williams' Company, March 3, 1776 (F-158, I-27). This or another Thomas Smith was a Private in Capt. Henry Dobson's Company in the 6th Maryland Line in North Carolina in October, 1780 (G-349).

SMITH, THOMAS LITTLETON. Captain in the Militia (C-87).

SMITH, WILLIAM. Private in Capt. John Oglevie's Co., July 25, 1776 (C-85, G-647). Oath of Allegiance, 1778 (A-14). This (or perhaps another) William Smith was recruited on October 16, 1780 and sent to Chester Town (G-345). One William Smith md ELizabeth Oldham, June 17, 1795 (O-15).

SOPER, ROBERT. Oath of Allegiance in 1778 (A-14).

SOUTH, HEZEKIAH. 1st Lieutenant in the 2nd Battalion under Col. Henry Hollingsworth in 1777 and Captain in the Elk Battalion under Colonel Edward Parker on April 21, 1778 (E-37, E-54, S-MdHR6636-9-93, S-MdHR6636-12-37A). He took the Oath of Allegiance in 1778 (A-16). Listed among those due a military clothing allowance, March 6, 1779 (L-38).

SPEER, JOHN. Oath of Allegiance in 1778 (A-7).

SPENCER, EDWARD. Oath of Allegiance in 1778 (A-12).

SPLANE, WILLIAM. Oath of Allegiance in 1778 (A-10).

SPRINGER, PETER. Oath of Allegiance in 1778 (A-7). Peter Springer md Mary Ann Pennington, June 18, 1792 (O-13).

STACKHOUSE, JOHN. Private in Capt. Henry Dobson's Company in the 6th Maryland Line in North Carolina in 1780 (G-348).

STALCOB, HENRY. Oath of Allegiance in 1778 (A-8).

STANLEY, MICHAEL. Private in Capt. Henry Dobson's Company in the 6th Maryland Line. Hospitalized at Hillsborough, North Carolina in October, 1780 (G-349).

STARN, FREDERICK. Oath of Allegiance in 1778 (A-2).

STARN, JOHN.  Oath of Allegiance in 1778 (A-2).

STARN, JOSEPH.  Oath of Allegiance in 1778 (A-2).

STARNES, NICHOLAS (1756, Cecil Co., MD - 1835, Talladega Co., AL). Sergeant in 1775 in Capt. Crabtree's Company of Mountaineers under Col. William Campbell.  Married Mary--- and had a son George (married Mary Nancy Buford) (U-677).

STEEL, ALEXANDER.  Born before 1730 in White Clay Creek, DE and died there on August 9, 1783.  He married Sara----- and had three children: Allen (married Ruth Sharp); James (married Ann-----); and, Ruth (married a Butler).  Took Oath of Allegiance in 1778, Cecil Co., MD (A-16, V-270).

STEEL, JAMES (c1750 - September 17, 1798). Married Mary----- and had three children: Hugh (married Hester Boyd); Jane (born 1773, married Hugh Boyd); and, John (V-270).  Oath of Allegiance in 1778 (A-10).  First Lieut. in Capt. James Mackey's Co., 2nd Battalion, 1777-1778 (S-MdHR6636-9-93).

STEEL, JAMES JR.  Oath of Allegiance in 1778 (A-6).  James Steel md ELizabeth Mahaffey, July 29, 1777 (O-1, R-170).

STEEL, JAMES SR.  Oath of Allegiance in 1778 (A-6).

STEEL, WILLIAM.  Oath of Allegiance in 1778 (A-6).

STEEN, JOHN.  Oath of Allegiance in 1778 (A-16).

STEPHENSON, ALEXANDER.  Drum and Fifer in Capt. Henry Dobson's Company in the 6th Maryland Line, in North Carolina in October, 1780 (G-347).

STEPHENSON, JOSEPH.  Private in Capt. Jeremiah Baker's Company, August 1, 1775 and in Capt. Baruch Williams' Company, March 3, 1776 (F-158, I-27).  Took the Oath of Allegiance in 1778 (A-6).

STEPHENSON, WILLIAM.  Two men with this name took the Oath of Allegiance in 1778 (A-5, A-6).

STERLING, JACOB.  Oath of Allegiance in 1778 (A-4).

STERLING, EPHRAIM.  Oath of Allegiance in 1778 (A-4).  Ephraim Sterling married Ann Carty, February 17, 1789 (O-10).

STERLING, WILLIAM.  Took Oath of Allegiance in 1778 (A-4).  Recruit, October 16, 1780; sent to Chester Town (G-345).

STERRETT, JOHN.  Oath of Allegiance in 1778 (A-10).  John Sterrett married Sarah Finley, August 23, 1781 (O-5).

STERRETT, SAMUEL.  Oath of Allegiance in 1778 (A-9).

STEUART, WILLIAM. Born in Anne Arundel County, Maryland on February 25, 1760 and served as an Ensign in Capt. Samuel Evans' Company, Flying Camp, commissioned September 28, 1776 (J-322, W-306). He became Second Lieutenant, 6th MD Regiment, December 10, 1776, and First Lieutenant, Capt. John Evans' Co. in 1777 (S-MdHR6636-9-93). Transferred to 3rd MD Regiment, January 1, 1781 and served to the close of the war. He died July 17, 1846 in Baltimore and is buried in Old St. Paul's Cem. (C-82, G-63, G-74, D-135, E-54). (Ed.: His name is often misspelled as "Stewart.")

STEVENSON, JAMES. Private in Capt. John Oglevie's Company, July 25, 1776 (C-85, G-647). James Stevenson married Abigal Wilson by license dated February 25, 1789 (O-9).

STEVENSON, JOHN. Private in Capt. Jeremiah Baker's Company, August 1, 1775 and in Capt. Baruch Williams' Co., March 3, 1776 (F-158, I-27). Oath of Allegiance in 1778 (A-13).

STEWARD, GEORGE. Drum and Fifer in Capt. Henry Dobson's Co., 6th Maryland Line in N. C. in October, 1780 (G-347).

STEWART: See "Steuart."

STEWART, ROBERT. Oath of Allegiance in 1778 (A-2).

STEWART, WILLIAM. Oath of Allegiance in 1778 (A-7). William Stewart married Deborah Miller, August 1, 1781 (O-5).

STIDHAM, HENRY. Oath of Allegiance in 1778 (A-7).

STILES, LAWRENCE. Oath of Allegiance in 1778 (A-2).

STILES, MICHAEL. Oath of Allegiance in 1778 (A-2).

STITT (STETT), THOMAS. Oath of Allegiance in 1778 (A-17).

STOCKTON, JOHN. Oath of Allegiance in 1778 (A-14). One John Stockton md Elizabeth Aldredge, November 5, 1745 (R-172).

STOCKTON, JOHN JR. Commissioned Second Lieutenant in Capt. Joshua George's Company, 18th Battalion, July 20, 1776 (C-84, G-61, G-62, W-157). Served as an Election Judge to elect representatives to the Maryland Convention on Nov. 8, 1776 (K-55). Oath of Allegiance, 1778 (A-14).

STOCKTON, JOSEPH. Oath of Allegiance in 1778 (A-14).

STONESTREET, WILLIAM. Private in Capt. Henry Dobson's Co. in the 6th Maryland Line in North Carolina, 1780 (G-349).

STOOPS, JOHN. Oath of Allegiance in 1778 (A-17). John Stoops married Susannah Ward, January 25, 1778 (O-1).

STOOPS, PHILIP. Oath of Allegiance in 1778 (A-2). Phillip Stoopes married Sarah Lland(?), April 20, 1782 (O-5).

STOOPS, WILLIAM. Oath of Allegiance in 1778 (A-12). William Stoops married Rachel Ford, February 28, 1778 (O-1).

STORMONT, NATHANIEL. Oath of Allegiance in 1778 (A-5).

STRAGHIN, WILLIAM. Oath of Allegiance in 1778 (A-6).

STRAHAN, JOHN. Quartermaster Sergeant in Major Henry (Col. Harry) Lee's Partizan Corps on February 17, 1780 (K-156).

STRAWBRIDGE, JAMES. Oath of Allegiance in 1778 (A-16).

STRAWBRIDGE, JOHN. Second Major in the Elk Battalion under Col. Charles Rumsey on January 6, 1776 and under Colonel Henry Hollingsworth in 1777, and Lieutenant Colonel under Colonel Edward Parker on April 21, 1778. He resigned on October 20, 1778 (E-38, E-54, J-323, S-MdHR6636-9-93). John Strawbridge also served as Sheriff of Cecil County, but resigned from that office on March 17, 1778 (I-151).

STREAN, WILLIAM. Private in Capt. John Oglevie's Company, July 25, 1776 (C-85, G-647).

STRIKEINGBURG, JOHN ANDREW. Private in Capt. W. Alexander's Co., 30th Battalion, enrolled Aug. 3, 1776 (C-86, G-63).

STRONGE, LEONARD. Oath of Allegiance in 1778 (A-7).

STUART, ALEXANDER. Oath of Allegiance in 1778 (A-17).

STUDSILL, CHRISTOPHER. He reportedly fled the state and was "supposed to be gone to the British Army" on November 15, 1777 (K-121, S-MdHR4570-88).

STUMP, GEORGE. George "Stumm" was a Drum and Fifer in Capt. Henry Dobson's Company in the 6th Maryland Line in North Carolina in October, 1780 (G-347).

STUMP, JOHN. Oath of Allegiance in 1780 (B-121). Received a certificate for wheat on March 20, 1780 (I-277). One John Stump married Hannah Stump, December 15, 1785 (O-7).

STUMP, JOHN JR. Oath of Allegiance in 1778 (A-15).

STUMP, WILLIAM, JR. Oath of Allegiance in 1778 (A-7).

STURGIS, JOB. Oath of Allegiance in 1778 (A-12).

SUGARS, PETER. Corporal in Capt. Henry Dobson's Company in the 6th Maryland Line in North Carolina in 1780 (G-347).

SUMMERS, JOHN. Private in Capt. Henry Dobson's Company in the 6th Maryland Line in North Carolina in 1780 (G-347).

SUTTON, ABRAHAM.   Fife Major in Col. Henry (Harry) Lee's Legion (Partizan Corps) in 1780 (G-587).

SUTTON, ASHBERRY.   Oath of Allegiance in 1778 (A-12).

SWAN, BAZEL.   Private in Capt. Jeremiah Baker's Company, August 1, 1775 and in Capt. Baruch Williams' Co., March 3, 1776 (F-158, I-27).  Oath of Allegiance in 1778 (A-5).

SWINK, ABRAHAM.   Private in Capt. Henry Dobson's Company in the 6th Maryland Line serving "On Guard" in Hillsborough, North Carolina in October, 1780 (G-349).

SWINK, GEORGE.   Oath of Allegiance in 1778 (A-2).

SWINK, JACOB.   Oath of Allegiance in 1778 (A-2).

TAGART, JOHN.   Oath of Allegiance in 1780 (B-121).

TALEN, JOSEPH.   Private in Capt. Walter Alexander's Company, in 30th Battalion.  Enrolled July 9, 1776 (C-86, G-63).

TALLUM, ADAM.   Oath of Allegiance in 1778 (A-5).

TALLUM, JOHN.   Oath of Allegiance in 1778 (A-5).

TANNER, JOSEPH.   Second Lieutenant in Capt. John Oglevie's Company on April 10, 1776 (C-85, G-647, P-320) and First Lieutenant in 1777 in the 2nd Battalion under Col. Henry Hollingsworth (S-MdHR6636-9-93).  He took the Oath of Allegiance in 1778 (A-6).

TATE, JOHN.   Oath of Allegiance in 1778 (A-7).

TAYLOR, BENJAMIN.   Oath of Allegiance in 1778 (A-2).  Private in Capt. Henry Dobson's Company in the 6th Maryland Line. Hospitalized at Hillsborough, N.C. in Oct., 1780 (G-349).

TAYLOR, EDWARD.   Oath of Allegiance in 1778 (A-6).  Edward Taylor married Mary----- in May, 1735 (R-176).

TAYLOR, JEREMIAH.   Second Lieutenant in Capt. Andrew Miller's Company, Elk Battalion, April 21, 1778 (E-54). Took the Oath of Allegiance in 1778 (A-2).

TAYLOR, JAMES.   Oath of Allegiance in 1778 (A-7).  He appears to have served because he is among those due a military clothing allowance on March 6, 1779 (L-38).  One James Taylor married Catherine Smith, Feb. 26, 1741 (R-176).

TAYLOR, JOHN.   Three men with this name took the Oath of Allegiance in 1778 (A-5, A-6, A-11).

TAYLOR, JOSEPH.   Oath of Allegiance in 1778 (A-2).

TAYLOR, MARLOW.   Private in Capt. Joshua George's Company in the

18th Battalion on August 18, 1776 (C-84, G-61).

TAYLOR, MATTHEW. Oath of Allegiance in 1778 (A-6).

TAYLOR, RICHARD. Two men with this name took the Oath of Allegiance in 1778 (A-4, A-7). One Richard Taylor married Anne Perrey in June, 1716 (R-176).

TAYLOR, RICHARD JR. Oath of Allegiance in 1778 (A-4).

TAYLOR, ROBERT. Sergeant in Capt. Henry Dobson's Company in the 6th Maryland Line. Recruiting in Oct., 1780 (G-347).

TAYLOR, SAMUEL. Oath of Allegiance in 1778 (A-17).

TAYLOR, THOMAS. Oath of Allegiance in 1778 (A-5). Private in Capt. Stephen Hyland's Company of Militia, September 8, 1775 (T-MS.1814). Thomas Taylor married Deborah Leffler by license dated July 25, 1781 (O-5).

TAYLOR, WILLIAM. Ensign in Capt. Samuel Veazey's Company, 18th or Sassafrass Battalion, by June 22, 1778 (E-56, S-MdHR6636-9-93). Three men by this name took the Oath of Allegiance in Cecil County in 1778 (A-2, A-4). One William Taylor md Rachel Brevard, Jan. 28, 1788 (O-9).

TEADLY, EDWARD. Corporal in Capt. Henry Dobson's Company in the 6th Maryland Line in North Carolina in 1780 (G-347).

TENKINS, SAMUEL. Private in Col. Harry Lee's Partizan Corps from January 1, 1779 through December, 1780 (G-587).

TERRY, JOSEPH. Private in Capt. Joshua George's Company in the 18th Battalion on August 18, 1776 (C-84, G-61).

THACKERY, JAMES. Oath of Allegiance in 1778 (A-8). James "Thackray" was a Private in Capt. Stephen Hyland's Co. of Militia on Sept. 8, 1775 (T-MS.1814). James Thackery married Ann Hart by license Nov. 16, 1777 (O-1, R-177).

THISTLOW, GEORGE. Oath of Allegiance in 1778 (A-10).

THOMAS, ------. Ensign in Capt. Andrew Miller's Company in the 2nd Battalion of Col. Henry Hollinsgworth, c1777, but his first name was not given on roster (S-MdHR6636-9-93).

THOMAS, AQUILA. Oath of Allegiance in 1778 (A-18).

THOMAS, BENJAMIN. Oath of Allegiance in 1778 (A-18).

THOMAS, CHRISTAIN. Oath of Allegiance in 1778 (A-7).

THOMAS, HENRY. Oath of Allegiance in 1778 (A-6). He appears to have served because he is among those due a military clothing allowance on March 6, 1779 (L-38).

THOMAS, ISAAC. Oath of Allegiance in 1778 (A-15). He appears to have served because he was due a military clothing allowance on March 6, 1779 (L-38). Isaac Thomas married Naomi Boggs by license October 3, 1791 (O-12).

THOMAS, JAMES. Oath of Allegiance in 1778 (A-14). Recruited October 16, 1780, and "sent to Chester Town" (G-345).

THOMAS, JOHN. Private in Capt. Henry Dobson's Company in the 6th Maryland Line, in N.C. in October, 1780 (G-348).

THOMAS, JOHN GERMAIN (JARMAN). Private in Major Henry (Col. Harry) Lee's Partizan Corps from April 7, 1778 through December, 1780 (C-83, G-586, G-587, K-156). Order was passed on March 16, 1836, for the "Treasurer, Western Shore, to pay to John Jarman Thomas, a soldier of the Revolution, half pay of a Private during life." (N-398)

THOMAS, JOSEPH. Two men with this name took the Oath of Allegiance in 1778 (A-15, A-18).

THOMAS, SAMUEL. Oath of Allegiance in 1778 (A-5).

THOMAS, WILLIAM. Three men with this name took the Oath of Allegiance in 1778 (A-5, A-6, A-7). One married Mary Ball by license dated January 23, 1778 (O-1). Another (born on June 6, 1729) married Sarah Kennerly (born April 4, 1742) on March 2, 1762 (R-178).

THOMPSON, ABRAHAM. Oath of Allegiance in 1778 (A-18).

THOMPSON, ALEX. Private in Capt. John Oglevie's Company on July 25, 1776 (C-85, G-647).

THOMPSON, ANDREW. Private in Capt. John Oglevie's Company, July 25, 1776 (C-85, G-647). Took the Oath of Allegiance in 1778 (A-6).

THOMPSON, EDWARD. Oath of Allegiance in 1778 (A-5).

THOMPSON, EPHRAIM. Oath of Allegiance in 1778 (A-18).

THOMPSON, EPHRAIM JR. First Lieutenant in Capt. John Leach Knight's Company, 18th or Sassafrass Battalion c1777 and in 2nd or Elk Battalion prior to April 21, 1778 (C-55, S-MdHR6636-9-93). Took Oath of Allegiance in 1778 (A-4).

THOMPSON, JOHN. Private in Capt. Jeremiah Baker's Company, August 1, 1775, and in Capt. Baruch Williams' Company, March 3, 1776 (F-158). Two men with this name took the Oath of Allegiance in 1778 (A-6, A-13). There were many John Thompsons in Cecil County: One married Hannah Evans, March 23, 1790 (O-11); another married Mary Griffith of Annapolis, March 12, 1739/1740 (R-178); another married Mary Julian, August 19, 1739 (R-178); another married Jane Houston, April 17, 1748 (R-178); and another John, son of John, married Mary

Haly of Philadelphia on May 4, 1765 (R-178). (Ed.: Obviously, additional research is required to determine which men gave partiotic service.)

THOMPSON, JOHN DOCKERY. Attended the Maryland Convention from April 24 to May 3, 1775 (K-1). He also signed the Declaration of Freemen of Maryland in 1775 (J-322) and was a Deputy to the Maryland Convention on May 16, 1775 and again on June 21, 1776 (I-2, K-2, K-28, P-3). Became Lieutenant Colonel in 18th Battalion under Col. Charles Rumsey on January 6, 1776 (C-84, G-61, I-323), and then Colonel of the 18th Battalion circa April 21, 1778 (E-55, H-540, S-MdHR6636-9-93). He was one of the Justices who administered the Oath of Allegiance, March, 1778 (A-17). Recommended for County Lieutenant, March 3, 1780 (I-273).

THOMPSON, RICHARD. Oath of Allegiance in 1778 (A-4).

THOMPSON, RICHARD JR. Oath of Allegiance in 1778 (A-4). Richard Thompson, Jr. married Mary Alman, daughter of Abraham Alman, on November 12, 1739 (R-178).

THOMPSON, ROBERT. Two men with this name took the Oath of Allegiance in 1778 (A-18).

THOMPSON, SAMUEL. Private in Capt. John Oglevie's Company on July 25, 1776 (C-85, G-647). Oath of Allegiance in 1778 (A-15). Private in Col. Harry Lee's Partizan Corps in 1780 (G-587).

THOMPSON, THOMAS. He fled the state on September 1, 1777, "supposedly gone to the British army" (S-MdHR4570-88).

THOMPSON, WILLIAM. Sergeant in Capt. James Mackey's Militia Company, July 25, 1776 (C-85, G-647). Two men with this name took the Oath of Allegiance in 1778 (A-15, A-18). One William Thompson married Hosannah Pennington by license December 23, 1794 (O-15).

THOMSON, WILLIAM. Oath of Allegiance in 1778 (A-6). Private in Capt. Stephen Hyland's Company of Militia on September 8, 1775 (T-MS.1814).

TIBBS, JOHN. Private in Capt. Walter Alexander's Company, in 30th Battalion. Enrolled July 27, 1776 (C-86, G-62).

TIDBALL, ABRAHAM. Oath of Allegiance in 1778 (A-10).

TIGNER, JAMES. Oath of Allegiance in 1778 (A-14).

TILLEY, WILLIAM. Oath of Allegiance in 1778 (A-10).

TILYARD, WILLIAM. Private in Capt. John Oglevie's Company on July 25, 1776 (C-85, G-647).

TOOLE (TOOL), ANDREW. Oath of Allegiance in 1778 (A-16).

TOOLE, JOHN. Recruit, October 16, 1780 (G-345).

TOUCHSTONE, CHRIS. Private in Capt. Henry Dobson's Company in the 6th Maryland Line. Hospitalized at Hillsborough, North Carolina in October, 1780 (G-349).

TOUCHSTONE, SAMSON. Oath of Allegiance in 1778 (A-9).

TOULSON, JOHN. Recruit, October 16, 1780 (G-345).

TOWER, JOHN. Private in Capt. Walter Alexander's Company, 30th Battalion. Enrolled July 27, 1776 (C-86, G-62).

TOWLAND, JAMES. Oath of Allegiance in 1778 (A-4).

TOWLIN, JOHN. Private in Col. Harry Lee's Partizan Corps from March 16, 1780 to at least December, 1780 (G-587).

TREMBLE (TRIMBLE), HANCE. Oath of Allegiance in 1778 (A-16).

TREMBLE (TRIMBLE), JACOB. Oath of Allegiance in 1778 (A-9).

TREMBLE (TRIMBLE), JOSEPH. Oath of Allegiance in 1778 (A-9).

TROATTLE, ALEXANDER. Oath of Allegiance in 1778 (A-8).

TUCKER, JAMES. On February 12, 1776 he was recommended by Lt. Col. Hollingsworth for commission as Adjutant (I-25).

TUCKER, WILLIAM. "A recruit, deserted" Oct 16, 1780 (G-346).

TULL, THOMAS. Oath of Allegiance in 1778 (A-4).

TUNSTILL, JOHN. Recruit, October 16, 1780 (G-345).

TURNBEL (TUMBEL?), WILLIAM. Oath of Allegiance, 1778 (A-7).

TURNER, MATTHEW. Oath of Allegiance in 1778 (A-10). Mathew Turner md Sarah Maybury, August 15 or 17, 1734 (R-182).

TUTON, GEORGE. Oath of Allegiance in 1778 (A-16).

TYSON, MATHIAS (July 20, 1754, Pennsylvania - March 25, 1829 Cecil County, Maryland). Married Jane Lewis (1754-1811) and had seven children: Tacy (born 1777); Elizabeth (born 1779); William (born 1781, married Hannah Taylor); Thomas (born 1784); Beulah (born 1785); Eliza (born 1787); and, Mathias (born 1795, married Ann Mingling). He was a Private in Capt. Curtis Lomnes Company under Lt. Col. Caleb Davis, Chester Co., Pennsylvania Militia (V-289).

VAIL, JOHN. Oath of Allegiance in 1778 (A-1).

VANSANT (VANSANDT), JOHN. Oath of Allegiance in 1778 (A-14).

VEAZEY, EDWARD. The uncle of Colonel John Veazey of Cecil County, Edward was a Captain who was killed at the Battle of Long Island on August 27, 1776 (C-85, I-16, J-326). Another Edward took the Oath of Allegiance, 1778 (A-12). Edward Veazey, son of John, married Elizabeth Coursey on June 19, 1755 (R-184).

VEAZEY, ELISHA.  Oath of Allegiance in 1778 (A-4).

VEAZEY, JAMES. Took the Oath of Allegiance in 1778 (A-2). Private in Col. Harry Lee's Partizan Corps, March, 1780 serving to at least December, 1780 (G-587). (Ed. Note: As records oftentime drop "Jr." or "Sr." or "III" from the end of names it is possible that the information that follows in the case of John Veazey, John Veazey, Jr. and John Veazey III could be assigned to one or the other of these three men by unintentional error. Additional genealogical research may be necessary in order to best determine which man goes with which historical event.)

VEAZEY, JOHN. Attended the Maryland Convention on June 21, 1776 (K-28). (Ed.: See information on John Veazey, Jr.)

VEAZEY, JOHN JR. "John Veazey" was a Lieutenant Colonel in the Militia (C-87) and also was one of the Justices who administered the Oath of Allegiance in March, 1778 (A-4). "John Veazey, Jr." was a Signer of the Declaration of Freemen of Maryland in 1775. He was elected a delegate to the Maryland Convention on May 16, 1775 (I-2, J-321, K-28, P-3), and Colonel of the Bohemia Battalion on January 6, 1776 (J-322, J-323. He was Chairman of the Committee of Safety on August 6, 1776 (W-178).

VEAZEY, JOHN III. Attended the Maryland Convention from April 24 to May 3, 1775 (K-1). Acting Clerk during the election of Deputies to the Maryland Convention, May 16, 1775 (I-2, K-2).

VEAZEY, JOHN WARD (1732 - 1790). Married first Sarah----- and second Mary Wilmer (1748-c1790) in 1767. Children were Hester (born 1764), John (born 1767), and Rebecca (1778-1855, married Thomas C. Cockrill, 1768-1815, of Ireland). John Ward Veazey was a Captain in Col. John D. Thompson's 18th Battn., June 22, 1778 (S-MdHR6636-9-93, E-56). He was one of the Justices who administered the Oath of Allegiance in 1778 (A-12) and was appointed Agent to purchase provisions in Cecil County in 1779 (U-723, V-293, and MD Society, Sons of the American Revolution application of descendant Wilson K. Barnes, Jr., National No. 89073, State No. 1822-L, approved October 21, 1983).

VEAZEY, JOSEPH. Private in Capt. Joshua George's Company in the 18th Battalion on August 18, 1776 (C-84, G-61). Took the Oath of Allegiance in 1778 (A-2).

VEAZEY, ELI. (Elk Neck). Private in Capt. Walter Alexander's Company, 30th Battn. Enrolled Aug. 3, 1776 (C-86, G-63).

VEAZEY, NOBLE. Private in Capt. Joshua George's Company in the 18th Battalion on August 18, 1776 (C-84, G-61). Took Oath of Allegiance in 1778 (A-2). Noble Veazey married Elizabeth Biddle by license dated Feb. 24, 1781 (O-4).

VEAZEY, ROBERT.  Oath of Allegiance in 1778 (A-4).

VEAZEY, SAMUEL.  Captain in Colonel John D. Thompson's Sassafrass Battalion, June 22, 1778 (E-56).

VEAZEY, THOMAS.  Oath of Allegiance in 1778 (A-2).

VEAZEY, THOMAS B.  Oath of Allegiance, 1778 (A-14). "Thomas Brookes Veasey" md Mary Thompson, March 24, 1781 (O-4).

VEAZEY, WILLIAM.  Two men with this name took the Oath of Allegiance in 1778 (A-7, A-14). One was a 1st Lieutenant in Capt. Stephen Hyland's Company on September 8, 1775 (T-MS.1814) and May 23, 1776 (P-430) and 1st Lieutenant in Capt. George's Company in the 18th Battalion on August 18, 1776 (C-84, G-61). William Veazey was an Ensign in Capt. J. W. Veazey's Co. in 1777-1778 (S-MdHR6636-9-93) and William Veazey was a Second Lieutenant in Capt. Samuel Veazey's Company, under Col. John D. Thompson, June 22, 1778, and "Will Veazey" was Captain in the 30th or Susquehanna Battalion under Col. Joseph Baxter in 1777 (S-MdHR6636-9-93) and under Col. Stephen Hyland on Sept. 9, 1778 (E-56, H-560, K-116, S-MdHR4570-72). One William Veazey was a Recruiting Officer on July 23, 1778 (I-182). There were several William Veazey's who married in Cecil County: One married Mary Louttit, October 23, 1778 (O-2); another married Sarah Lewis, October 12, 1781 (O-5); another married Mary Carr, May 16, 1758 (R-184); and, another married Mary Rock, March 1, 1771 (R-184). (Ed.: Further research may be necessary in order to determine which men rendered patriotic service.)

VEAZEY, WILLIAM 3RD.  Oath of Allegiance in 1778 (A-4). He was commissioned 1st Lieutenant in Capt. Joshua George's Company on July 20, 1776 (W-157).

VICKERS, BENJAMIN.  Oath of Allegiance in 1778 (A-12).

VICKERS, GEORGE.  Oath of Allegiance in 1778 (A-17).

WAGONER, JOHN.  Oath of Allegiance in 1778 (A-16).

WAKEFIELD, WILLIAM.  Private in Capt. Jeremiah Baker's Company, August 1, 1775, and in Capt. Baruch Williams' Company, March 3, 1776 (F-158).

WALKER, ANDREW.  Oath of Allegiance in 1778 (A-13).

WALKER, JOHN.  Oath of Allegiance in 1778 (A-10).

WALKER, ROBERT.  Oath of Allegiance in 1778 (A-1).

WALKER, WILLIAM.  Recruit, October 16, 1780 (G-345).

WALLACE, ADAM.  Took the Oath of Allegiance in 1778 (A-2).

WALLACE, ADAM JR. Private in the Militia on October 1, 1778 (S-MdHR6636-12-37A). Took Oath of Allegiance, 1778 (A-2). Adam Wallace md Fanny Henderson, April 25, 1787 (O-8).

WALLACE, ANDREW. Two men with this name took the Oath of Allegiance in 1778 (A-4, A-16).

WALLACE, DAVID. First Lieutenant in Capt. Samuel Maffitt's Company in the 2nd or Elk Battalion on April 21, 1778 (S-MdHR6636-9-93, E-54), but then resigned his commission some time after October 1, 1778, stating, "I am about to leave the State, and being of a weakley constitution, is the reason of this my resignation." (S-MdHR6636-11-52, S-MdHR6636-12-37A, I-136). He had also taken the Oath of Allegiance in March, 1778 (A-6). David Wallace married Eleanor Alexander by license dated May 21, 1782 (O-5).

WALLACE, GEORGE. Took the Oath of Allegiance in 1778 (A-16). He was from New Munster in Cecil County, Maryland, but served in the Delaware Regiment (C-83).

WALLACE, HUGH. Oath of Allegiance in 1778 (A-7).

WALLACE, JAMES. Two men with this name took the Oath of Allegiance in 1778 (A-7, A-8). One was a Private in Capt. Walter Alexander's Company, 30th Battalion, enrolled on August 3, 1776 (C-86, G-63). One was a Private in Major Henry (or Col. Harry) Lee's Partizan Cavalry in June, 1778 and on February 17, 1780 (C-83, G-586, K-156).

WALLACE, JOHN. Oath of Allegiance in 1778 (A-2).

WALLACE, THOMAS (1748 - March 31, 1812). Married Esther Patterson in 1770 and had eight children: Samuel (born 1771, married Frances McCoy); Michael (born c1777); Sarah (died 1819, unmarried); Esther (married Thomas Boyer); Rachel (born 1780, married Andrew Cross); Catherine (born 1786, married Joseph Jamison); Thomas (married Mary Jackson); and, Elizabeth (U-731). Thomas Wallace took the Oath of Allegiance in 1778 (A-6).

WALLACE, MICHAEL. (New Munster). Surgeons Mate in the Maryland Line (C-82).

WALLIS, THOMAS. Oath of Allegiance in 1778 (A-7).

WALMSLEY, BENJAMIN. Ensign in Capt. John Cox's Company in the 18th or Sassafrass Battalion prior to April 21, 1778 (E-55, S-MdHR6636-9-93). Oath of Allegiance, 1778 (A-11). Benjamin Walmsley md Rachel Money, July 6, 1780 (O-4).

WALMSLEY, JOHN. Oath of Allegiance in 1778 (A-14).

WALMSLEY, ROBERT. Private in Capt. Joshua George's Company in the 18th Battalion on August 18, 1776 (C-84, G-61). Took Oath of Allegiance in 1778 (A-14). There were several Robert Walmsley's in Cecil County: One Robert Walmsley married Elizabeth Vanhorn,

February 20, 1734/5; another Robert married Temperance Brewer on August 16, 1780 (O-4); and Robert Walmsley, Jr. married Margaret Gooding on November 12, 1787 (O-8).

WALMSLEY, WILLIAM. Oath of Allegiance in 1778 (A-11). William Walmsley married Sarah Ward, daughter of John, in November, 1740 (R-186).

WALTER, CHRISTOPHER. Oath of Allegiance in 1778 (A-7).

WARAM (WORAM), JAMES. Oath of Allegiance in 1778 (A-8). Private in Capt. Stephen Hyland's Company of Militia on September 8, 1775 (T-MS.1814).

WARD, GEORGE. Oath of Allegiance in 1778 (A-11).

WARD, HENRY. Oath of Allegiance in 1778 (A-12).

WARD, JOHN. On February 17, 1776 he was recommended by John Veazey, Jr. and John Dockery Thompson for an officer's commission (I-25). He was a Justice who administered the Oath of Allegiance in March, 1778 (A-14). He was probably the "John Ward, Sr." who was a First Lieutenant in Capt. John Cox's Company in the 18th Battalion c1777 and in the Elk Battalion by April 21, 1778 (E-55, S-MdHR6636-9-93).

WARD, JOHN. Two men with this name took the Oath of Allegiance in 1778 (A-7, A-11). One was a Private in Major Henry (or Col. Harry) Lee's Partizan Corps in June, 1778 and on February 17, 1780 (C-83, G-586, K-156). One was probably the "John Ward, Jr." who was 2nd Lieutenant in Capt. John Cox's Company in the 18th Battalion c1777 and in Elk Battalion by April 21, 1778 (S-MdHR6636-9-93, E-55). John Ward, son of John Ward, Sr., was recommended to be an officer in the Second Battalion on February 17, 1776, being "a young man of very respectable parents, of an exceeding good character, well attached to the cause." (P-167). One John Ward (1730-1787) married Elizabeth---- and had four children: Robert (died 1805), Joshua, George and Deborah. This John enlisted January 24, 1776 (U-734). One John Ward married Elizabeth Pennington, February 20, 1782 (O-5) and another John Ward married Sarah Walmsley, March 22, 1786 (O-7).

WARD, JOHN (SON OF PEREG.) Oath of Allegiance, 1778 (A-14).

WARD, WILLIAM. Attended the Maryland Convention from April 24 to May 3, 1775 (K-1) and Deputy to the Convention on May 16, 1775 (I-2, K-2). He took the Oath of Allegiance in 1778 (A-17). There were several William Ward's married in Cecil County: One William Ward married Martha Doughety on February 5, 1765 (R-187); another William Ward married Rachel Ricketts by license dated February 10, 1779 (O-2); another William Ward married Ann Veazey by lic. November 19, 1784 (O-6); and, William Ward, Jr. married Rachel Walmsley, November 30, 1791 (O-12). (Ed.: Additional research is required to determine which were patriots.)

WATERS (?), ALLEN. Oath of Allegiance in 1778 (A-1).

WATSON, ISAAC DEAN. Oath of Allegiance in 1778 (A-13).

WATSON, JOSEPH. Oath of Allegiance in 1778 (A-5). Ensign in the Militia (C-87).

WATSON, WILLIAM. Oath of Allegiance in 1778 (A-6). William Watson married Alicia Denlon, February 12, 1731 (R-188).

WATT, JOHN. Oath of Allegiance in 1778 (A-4). John Watt married Elizabeth Colvin by lic. April 22, 1778 (O-1).

WEIR, ANDREW. Oath of Allegiance in 1778 (A-5).

WEIR, EDWARD. Oath of Allegiance in 1778 (A-16).

WEIR, ROBERT. Oath of Allegiance in 1778 (A-5).

WELCH, GEORGE JR. Oath of Allegiance in 1778 (A-10).

WELCH, GEORGE SR. Oath of Allegiance in 1778 (A-10).

WELCH, JAMES. Private in Capt. John Oglevie's Company on July 25, 1776 (C-85, G-647). Took the Oath of Allegiance in 1778 (A-6).

WELCH, JOHN. Oath of Allegiance in 1778 (A-10).

WELCH, ROBERT. Oath of Allegiance in 1778 (A-10).

WELCH, ROBERT SR. Oath of Allegiance in 1778 (A-10).

WELLS, JOHN. Private in Capt. Henry Dobson's Company in 6th Maryland Line, serving in North Carolina in October, 1780 (G-348). John Wells, son of John, married Mary Riley, of County Donegal, Ireland, on January 26, 1773 (R-190).

WELSH, ANDREW. Oath of Allegiance in 1778 (A-5).

WELSH, JAMES. Oath of Allegiance in 1778 (A-13).

WENNER, JACOB. Oath of Allegiance in 1778 (A-7).

WESTWOOD, WILLIAM. Private in Capt. Henry Dobson's Company in the 6th Maryland Line in North Carolina, 1780 (G-347).

WHAN, JAMES. Oath of Allegiance in 1778 (A-16).

WHAN, SAMUEL JR. Oath of Allegiance in 1778 (A-16).

WHAN, WILLIAM. Oath of Allegiance in 1778 (A-16). William "Whann" md Jane Maffitt by lic. May 21, 1794 (O-14).

WHATTSON, JOSEPH. Oath of Allegiance in 1778 (A-7).

WHITE, ABNER. Oath of Allegiance in 1780 (B-123). Abner White married Margaret Johnson, October 1, 1782 (O-5).

WHITE, JOHN. Took the Oath of Allegiance in 1780 (B-123). John White married Sarah White (sic) "his present wife" on October 16, 1771 (R-193).

WHITE, JONATHAN. Oath of Allegiance in 1778 (A-9).

WHITE, PETER. Oath of Allegiance in 1778 (A-13).

WHITE, WILLIAM. Oath of Allegiance in 1778 (A-16).

WHITEACRE, RALPH. Oath of Allegiance in 1778 (A-6).

WHITEACRE (WHITESIER?), WILLIAM. He appears to have served because he is listed among those who were due a military clothing allowance on March 6, 1779 (L-38).

WHITELOCK, CHARLES JR. Oath of Allegiance in 1778 (A-5).

WHITELOCK, CHARLES SR. Oath of Allegiance in 1778 (A-5).

WHITELOCK, PATRICK. Oath of Allegiance in 1778 (A-5).

WHITTAM, PEREGRINE. Oath of Allegiance in 1778 (A-2).

WHITTAM, BENJAMIN. Oath of Allegiance in 1778 (A-18).

WHITTAM, WILLIAM. Two men with this name took the Oath of Allegiance in 1778 (A-2, A-18). One William Whittam married Augustua Heawking by lic. July 17, 1779 (O-3) and one married Margaret Moore by lic. April 9, 1792 (O-13).

WILCOX, JOSEPH. Oath of Allegiance in 1778 (A-2).

WILEY, JOHN. Oath of Allegiance in 1778 (A-12).

WILKINSON, JOHN. Oath of Allegiance in 1778 (A-6).

WILLCROFT, JAMES. He appears to have served because he was due a military clothing allowance on Mar. 6, 1779 (L-38).

WILLIAMS, BARUCH (Of Charlestown). Captain in the 30th or Susquehanna Battalion on March 3, 1776 and resigned his commission on March 24, 1776 (I-29, P-419). Later he was apparently commissioned again and promoted to the rank of Major, Susquehanna Battalion on September 9, 1778, and subsequently became a Lieutenant Colonel (C-87, F-157, I-27, I-29, K-116, S-MdHR4570-72). He was Clerk of the Cecil County Committee on August 7, 1780 (I-307). One marriage record indicates that Baruch Williams, late of Prince George's County, married Rachel Baxter, daughter of Col. James and Elizabeth, on May 7, 1771 (R-195).

WILLIAMS, BASIL. 1st Lieutenant in Capt. James Pritchard's Company, 30th or Susquehanna Battalion under Col. Joseph Baxter, by April 21, 1778 (E-58, S-MdHR6636-9-93). Also took the Oath of Allegiance in March, 1778 (A-5). Basil Williams married Jane Barret, daughter of Andrew Barret, on April 6, 1775 (R-195).

WILLIAMS, BENJAMIN. Private in Capt. Henry Dobson's Company in the 6th Maryland Line in North Carolina, 1780 (G-347).

WILLIAMS, CHARLES. Oath of Allegiance in 1778 (A-6). He appears to have served because he is among those due a miitary clothing allowance on March 6, 1779 (L-38).

WILLIAMS, ELIOT. Private in Capt. Joshua George's Company on July 25, 1776 (C-85, G-647).

WILLIAMS, JOSEPH. Oath of Allegiance in 1778 (A-3).

WILLIAMS, RICHARD. Oath of Allegiance in 1778 (A-7).

WILLIAMS, ROBERT. First Lieutenant in Capt. Robert Porter's Company, 30th or Susquehanna Battalion under Col. Joseph Baxter prior to Sept. 9, 1778 (E-57, S-MdHR6636-9-93). Took the Oath of Allegiance in March, 1778 (A-4). Robert Williams married Mary Kirkpatrick, Feb. 28, 1786 (O-7).

WILLIAMS, THOMAS. Oath of Allegiance in 1778 (A-5). One Thomas Williams md Agnes Hartshorn, Aug 20, 1800 (Q-126).

WILLIAMSON, ALEXANDER. Oath of Allegiance in 1778 (A-4).

WILLIAMSON, DANIEL. Private in Harry (or Henry) Lee's Partizan Cavalry in June, 1778 (C-83, G-586).

WILLOCK, ANDREW. Oath of Allegiance in 1778 (A-6).

WILLOCK, JAMES. Oath of Allegiance in 1778 (A-6).

WILLSON, ANDREW. Oath of Allegiance in 1778 (A-10). Andrew "Wilson" married Ann McCoy by license Oct. 6, 1786 (O-8), and Andrew "Wilson" md Sarah Miller, Apr. 10, 1788 (O-9).

WILLSON, GEORGE. Oath of Allegiance in 1778 (A-7).

WILLSON, JOHN. Private in Capt. Jeremiah Baker's Company, August 1, 1775, and in Capt. Baruch Williams' Company, March 3, 1776 (F-158). Two men with this name took the Oath of Allegiance in 1778 (A-5, A-7).

WILLSON, PETER. Oath of Allegiance in 1778 (A-9).

WILLSON, SAMUEL. Two men with this name took the Oath of Allegiance in 1778 (A-5, A-10).

WILSON, ALEXANDER. Ensign in Capt. Samuel Evans' Company, Elk Battalion, April 21, 1778 and Lieutenant in Capt. Samuel Maffitt's Company, October 1, 1778 (C-87, E-43, E-54, S-MdHR6636-9-93,

S-MdHR6636-12-37A). He took the Oath of Allegiance in 1778 (A-16).

WILSON, DANIEL. Private in Capt. Setphen Hyland's Company of Militia on September 8, 1775 (T-MS.1814). Private in Capt. Joshua George's Company, 18th Battalion on August 18, 1776 (C-84, G-61). Oath of Allegiance in 1778 (A-17).

WILSON, GEORGE. Private in Capt. Jeremiah Baker's Company, August 1, 1775, and in Capt. Baruch Williams' Company, March 3, 1776 (E-158). Two men with this name took the Oath of Allegiance in 1778 (A-5, A-6).

WILSON, JAMES. Oath of Allegiance in 1778 (A-5).

WILSON, JOHN. Private in Capt. Jeremiah Baker's Company, August 1, 1775, and in Capt. Baruch Williams' Company, March 3, 1776 (E-158). Oath of Allegiance in 1778 (A-6).

WILSON, JOHN (QUAKER). Oath of Allegiance in 1778 (A-2).

WILSON, JOHN (WEAVER). Oath of Allegiance in 1778 (A-5).

WILSON, THOMAS. Two men with this name took the Oath of Allegiance in 1778 (A-6).

WILSON, WILLIAM. Two men with this name took the Oath of Allegiance in 1778 (A-2, A-15). One William "Willson" married Elizabeth Cammoran by lic. March 1, 1791 (O-123).

WINCHESTER, WILLIAM. Oath of Allegiance in 1778 (A-6).

WINDLE, JONA. Private in Capt. Henry Dobson's Company in the 6th Maryland Line. Enlisted April 24, 1778 for three years. Serving in North Carolina in Oct., 1780 (G-348).

WINKELES, GEORGE. Oath of Allegiance in 1778 (A-6).

WINKET (WINKERT), SAMUEL. Oath of Allegiance in 1778 (A-7).

WINKET, THOMAS. Oath of Allegiance in 1778 (A-15).

WINTERS, ELISHA. Assisted Henry Hollingsworth in mounting 200 gun barrels under an order of July 5, 1776. His shop was used to fit bayonets on July 12, 1776 (I-42, K-38).

WINTGAGE, HEZEKIAH. Oath of Allegiance in 1778 (B-124).

WIREY, MICHAEL. Private in Capt. Henry Dobson's Company in the 6th Maryland Line in North Carolina in 1780 (G-348).

WIRTS (?), THOMAS. Oath of Allegiance in 1778 (A-18).

WISHAM, JOHN. Private in Major Henry Lee's Partizan Corps on February 17, 1780 (K-156). Granted leave of absence "till called for" on June 17, 1783 (G-588).

WOOD, JOHN. Oath of Allegiance in 1778. (A-16) Another John Wood (or possibly the same one) took the Oath of Allegiance in 1780 (B-124). There were several John Woods married in Cecil County: One married Elizabeth Watson by license dated May 17, 1779 (O-3); another married Rebecca Eliason, daughter of Corenlias, on Dec. 19, 1737 (R-199); another married Francis Flintom on Dec. 20, 1737 (R-199); and, another married Rachel Death, Jan. 20, 1755 (R-199). (Ed.: Obviously, further research is required in order to determine which men actually rendered patriotic service.)

WOOD, WILLIAM. One William Wood took the Oath of Allegiance in March, 1778 (A-4). Another William Wood was reported to have fled the state on September 1, 1777 and "supposed to be gone to the British Army" (S-MdHR4570-88, K-121).

WORK, ALEXANDER. Private in Capt. Walter Alexander's Company, 30th Battalion. Enrolled on July 24, 1776 (C-86, G-62). Took the Oath of Allegiance in 1778 (A-16).

WORK, ANDREW. Oath of Allegiance in 1778 (A-10).

WORK, JAMES. Oath of Allegiance in 1778 (A-16). Private in the Militia on October 1, 1778 (S-MdHR6636-12-37A).

WORK, SAMUEL. Oath of Allegiance in 1778 (A-16).

WORK, WILLIAM. Oath of Allegiance in 1778 (A-10). William Work married Ann Meeck by license April 12, 1779 (O-3).

WRIGHT, JAMES. Private in Capt. John Oglevie's Company on July 25, 1776 (C-85, G-647).

WRIGHT, JOHN. Oath of Allegiance in 1778 (A-15).

WROTH, JAMES. Private in Capt. Joshua George's Company, 18th Battalion, August 18, 1776 (C-84, G-61). Ensign in Capt. Samuel Veazey's Company, Sassafrass Battalion, June 22, 1778 (E-56). Took Oath of Allegiance in 1778 (A-14). James Wroth md Ann Severson by lic. May 19, 1778 (O-2).

WROTH, JAMES JR. Oath of Allegiance in 1778 (A-12).

WROTH, THOMAS. Oath of Allegiance in 1778 (A-14). Thomas Wroth married Mary Pennington, widow of John Pennington, on January 12, 1747 (R-202).

YARDLEY, WILLIAM. Oath of Allegiance in 1778 (A-11).

YEOMANS, JOSHUA. Oath of Allegiance in 1778 (A-8).

YEOMANS, SAMUEL. Oath of Allegiance in 1778 (A-8).

YEOMANS, THOMAS. Oath of Allegiance in 1778 (A-8). Thomas "Yeoman" md Elizabeth Cunningham, July 5, 1791 (O-12).

YOUNG, GODFREY. Private in Capt. Henry Dobson's Company in 6th Maryland Line in North Carolina in 1780. Transferred to the Invalids Corps on October 23, 1780 (G-349).

YOUNG, JOHN. Recruited, October 16, 1780 (G-345). This or another John Young was a Corporal in Capt. Henry Dobson's Company, 6th Maryland Line, serving in North Carolina in October, 1780 (G-347).

YOUNG, ROBERT. Oath of Allegiance in 1778 (A-6). Robert Young married Rebecca Taylor by license dated February 19, 1781 (O-4).

YOUNG, SAMUEL. Two men with this name took the Oath of Allegiance in 1778 (A-7, A-17). One was a Quartermaster in the Militia (C-87) and another was a Private in Capt. Henry Dobson's Company in the 6th Maryland Line in North Carolina in October, 1780 (G-347). One Samuel Young married Elenor Johnson on February 2, 1730 (R-203).

YOUNG, WILLIAM. Oath of Allegiance in 1778 (A-13). William Young married Ann Brown by license August 24, 1778 (O-2).

# INDEX

ABRAEM Richard 1
ADAIR Elizabeth 5
ADAMS Hester 66
  William 1
ADARE John 1
  William 1
AGNEW Michael 1
AIKEN Elizabeth 93
AIRES Rebecca 97
AKEN Robert 1
ALDREDGE Elizabeth 108
ALDRIDGE Fredus 1
  Fredus 53
  Sarah 66
ALEXANDER Abigail
  Amos 1, 2
  Amos, Jr. 1
  Arthur 1
  Caleb 1
  Capt. 67
  Charles G. 2
  David 1
  Dorcas 2
  Dorcas R. 2
  Edward 1
  Eleanor 117
  Eli 1
  Ester 38
  Ezekiel 1
  George 2
  Hannah 2
  Hezekiah 2
  Isaac 1
  James 1, 2
  James R. 2
  James, Jr. 2
  Jemima 1
  John 2
  John G. 2
  John McKnitt 2
  John, Jr. 2
  Josiah 2
  Margaret 1
  Mark 1, 2, 41
  Mary 1, 33
  Mary S. 2
  Moses 2
  Priscilla 1
  Rachel 1
  Rebecca 66
  Robert 3, 41
  Ruth 1
  Silas 2
  Walter 1-9, 15, 17, 18, 20-23, 25, 27-34, 38, 40, 42, 45, 47, 48, 49, 51, 58, 59, 61, 62, 64, 68, 70-75, 79, 82, 86, 87, 89, 90-92, 94-98, 100, 101, 104, 105, 109, 110, 113-115, 117, 123
  William 3
ALIE Burnet 3
ALLEN Mary 17
  Robert 3
ALLIT Joseph 3
ALMAN Abraham 113
  John 3
  Mary 113
ANDERSON Henry 3
  Jacob 3
  James 3
  John 3
ANDREW James 3
ANDREWS James 3
ANKRIM James 3
ARBUCKLE Elizabeth 72
ARGUCKLE Elizabeth 72
ARMSTRONG Alexander 4
  Edward 4
  Edward, Jr. 4
  John 4
  William 4
ARNIT Alexander 4
ARNO William 4
ARRANTS Ann 64
  Harman 4
  James 4
  Juliana 53
  Nathan 4
  William 4
ARRATS Harman 4
ARTHERGE John 4
ASH George 4
  Nicholas 4
ASKIN Henry 4
  Michael 4
ASPARAGOR Johannes 4
AUREN Sarah 31
  Thomas 4

AVREN Thomas 4

BAAL George 5
BADDERS John 5
BAKER Ann 56
  Capt. 42-45, 48
  Charlotte 5
  Elizabeth 5
  Francis 5
  Henry 5
  Jeremiah 1, 2, 5, 15, 16, 18, 19, 24, 30, 39, 40, 57, 58, 59, 60, 70, 71, 73, 74, 76, 77, 78, 81, 83, 101, 103, 106, 107, 108, 110, 112, 116, 121, 122
  Jethro 5
  John 5, 99
  Lydia 5
  Marcie 5
  Mary Ann 5
  Nathan 5
  Sarah 5, 99
  Siney 5
  Thomas 5
BALDIN Peter 5
BALL George 5
  Mary 112
BALLINTINE Hugh 6
BANBURY John 6
BANKHEAD John 6
BARCKLEY James 6
BARCLAY William 6
BARCLEY James 6
  James, Sr. 6
BARE Thomas 6
BARFORD William 6
BARNABY John 6
BARNEBY Mary 18
BARNES James 6
  James, Jr. 6
  Joseph 6
  Thomas 6
  Wilson K., Jr. 115
BARNETT Debrah 89
BARNIT John 6
BARNS James 6
  James, Jr. 6
  Joseph 6
  Thomas 6
BARR David 6

John 6
Mary 96, 97
Robert 6
BARRET Andrew 121
Jane 121
BARRETT Andrew 6
Jane 91
Philip 91
BARRY John 6
Thomas 6
BARWICKE James 11
BASSETT Michael 6
Richard 6
BATEMAN William 7
BATH Joseph 8
BAVINGTON John 7
BAXTER Col. 87, 91
Elizabeth 58, 120
James 58, 120
Joseph 7, 28, 79, 92, 116, 120, 121
Rachel 120
BAY Kenniday 7
BAYARD Ann 35
Benjamin 7
Col. 95
John, Jr. 7
Mary 11
Peter 7
Samuel 7
Sarah 88
BAYLES John 13
BAYTHORN James 7
BEADLE Sarah 88
BEALL Evan 7
BEAN William 7
BEARD Elizabeth 18
Hugh 7
James 7
Lambert 7
Lewis 7
William 7
BEARE Lawson 7
BEASTIN Andrew 7
Elizabeth 88
George 7
Richard 7
William 88
Zebulon 7
BEASTON Ann 28
Jeremiah 8
Joseph 8
BEATH Joseph 8

BEATY Samuel 8
BEAZLY Edward 8
BECK Mary 38
William 8
BECKELL Isaac 8
BECKETT Isaac 8
BEEDLE Andrew 9
Harman 8
Henry 8
Hyland 8
John 8
Noble 8. 9
Peregrine 8
Raman 8
Rebecca 8
Samuel 8
Sarah 10, 32
Thomas 8
BEEDLEE Henry 8
BEEK William 8
BEETH Joseph 11
BEETLE Tobias 12
BELEW Tile 8
BELL John 8
Robert 8
BENJAMIN Joseph 8
BENNET John 9
Nathan 9
BENNETT John 9
Richard 9
BERRY James 9
BETHELL John 9
BEVERLY James 9
BEYTHORN James 7
BIDDLE Andrew 9
Elizabeth 115
Noble 9
Stephen 9
Susan Ann 85
BIGGS Nathan 9
BILLIP Harry 9
BING Bethen 9
John 9
Oliver 9
Samuel 9
BIRD Empson 9, 27
George 9
George R. 55
Mary 27
Richard 9
Susanna 27
Thomas 10
BITTLE Thomas 10
Thomas, Jr. 10
BLACK Ann 50

David 10
Sally 95
BLAKE Isaac 10
Martha 3
Solomon 10
BLANEY John 10
BLANSFORD John 10
Joseph 10
BLEW Sarah 5
BLUE Sarah 5
BLUNDELL Charles 10
BOGGS Archibald 10
James 10
Naomi 112
BOICE George 12
BOING Isaac 10
BOLTERMON John 10
BOLTON Robert 10
BOME Bartle 10
BOMGARDNER George 10
BOND Levi 10
Lidya 56
Lydia 56
Richard 10
Richard, Jr. 10
Samuel 11
Samuel, Jr. 11
BONDWICKE Walter 11
BONNEDY John 11
BONSALL Enoch 11
BONWICKE James 11
BOON Joseph 11
BOOTH Ebenezer 11
Edward 11
Jonathan 11, 50, 96, 99
Joseph 11
BORLAND James 11
John 11
BORRIS Edward 11
BOUCHALL S. G. 11
BOUCHELL John 11
Sluyter 11
Slyter, Jr. 11
Thomas 11
BOUCHING Mary 102
BOULDEN Sarah F. 22
Thomas, Jr. 12
Thomas, Sr. 12
BOULDIN Andrew 12
Augustine 12
Dorcas 12
Ephraim 12
Francina 12
Herman 12

James 12
Jane 12
John 12
Joseph 12
Lewis 11
Mary 9, 12
Mary N. 11
Reuben 12
Richard 11, 12
Samuel 12
Sophia M. 66
Tamar 12
Thomas 8, 12
Thomas, Jr. 12
William 12
Wood 12
BOULDING Nathan 35
BOWARD Leonard 12
BOWEN Jonathan 12
Thomas 12
BOWERS George 12
BOWMAN Mary 44
BOYCE Alexander 12
Catherine 37
Francis 12
George 12, 13
BOYD Alexander 13
Francis 13
Hester 107
Hugh 55, 107
John 13, 55
Nathan 13
Robert 13
Susannah 53
BOYLE John 13
BOYLES Adam 13
John 13
Robert 13
Timothy 13
BOYS Alexander 12
BRACKLEY Joackin 13
BRADDOCK Johnson 13
BRADFORD Rebecca 79
BRADLEY Cornelius 13
George 13
Neal 13
BRAZIER W. F. 13
BREVARD Benjamin 13 Capt. 53
Rachel 111
Thomas 12, 13

BREWER Temperance 118
BRICEN Thomas 15
BRIDGE Daniel 13
BRIGHLEY Joakim 13
BRIND Isaac 14
BRISLAND William 14
BRISON Thomas 15
William 15
BRISTOW John 14
John, Jr. 14
William 14
BROCKELL Richard 14
BROOKINGS Charles 14
BROOKS Rebecca 106
Thomas 14
BROOM Abraham 14
Thomas 14
BROOME Abraham 14
Thomas 14
BROWN Ann 124
Catherine 14
Daniel 14
George 14
Hannah 39
Jacob 14
James 14
Jessee 14
John 14
John H. 36
Joseph, Jr. 15
Joshua 14
Mary 15
Messer 15
William 15
BROWNE Hugh 15
BRUMFIELD Daniel 15
Francis 15
James 15
John 15
Mary 11
Nathan 15
William 15
BRUNFIELD Mary 15
BRYAN Ann 8
Augustine 15
Mary 25
BRYON Sarah 81
BRYSON Daniel 15
Richard 15
Sarah 62
Thomas 15
William 15
BUCHANAN James 15

Robert 15
William 15
BUCKWORTH Samuel 15
BUFORD Mary N. 107
BULTEEL Henry 15
BURK James 16
Richard 16
BURKE William 16
BURLEY Neal 16
BURLIN John 65
BURNHAM Thomas 16
BURNS Annie W. 59, 68, 89, 96
BUTLER John 16
Richard 16
Ruth 107
BYARD Samuel, Jr. 7
BYERS Stanly 16

CACKEY Hector 16
CADLE Elizabeth 100
CADWELL Elizabeth 27
CAHOE Thomas, Jr. 16
CALDWELL Betsey Ann 68
John 68
Mary H. 68
Rachael 68
Robert 16, 68
CALHOUN William 16
CALLENDAR Jane 87
CALWELL James 16
William 16
CAMERON John 16
CAMMORAN Elizabeth 122
CAMPBELL Alexander 16
Archibald 16
George 16
George H. 16
Henry 17
Iliander 16
James 17
James, Jr. 17
Jane 17
John 17
John, Jr. 17
John, Sr. 17
Joseph 17
Mary 5
Thomas 17
William 107
CAMPBLE Henry 17
James 17

CAN Augusteen 17
  Elizabeth 70
  John 17
CANN John 17
  Rachel 90
  Robert 17
CANNON Moses 17
CANTWELL Paterson 17
CARAVELL John 17
CARBERRY Peter 17
CARITHERS James 17
  Robert 18
CARLIN George 18
CARLON George 18
CARMOTHAN James 18
CARPENTER
  Valentine 18
CARR Mary 116
CARRIL Daniel 18
CARRIL John 18
CARROLL Anna
  Statia 87
  Dominick 87
CARSON John 18
  Robert 18
CARSWELL John 18
CARTER Noah 18
CARTY Ann 107
  John 18
CARUTHERS Francis 18
  John 18
  Lavinia 103
  Walter 18
  William 18
CASHIRE William 18
CASHNE William 18
CASSADY William 18
CASSE Robert 18
CASWELL Anne 18
  Calpam 18
  Christian 18
  John 18
  Mary 18
  Richard 18
  Sarah 18
  Susannah 18
  William 18
  Winston 18
CATHCART David 18
CATHER Ann 98
  David 19
  George 19
  Robert 19, 96

CATO George 19
CATTO George 19
CAUGHEY Patrick 19
CAULK Thomas W. 19
CAVENDER Ann 49
  Rachel 101
CAVINDER James 19
  John 19
CAYHAN Hannah M. 63
CAZIER Abraham 4, 19, 66, 92
  Capt. 44
  James 24
  John 24, 36
  Thomas 36
CHAMBERS John 19
  John C. 19
  Jonas 19
  Nicholas 19
  Sarah 61
  William 19
CHANDLEE Benjamin 19
  Benjamin, Jr. 19
CHANDLER Thomas 19
CHAPPELL John 20
CHARLOTON Ann P. 60
CHEETHAM Nancy 12
CHESNEY William 20
CHESNUT William 20
  Benjamin 20
CHEW Anne 106
  Sarah 26
CHICK Nathaniel 20
  Peregrine 20
CHILDS Nathaniel 20
CHILES Tamor 29
CHISNUT William 20
CHRISFIELD Cornelia 26
CHURCH Abraham 20
CHURCHMAN Catherine 44
  Elijah 20
CHURN Michael 20
CITELY Thomas 20, 59
CLARK Ann 12
  Frances 39
  James F. 20
  John 20
  John B. 20
  Keesy 4
  Michael 20
  Robert 20

  Samuel 20
  Thomas 20
CLAYTON James L. 20
  Joshua 20
  Richard 20, 21
  Thomas 20
CLEAVER Benjamin 21
CLEESE John 21
  Peter 21
CLEEVES Hannah 26
CLENDENIN James 21
  John 21
CLENDENNIN Mary 1
CLENEHAN Robert 21
CLENSHEY James M. 21
CLOOSE John 21
  Peter 21
CLOWARD William 21
COALE Philip 21
  William 22
COARD James 21
  William 21
COCH James 21
COCHRAN James 21
  John 21, 66
  Moses 21
  Patrick 21
  Robert 21
  Willam 21
COCK James 21
COCKRILL Thomas C. 115
COHOUND Wadley 21
COHRAN John 21
  Robert 21
COLE Abigail F. 22
  Elijah 22
  Hannah 22
  Mary 22
  Philip 13, 22, 25, 59
  Sarah 22
  William 22
COLLINS Edmond 22
  John 22
  Solomon 22
  Timothy 22
COLVIN Elizabeth 119
COMEGYES Jesse 22
COMEGYS Alphonso 22
  Jesse 22
  Jonathan 22
CONCAU John 22
CONNALLY Cornelius 22

CONNELLY Gustain 22
  James 22
  Jeremiah 22
  John 22
  Mary 59
  Michael 23
  Rebecca 105
  Samuel 23
CONNER Cornelius 23
  James 23
CONNOLEY John 23
CONNOLLY Mary 69
CONNOR Catharine 31
  James 23
CONWAY William 23
COOCH William 51
COOPER Ann 96
  Ephraim 23
  Hezekiah 23
  John 23
  Jonas 23
  Thomas 23
COPPEN Sarah M. 91
CORBALLY Richard 23
CORBET David 23
  Joseph 23
  William 23
CORBIT Ester 23
CORBITT David 23
CORCAU John 22
CORD Thomas 24
CORLET John 24
COSDEN Aletha 80
  Catherine 1
  James 24
  Thomas 24
COSNER Daniel 24
COTHER George 19
  Robert 19
COUCH William 26
COUDEN Anna 103
COULSON Nathaniel 24
COULTER Samuel 24
COURSEY Elizabeth 115
COVENHOVEN Gertrude 44
COWEN John 24
COX Alice 24
  Benjamin 24
  Elijah 24
  George 24
  John 24, 117, 118
  Rebecca 24
  Samuel 24
  Sophia 24
  Susannah 69
  Thomas 12, 24
  William 24
COZIER Abraham 19
  James 24
  John 24
CRABSON Moses 24
CRABSTON Moses 24
CRABTREE Capt. 107
CRAFORD James 25
CRAGE George 25
  James 24
CRAIG George 25
  Grissell 55
  James 24
  John 25
  Robert 24, 25
  William 54
CRAIGE John 25
  William 25
CRAIGIE James 25
  James, Jr. 25
CRAMAR Philip 25
CRASBY Jesse 25
CRAWFORD James 25
  John 25
CREAGHTON William 25
CREAIGHTON William 25
CREATON William 25
CRESSWELL Mary 46
CRESWELL James 25, 59
CRIME Michael 25
CRISWELL James 25
CROCKETT Ann 26
  Elizabeth 19
  Samuel 25
CROCKIT Samuel 25
CROMBERS Jonas 25
CROMWELL John 25
CROOKSHANKS Isabel 53
  William 25, 26
CROSBY Hugh 26
  Jesse 25
  Nathaniel 26
CROSS Andrew 117
  John 26
CROUCH Elizabeth 53
  Hannah 6
  Isaac 26
  James 26
  John 26
  John D. 26
  Margaret 53
  Peggy 104
  Robert 26
  William 26
CROW Andrew 26
  Andrew, Jr. 26
CROWL Alexander 26
CROWLEY John 26
CROZEN Robert 26
CROZIER James 26
CRUCKSHANKS William 25
CRUTHERS Elizabeth 3
CULLEY George 27
CUMMINGS James 27
  John 27
  Samuel 27
CUMMINS John 27
CUNNINGHAM Carbery 27
  Elizabeth 123
  George 27
  Hugh 27
  James 27
  John 27
  William 27
CURRANT James 27
CURRER Mary 80
  Sampson 27
  William 27
CURRIER Benoni 27
  Mary 19
  Sampson 27
  Sara 39
  William 27
CUSEX Elizabeth 65
CUSTCK Chris. 27

DAGG James 28
DALEY Daniel 28
DALLAM Col. 59, 64
DANLEY Edward 28
DANUEL John 28
DAUGHERTY Edward 13, 25, 28, 59
  Roger 28
DAVIDSON James 28
  James, Jr. 28

John 28
William 28
William, Jr. 28
DAVIS Amos 28
  Caleb 114
  Frances 45
  Henry 28
  John 28
  Margaret 35
  Morris 28
  Rebecca 79
  Robert 28
  Samuel 28
  William 28
DAWSON Joseph 28
  Nathaniel 28
  William 29
DAY George 29
DEAN Elizabeth 25
DEATH Jacob 29
  Rachel 123
  Randall 29
  Randle 29
DENLON Alicia 119
DENNEY John 29
DENNIS Capt. 42
  John 29
DENOON John 29
DERREL Sarah 65
DEVERICKS James 29
DEVLIN James 29
DICKSON Sarah 56
  Staford 29
  Thomas 29
DIXSON Thomas 29
DOBSON Adam 29
  Henry 3, 4, 6, 8-12, 14, 16-23, 25, 27-32, 35, 38, 40, 42, 43, 45, 47-51, 55, 56, 58, 64-67, 69-72, 74, 76, 77, 79, 81, 84, 85, 89, 92, 95, 98, 99, 103-112, 114, 119, 121, 122, 124
  Richard 29
DOGAN James 30
DOLLISON Mary 26
DOMAGAN William 30
DOMINICK Benjamin 30

DONAGAN William 30
DONAHO Joshua 30
DONALDSON David 30
DONLEY Edward 28
DONN John 30
DONNELEY Patrick 30
DONNOLLY Caleb 30
DONNOLLY Edward 30
DONOLY Caleb 30
  Edward 30
DONOVAN John 30
DOOGAN James 30
DORAN Patrick 30
DORMETT Rachell 17
DOROUGH John 30
DORSEY Ann 51
  Elizabeth Ann 36
DOUGHARTY James 20, 30, 60
  Mary 10
  Michael 30
DOUGHETY Martha 118
DOUGLAS Gray 30
DOWDLE William 31
DOWLIN Roger 31
DOWNEY Patt. 31
DOYAL Patrick 31
DOYL Thomas 31
DRAKE Elizabeth 56
DUFF Samuel 31
DUFFEY John 31
DUFFIELD Amanda 1
  William 31
DUFFY John 31
DUGIN James 31
DUNBARR Andrew 31
DUNN William 31
DURBIN Samuel 31
DURHAM William 31
DUTTON Mary 103
DUVALL Richard 31

EAKIN James 31
EDDY Anna 34
EDGE William 31
EDMISTON David 31
EGAN Patrick 31
EGANS James 54
EKEY Peter 31
ELEXSON Charles 31
ELIASON Cornelias 123
  Gertrude 24
  Mary 52
  Rebecca 1223

ELLERY John 32
ELLIET John 32
ELLIOTT Catharine 65
  James 32
  John 32
  Joseph 32
  William 32
ELLIS Richard 32
  Sarah 49
ELSBERRY Lambert 32
ELSBUREY Lambert 32
ELWOOD John 32
  Richard 32
  Richard F. 32
EMMITT Abram 32
  David 32
  John 32
ENGLAND George 32
  Richard 32
ENGLANG George 32
ENSOR Augusteen H. 32
  Mary 85
ETHERINGTON
  Bartholomew, Jr. 32
  Bartholomoew, Sr. 32
  Benjamin 33
  John 33
  Sarah 88
  Thomas 33
  Thomas, Jr. 33
EVANS Capt. 86
  Hannah 112
  James, Jr. 33
  James, Sr. 33
  Jane 50
  John 1, 33, 108
  Mary 51
  Polly 17
  Robert 33
  Samuel 29, 33, 93, 100, 102, 108, 121
EVERDSON Everd 33
  Jacob 33
EVERTSON Evert 33
  Jacob 33
EVERYT Mary 22
EWING Henry 33
  Mary 55
  Moses 33
  Nathaniel 33

Patrick 34
Peggy 34
Peter 34
Robert 34
Thomas 34
William 25, 34, 65, 90
EYANSON Ann 34
  John 34

FAIRBROTHER
  Francis 34
FALTON William 34
FARIAS James 34
FARIES Ann 12
  Margaret 12
FARIS James 34
FARMER Joseph 34
FARREL Francis 34
FARRIER Grace 16
FEDERY Richard 34
FEE John 34
FERGUSON Agnes 6
  Benjamin 34
  Mary 44
  Rebecca 98
  Samuel 34
  William 35
FERIS Adam R. 68
FERVOTT Peter 35
FIELDS James 35
FINLEY John 35
  John E. 35
  Margaret 6
  Robert 35
  Samuel R. 35
  Sarah 107
  William 35
  William, Jr. 35
FITSGARELD James 35
FITZGERALD Timy. 35
FLACK James 35
FLANNAGIN Mary 82
FLINTER Sarah 8
FLINTHAM Benjamin 35
  R. 35
FLINTOM Francis 123
FOARD Ann 35
  Hezekiah 35
  James 35
  John 35

Levi G. 35
Mary 35
Richard B. 35
William 35
FORD Araminta 36
  Charles T. 36, 70
  Cornelia 36
  Edward 35
  Frances 12
  George W. 36
  Hezekiah 36
  John 11, 35, 36, 49, 91
  John H. 36, 53
  Lambert 36
  Martha 24, 36
  Nathaniel 36
  Rachel 109
  Rebecca 36, 62
  Richard 36
  Richard B. 35
  Richard, Jr. 36
  Richard, Sr. 36
  Stephen H. 36
  Thomas 36
  William 36
  William W. 36
FORDIN Thomas 36
FOREACRES Joseph 36
FOREMAN Thomas M. 36
FORESTER Catherine 45
  Frances D. 52
  George W. 45
FORGESON Benjamin 34
FORRESTER Alex. 36
  Cornelius 37
  Frances 52
  John 37
FORSTER Alex. 36
  Cornelius 37
  Jesse 37
  John 37
  John, Jr. 37
  John, Sr. 37
  Thomas 37
  William 37
FOSTER Ann 15
  Archibald 37
  Benjamin 37
  Catherine 53
  Elenor 60
  Francis 37

131

Isaav 36
James 37
Jesse 37
Rachel 59
Sarah 24
FOX Margaret Ann 55
  Mary 55
FRAMPTON Moses 37
FRANKLIN Benjamin 37
FREEMAN Ephraim 37
FRENCH Thomas 38
  William 38
FREW David 38
  James 38
FRIER William 38
FULLAM James 38
FULLER William 38
FULTON Alexander 38
  Sarah 21
  William 38
FURNER Edward 38
FYFE James 38

GALE George 38
GALLIHER John 38
  John, Jr. 38
GALLINOUGH Edward 38
GALLOWAY James 38
GANTT James 38
GARDINER George 38
  William 39
GARMON Thomas 39
GARNER David 39
  James 39
GARRISH Edward 39
  William 39
GARRISON Dorcas 2
GARROTT William 39
GASTON James 39
GATCHELL Anne 39
  Elisha 39
  Elisha, Jr. 39
  Hannah 39
  Jeremiah 39
  Mary 39
  Samuel 39
GAULT James 38
GAUNCE Mary Ann 85
GEAR Peregrine 39
GEARS Peregrine 39
GEORGE Calvin S. 39
  Capt. 116
  Elizabeth 39
  John 39
  Joshua 5, 8, 9,

11, 13, 14, 17,
22-24, 27-29,
31-33, 36, 38-
40, 45-47, 51-
53, 55, 61-63,
69, 70, 72, 74,
75, 77, 78, 80,
82, 84-88, 91,
92, 96, 101-
103, 105, 108,
110, 111, 115-
117, 121-123
  Nicholas 40
  Rachel 69
  Sampson 39
  Stephen 39
  William 40
GERISH Edward 39
GETTRICK William
  40
GIBNEY Simon 40
GIBSON Andrew 40
  Elizabeth 15
  Mary 80
  Robert 40
  William 40
GILES Elizabeth 85
  Thomas 40
GILLASPY Francis
  40
GILLEN James 40
GILLES John 40
GILLESPIE George
  44
  James 40
  Mary 44
  Richard 40
GILLILAND Thomas
  40
GILLIS James 40
  John 40
GILMORE James 40
GILPIN Elizabeth
  1, 41
  Hannah 41
  Jane 41
  John 41, 50
  Joseph 40, 41
  Josiah 41
  Mary 41
  Rachel 41
  Samuel 11, 21,
    40, 41, 57
  Samuel, Jr. 41
  Sarah 41

GINN Ann 44
GIPSON Andrew 40
GLADEN Martha 89
GLASCOW Adam 41
GLASFORD Harry 41
GLASGOW Adam 41
  Ann 46
  James 41
  Mary 30
  Robert 41
  William, 3rd 41
  William, Sr. 41
GLASS Elizabeth 103
  George 41
  John 41
GLASSFORD Henry 41
GLENN John 42
  Samuel 42
GOFTON John 42
GOLD John 42
GOLDSBOROUGH Howes
  98
GONSEN Ann 5
GOOD Jannet 60
  John 42
GOODING Isaac 42
  Margaret 118
  William 42
GORDON Archibald 42
  David 42
  Elizabeth 44
  John 42
GORTRILL George 42
GOTTIER Francis 42
GRACE William 42
GRAHAM James 42
  Moses 42
  Rosanna 65
GRANT George 42
  Joseph 76
GRANTLY James 42
GRAVES Elizabeth 29
GRAY John 43
  Starret 43
GREAR William 43
GREAS William 43
GREAVES Isaac 43
GREEN Jane 74
  John 43
  William 43
GREENLAND Sarah 55
GREENTREE Isaac 43
GREENWOOD Alex. 43
GREHAMS William 43
GREY Andrew 98

GRIFFE William 43
GRIFFITH John 43
  Mary 112
  Thomas 43
GRIMES Richard 43
GROUCER Adam 43
GROVES Ann 78
GRUBB Andrew 43
GUFFEY James 43
  John 43
  Joseph 43
GUFFY Jean 44
GUTHRIE William 43
GUY Eleanor 87
  Richard 43
  Samuel 43
GUYE Robert 43

HADABUCK John 43
HAGAR Martha 13
HAGUE Joseph 44
HAINES Job 44
HALL Catherine 44
  Catherine O. 44
  Charles 44
  Eleanor 44
  Eleanor B. 93
  Elihu 44
  Elihu, III 44
  Elihu, Jr. 44
  Elihu, Sr. 44
  Elisha 44
  Elisha J. 44
  Elizabeth H. 44
  George W. 44
  Hannah 100
  Henry 44
  Isaac 44
  James 44
  John 44, 100
  John, Jr. 44
  Joseph 45
  Julia R. 44
  Mary 12, 100
  Nicholas 44
  Samuel C. 44
  Sarah 44
  Susan 44
  Susannah 67
  Washington 44
  William 45
HALLON Jacob 50
HALLURAN Thomas 45
HALTHAM Joseph 51
HALY Mary 113

HAMBLETON John 45
HAMILTON Ensign 5, 9
  George 45
  John 45, 59
  John, Jr. 45
  Patrick 45
  Samuel 45
  Thomas 59
HAMM Araminta 54
  Nancy 36
HANCE Martha 31
HANDY George 45
HARGAN John 45
HARLEY William 45
HARRIES John 45
HARRINGTON Mary Ann 12
HARRIS William 45
  William, Jr. 45
  William, Sr. 45
HARRISON Richard 46
  William 46
HARSON Benjamin 47
HART Ann 111
  Jane 53
  Mary 26
  Robert 46
  Robert, Jr. 46
  Thomas 46
HARTHORN John 46
  Joshua 46
HARTSHORN Agnes 46, 121
  Benjamin 46
  John 46
  Jonathan, Jr. 46
  Joshua 46
  Samuel 46
  Thomas 46
HARTSHORNE John 46
  Jonathan 46
HARVEY Arramantha 29
  Joshua 46
  Mathew 47
  Phineas 47
  William 47
HARVIE Robert 47
  Thomas 47
HARWARD Henry 47
HARWOOD Elizabeth 85
HASSON Benjamin 47

James 47
HATHORN John 46
  Joshua 46
HAYES Henry 47
  James 47
  Richard 47
HAYS James 47
  Richard 47
HEATH Charles 33, 47, 83, 84
HEAWKING Augustua 120
HEDRICK Catherine 36
  George 47
  Michael 47
HEGARTY Andrew 47
HEGON James 47
HELM Michael 47
HEMPHILL James 47
  Joseph 47, 48
  Robert 48
HENDERSON Capt. 42
  David 48
  Fanny 117
  Fresby 50
  Rachel 65
HENDRICKSON
  Augustine 48
  Ephraim 48
  Henry 48
  John 48
  Rebecca 15
HENECY Peter 48
HENERSON James 48
  William 48
HENNIE John 48
HENREY David 48
HENRY David 48
  Samuel 48
HERBERT James B. 5
HERITAGE Sarah 18
HERMAN Augustine 54
HERON J. G. 48
HERSEY Isaac 48
HERVIE Robert 47
HESSEY Isaac 48
  James 48
HEWIT James 48
HEWSTON William 53
HIBBETS Isaac 48
  James 48
HICKMAN William 48
HIGGINS Thomas 48
HILL Charles 49

133

David 49
George 49
James 49
John 49
Jonathan 49
Margaret 94
Samuel 49
HILLONS Abraham 49
HINDMAN James 49
HINMAN James 49
  Robert 49
  Samuel 49
HITCHCOCK Julia Ann 2
  Thomas 49
  William 49
HITCHMAN William 49
HODGSON Araminta 102
  Jonathan 49
  Jonathan, Jr. 49
  Richard 49
  Robert 49
HOGANS William 50
HOGG Samuel 70
HOLLADAY John 50
HOLLAN John 50
HOLLAND Jacob 50
  John 50
HOLLIDAY John, Jr. 50
HOLLINGS Esther 84
  Jonathan 50
HOLLINGSWORTH
  Abigail 29
  Betsy 50
  Col. 42, 86
  Evans 51
  George 50
  Hannah 50
  Henry 3, 11, 14, 16, 32, 40, 41, 50, 51, 67, 68, 79, 84, 102, 106, 109, 110, 111, 122
  Jacob 50
  James 50, 51
  John 51
  Levi 51
  Margaret 26
  Mary 41, 51
  Nancy 50
  Peggy 51
  Polly 50
  Robert 51

Samuel 50
Stephen 50
Thomas 51
William 50, 51
Zebulon 50, 51
HOLMS Abraham 51
HOLT George 51
  Isaac 51
HOLTHAM Joseph 51
  Spencer 51
HOLYDAY Hester 56
HOMES George 51
HONEYMAN Robert 51
HOOPER Abraham 51
  Isaac 51
HOPKINS John 51
HORLEY William 45
HOTTHAM Spencer 51
HOUSLY John 51
HOUSTON Jane 112
HOWARD John 51
HOWEL James 51
  William 51
HOWELL George 51
  James 51
  Mary 51
  William 51
HOWLAND Alias 51
  Richard 51
HUCANS Abiah 52
HUDDABUCK John 44
HUDSON Jacob 52
  John 52
HUGG Jacob 62
HUGGINS Charles 52
  Thomas 52
HUGHES Andrew 52
  Evin 52
  Roland 52
  Samuel 52
  Thomas 52
HUGHS Thomas 52
HUKILL Abiah 52
  Daniel 52
  James 52
  Jeremiah 52
  Jesse 52
  Joseph 52
  Peter 52
  Richard 52
  Spencer 53
HUKINS Joseph 52
HULET James 53
HULL Jane 102
  John 53

Sarah 26
William 53
HUNGARD Mary 20
HUNT Joseph 53
  Marshall 44
HUNTER James 53
  Mary 37
  William 37
HURLEY John 53
HURLY John 53
HUSBAND Sarah 50
HUSLER William 53
HUSLEY Rachel 80
HUSSA James 53
HUSSON James 47
HUSTON William 53
HUTCHESON Jesse 53
  Joseph 53
  Samuel 53
HUTCHINSON Samuel 53
HUTCHISON Mary 88
HYLAND Amelia 53
  Ann 46
  Araminta 53, 70
  Col. 87
  Edward 53
  Elizabeth 81
  Isaac 54
  Jacob 54
  John 54
  John, Jr. 53
  Johnson 53
  Joshua 53
  Lambert 54
  Margery 71
  Martha 54
  Mary 53, 54
  Millicent 36
  Milliscent 57
  Nicholas 53, 54
  Rachel 66
  Rebecca 53, 58
  Stephen 1, 6, 8,
    14, 22, 26, 31,
    32, 34, 36, 38,
    39, 40, 42, 43,
    46, 49, 53, 54,
    58, 61, 64, 70,
    75, 79, 81, 88,
    90, 94-97, 101,
    105, 111, 113,
    116, 118, 122
  Stephen, Jr. 54
  William 53

HYNSON Nathaniel 54

IGANS James 54
IRELAND Nathan 54
IRON Alexander 54
IRVAN Bazel 54
IRWIN John 54
IVORY Patrick 54

JACK John 54
JACKSON Daniel 54
  Edward 55
  Elizabeth 25
  Henry 55
  Hugh 55
  James 55
  John 55
  Margaret 55
  Mary 64, 117
  Robert 55
  Samuel 55
  Walter 55
  William 55
JACOBS J. 99
  Jesse 55
JACSON Walter 55
JAMES Morgan 55
  Seth 55
JAMESON John 55
  William 55
JAMISON Adam 55
  George 55
  John 55
  Joseph 117
  William 55
JANVIER Lidia 55
  Philip 55
JARALIMAN John 55
JARVIS John 55
  Mary 101
  William 55
JAVINS Daniel 56
JAVYR Lidia 55
  Philip 55
JEFFERSON Pres. 67
  William 56
JEFFRIS William 56
JENKINS Samuel 56
JEWELL Cornelius 56
JOB Archibald 56
  Daniel 56
  Elizabeth 56
  Enoch 56
  Margaret 56
  Morris 56

Sarah 56
Thomas 56
Thomas, Jr. 56
JOBE Morrico 56
JOBSON John 56
JOHNSON Amelia 62
　Ann 23, 25, 26
　Col. 67
　David 56
　Elenor 124
　Elisha 56
　George 45, 52, 56
　Isaac 56
　Jacob 56
　James 56
　John 56, 57
　Josiah 57
　Levi 57
　Margaret 120
　Mary 54
　Mary 104
　Mathias 57
　Robert 57
　Rozanna 6
　Simon 57
　Thomas 57
　William 57
JOHNSTON Isaac 57
　James 57
　John 57
　Thomas 57
　William 57
JOHNSTONE William 57
JONES Charles 57
　Jane 81
　John 57
　Mary 26
　Moses 58
　Nathaniel 58
　Rebecca 36
　Robert 58
　Samuel 58
　Thomas 58
　William 58
JONSON John 58
　Josiah 57
　William 58
JORDAN Hugh 58
　Thomas 58
JULIAN Mary 112
JULIUSTRA Mary 53
JUSTICE Edward 58
　Rebecca 2

William 58
KANKEY Ann 23, 54
　Elizabeth 89
　John 54, 58
　John, Jr. 58
　Margery 54
　Maria 53
　Marie 54
　Rebecca 23
KEARNES Thomas 58
KEATLY Thomas 59
KEELY Ann 5
KEITH Robert 58
KEITHLEY Mary 96
KEITLY Henry 58
　John 59
　Thomas 20
　Thomas 59
KELLER George 59
KELLEY John 59
　Nicholas 59
　Thomas 59
KELLY Ebenezer 59
　James 59
　John 59
　Nicholas 59
　Samuel 59
　Thomas 59
KELY Ann 5
KEMPHILL Joseph 47
KEMPTON Thomas 59
KENNERLY Sarah 112
KENT James 59
　Thomas 59
　William 59
KERR George 59
　Nathaniel 60
　Samuel 60
KERSY Honour 29
KEY Francis Scott 60
　James 60, 95
　John Ross 60
KIDD Andrew 60
　George 65
KIGHT John 60
KILGOUR James 60
KILLGORE James 60
　William 60
KILLPATRICK Samuel 60
　William 60
KILPATRICK Elenor 60

135

Elizabeth 41
Samuel 60
KIMBLE Elizabeth 99
　Sarah 48
KINARD John 60
KINCADE John 60
KINCAID John 60
KING Abna 60
　John 60
　Thomas 60
　William 60
KINKEAD John 60
KINNARD John 60
KIRK Abner 60
　Alexander 61
　Garratt 61
　Garret 61
　Jacob 61
　John 61
　Joseph 61
　Mary 93
　Timothy 61
　Zachariah 61
KIRKPATRICK John 61
　Mary 121
KITE William 61
KITELY Thomas 59
KITLEY Thomas 20
KLEINHOFF William 61
　William, Jr. 61
KNIGHT Elizabeth 58
　George 61
　John L. 32
　John Leach 10, 61, 112
KNOX Robert 61
　Sarah 79

LACKLAND James 61
　Mathew 61
　Nathan 61
LAFAYETTE Gen. 44
LAFFERTY William 61
LAING John 61
LANCASTER Elizabeth 62
　Jeremiah 62
　Samuel Sinclair 62
　Sinclair 62
　St. Clair 62
LANGLEY John 62
LANGVILL Hugh 62
　Robert 62
　William 62
LANGWELL Hugh 62

Robert 62
William 62
LASHLEY George 62
LASHLY George 62
Nancy 62
LASHU John 63
LASLEY John 62
LASLY George 62
LASSLIE John 62
Robert 62
Thomas 62
LATHAM Aaron 62
Susanna 4
Sylvester 62
LAUGHLIN Robert 62
LAURENCESON
Susannah 26
LAURENSON Mary 20
LAWIS John 62
LAWREMORE James 63
LAWRENCE Ann 7
Rachel 7
LAWRENSON James 62
Sarah 36
LAWSON George 63
John 63
Peter 63
LAYHUA John 63
LEE Ephraim 63
Harry 3, 4, 6,
9, 11, 12, 14,
20, 25, 26, 27,
31, 38, 42, 45,
46, 47, 47, 48,
49, 51, 52, 56,
56, 60, 63, 69,
73, 74, 85, 86,
96, 99, 100,
104, 109, 110,
111, 112, 113,
114, 115, 117,
118, 121
Henry 26, 40,
52, 63, 122
James 63
Mary 14
Richard 63
William 63
LEECH John 63
LEFFLER Deborah
111
LEHU John 63
LEMON Archibald 63
LEONARD James 63
William 63

LESLOW Peter 63
LESSLIE Daniel 63
William 64
LEWIS Araminta 20
David 64
Jane 114
John 62, 64
Richard 64
Samuel 64
Sarah 37, 116
LIGGET George 64
LIN Mathew 64
LINCH William 64
LINCOLN John 64
LINSEY Daniel 64
LINTON George 64
LISSEY Isabella 34
LITELL Nathaniel 64
LITTLE Christopher
5
James 64
Nathaniel 64
Robb 64
William 64
LIVEZEY Jon H. 9,
39, 76
LLAND Sarah 108
LLOYD Mary T. 60
LOCK William 64
LOCKRIDGE Elizabeth
68
LOGAN Hugh 64
Matthew 64
Samuel 64
William 64
LOGE Manasseh 65
LOGUE Ephraim 65
Isaac 65
James 65
Jamima 35
Manassa 65
LOMNES Curtis 114
LONG Alexander 65
Andrew 65
John 65
Joseph 65
LONGE Ephraim 65
LONGWELL Hugh 62
Robert 62
William 62
LONGWORTH Robert 1
LOPP John 89
LORAN Margaret 53
LORT Joseph 99
LOUTTIT James 65

Joshua 65
Mary 116
LOVE Ann 72
Anna 65
Elizabeth 65
James 65
Jane 65
John 65
Margaret 65
Mary 65
Robert 65
Rosanna 65
Samuel 65
LOW Isaac 65
William 65
LOWRY James 65
John 66
William 66
LUCKEY Robert 66
LUM Ann 66
Edward 66
Elizabeth 66
Hyland 66
Isaac 66
Jacob 66
John 66
Julia 66
Michael 66
Millicent 66
Rebecca 69
LUSBY Edward 66
Joseph 66
Robert 66
LUTTON James 66
Robert 66
LYNCH George 66
John 66
Sarah 58, 88
LYNN John 66
LYON Eleanor 84
Heetor 66
Hugh 66
James 66
James, Jr. 66
John 67
Joseph 67
Robert 44, 67

MACKELWEE John 67
MACKEY Catherine 67
David 67
James 34, 36, 38,
49, 67, 107, 113
James, Jr. 67
James, Sr. 67

John 67
Mary 67
Robert 67
Thomas 67
William 67
MACKY David 67
 James, Jr. 67
 James, Sr. 67
 John 67
 Robert 67
MACOMB Jeanette 20
MACY Col. 95
MADDOX Alexander 67
MAFFITT James 68
 Jane 119
 Samuel 68, 76, 94, 117, 121
MAGRUDER Zadok 65
MAHAFEY Joseph 68
MAHAFFEY Elizabeth 107
MAHANNY Thomas 68
MAHONEY Stephen 68
 William 68
MAJORS Rowland 68
MAKENNE Mary 66
MAKENS Richard 78
MALOAN John 68
 Rachael 68
MALONE Andrew 68
 Obediah A. 68
 Thomas 68
MANLEY Jacob 68
 Jesse 69
 John 69
 Rebecca 25
 Tesey 69
MANLY Elizabeth 49
 Jacob 68
 John 69
 Milicent 52
 Rebecca 49
 Thomas 69
MANSFIELD James 69
 Robert 69
 William 69
MANTLE George 69
 John 69
MANUEL Thomas 69
MARCER James 78
MARCHANT James 69
MARQUES John 69
 John, Jr. 69
 Robert 69

Robert, Jr. 69
Samuel 69
MARQUIS John, Jr. 69
 Samuel 69
MARR David 69
MARSHALL John 69
 William 70
MARTAIN Edward 70
MARTIN Edward 70
 Hugh 70
 James 70
 John 70
 William 70
MASON Rebecca 96
MATHEWS James 70
 William 70
MATTHEWS Charles 70
 James 70
 Robert 70
 William 70
MAULDEN Ann 50
 Benjamin 70
 Henry 70
 Marjorie 54
 William 70
MAULDIN Benjamin 53, 70
 Francis 70
 Henry 70
 James 70
 John 70
 Mary 36, 70
 Rebecca 5, 70
 Thomas 70
 William 70, 71
MAUNTETH William 71
MAXWELL James 27, 33, 46, 57, 71
 James, Jr. 71
 John 71
 William, Jr. 71
 William, Sr. 71
MAY Hugh 71
 John 71
 Thomas 71
MAYBEN Edward 71
MAYBERRY Benjamin 71
MAYBON Edward 71
MAYBURY Sarah 114
McALESTER Daniel 71
McBRIDE Hannah 71
 James 71
McBURNEY Mary 13

137

McCALL Ann 94
 John 71
McCALLOR Margaret 89
McCANE Patrick 72
McCANN Hugh 72
 Michael 72
 Patrick 72
McCARRAHAN Mary 55
McCARTNEY John 72
McCASHLIN William 72
McCASKER Michael 72
McCAULEY Daniel 72
 Henry 72
 James 72
 John 72
 Susannah 1
McCAY Agnes 72
 Alexander 72
 Ann 72
 Catherine 72
 Elizabeth 72
 Ester 72
 Frances 72
 Hugh 72
 James 72
 Jean 72
 John 72
 John, Jr. 72
 Joseph 72
 Margaret 72
 William 72
McCELVEY Owen 72
McCIBBINS James 72
McCLANE Margaret 66
McCLAREY Bassett 72
McCLEAN James 73
 John 73
 Robert 73
McCLEARY Rachael B. 20
 Thomas 73
McCLELLAND George 73
 Nathaniel 73
McCLELON James 73
 Robert 73
McCLINTOCK John 73
McCLOUD Alexander 73
 John 73
McCLUAR Margaret 19
McCLUER William 73
McCLURE Charles 73
 William 73
McCLUREY John 73
 Samuel 73
McCOLLA John 73

McCOLLACH John 73
　Samuel 73
　Samuel, Jr. 73
McCOLLAGH Samuel 73
McCOLLOCK John 73
McCOLLOM James 73
McCOLLOUGH John 74

McCOLVEY Owen 72
McCONKEY John 74
　William 74
McCONN Hugh 72
McCONNELL Rebecca 37
　Samuel 74
　Stephen 74
McCOOLE John 74
McCORMICK
　Catherine 14
McCOULOUGH
　Alexander 74
　James 74
　William 74
McCOY Ann 65, 121
　Catherine 65
　Esther 99
　Frances 117
　Henry 1
　Hugh 65
　John 72
McCRACKEN James 74
　James 74
　Ruth 53
McCRAY Margaret 79
McCREA Ann 106
　Hugh 74
McCRERY John 74
　Thomas, Sr. 74
McCULLEY Henry 72
McCULLOCH John 73
　William 74
McCULLOUGH
　Elizabeth 95
　James 74
　Rebecca 46
McCULOGH William 74
McCURDEY Daniel 75
　David 75
　John 75
McCUTCHEN Francis 75
　John 75
McDEAD John 75

McDONALD Patrick 75
McDOWELL Ann 14
　Benjamin 75
　Hugh 75
　John 75
　Joseph 75
　Matthew 75
McDUGAL Joseph 75
McELPIN Thomas 75
McELWAIN Mary 18
McFADEN Patrick 75
McFALL Daniel 75
McGAHAN Henry 75
McGARRETY James 75
　Richard 75
McGAUGHEY Alexander 75
McGIFFIN Nathaniel 76
McGILLAN Michael 76
　Michael, Jr. 76
McGLOCHLIN Owen 76
McGOWEN Heket 76
　James 76
　John 76
McGOWNE Hackrey 76
McGREAGOR William 76
McGUFFIN Daniel 76
McGUIRE Hugh 76
　Patrick 76
McHENDRICKS James 76
McHERD Alexander 76
McHUGH William 76
McINTIRE Sophia 12
McINTYRE John 76
　Samuel 103
McKAY John 72
　William 72
McKEOWN Elizabeth 76
　John 76
　Samuel 76
　William 76
McKEY John A. 76
McKIBBIN James 77
McKINLEY Alexander 77
McKINLY John 94
McKINSEY John 77
McKNIGHT Grace 38
McLAUGHLIN James 77
　Matthew 77
McLEAN James 77

McLOUGHLIN Matthew 77
McMAHON Benjamin 77
　Morris 77
McMASTER Robert 77
McMIN Lydia 42
McMONAGLE Joseph 22
McMULLAN John 77
McMULLEN John 77
　Margaret 55
　Robert 77
　Samuel 77
McMULLIN Samuel 77
　Samuel, Jr. 77
McMULLON Daniel 77
　Robert 77
McNAMARA George 77
　Patrick 77
McNAMARR George 77
McNAUGHT Hugh 77
McNEELY Joseph 77
McNEIL William 77
McNINEH James 77
McNINEK James 77
McSHEEHY Eugene L. 77
　Marmaduke 77
McVEA Elizabeth 11
McVEGH Jacob 78
　John 78
　John, Sr. 78
McVEY Benjamin 77, 78
　Jacob 78
　John 78
　John, Sr. 78
McVINCHY Edward 78
McWHIRTER John 78
McWILLIAMS William 78
MEAK Eleanor 69
MEANS Benjamin 78
　John 78
MEAS Robert 78
MEDLICOTT James 78
MEECK Ann 123
MEEKINS Joshua 78
MEGLOHLAND Mathew 78
MEGREDY John 56
　Mary 56
MEKENS Joshua 78
MEKINS Joshua 78
　Richard 78
　Richard, Jr. 78
MELOAN Alex 68

Andrew 68
Andrew, Jr. 68
Elizabeth 68
Isabel 68
Obadiah 68
P. O. 68
Permile 68
Sally 68
Thomas 68
MELONE Andrew 68
MENE Benjamin 78
MENTEHEN James 78
MENTEKEN James 78
MERCER James 78
   Thomas, Sr. 79
   William 79
MERDITH Martha 94
MERIT William 79
MICHELL William 79
MIDDLECUT James 78
MILBURN Nicholas 79
MILLBOURN Nicholas 79
MILLER Agnes 46
   Andrew 15, 19, 79, 110
   Benjamin 79
   Capt. 42
   Deborah 108
   Henry 79
   Henry, Jr. 79
   James 79
   John 79
   Margaret 84
   Samuel 19, 23, 79, 81, 94, 96
   Sarah 52, 121
   Thomas 79
   William 79
MILLIGAN James 79
MILLS John 79
Mills Milicent 104
   Robert 79
MINGLING Ann 114
MINOR John 79
MITCHELL Abraham 79
   Abraham D. 80
   Andrew 80
   Ephraim T. 80
   George E. 80
   John 80
   John, Jr. 80
   Mary 40

Oliver 22
Robert 80
William 80
MOFFITT Samuel 68
MONEY Aletha 80
   Anne 90
   Catherine 88
   Hyland 80
   Isaac 80
   John 80, 90
   Mary 80
   Rachel 90, 117
   Robert 80
   Samuel 80
   Susan 80
   William 80
MONTGOMERY Hugh 80
   Jane 93
   John 80
   John H. 80
MONTLE George 69
MOODY Alexander 80
   Benjamin 81
   Catharine 59
   Elizabeth 34, 88
   Jane 48
   Jane 79
   John 81
   Leah 80
MOONEY John 80
MOOR Alexander 81
   Hugh 81
MOORE Alexander 81
   Elizabeth 42
   Ferdinand 81
   George 81
   Hugh 81
   Margaret 120
   Robert 81
   Robert, Jr. 81
   Robert, Sr. 81
   Sarah 58
MORAN Benjamin 81
   William 81
MORGAIN Dorety 97
   John 97
MORGAN Abigail 81
   Ann 81
   Araminta 81
   Daniel 95
   David 81
   Elizabeth 81
   James 81
   John 81
   Matthew 81

Rebecca 81
Rulif 81
Rulof 81
Sarah 81, 97
Susan 44
Thomas 81
William 81
MORLEDGE Samuel 82
MORRAU John 82
MORREY Mary 70
MORRISON David 82
   Elizabeth 51
   Michael 82
   Samuel 82
   William 82
MORROW James 82
   John 82
MORYNIN Jacob 82, 83
MOSELEY Betty 12
   Martha 12
MOSS Joseph 82
MOTT John 5
MUIR John 82
MULLAN Charles 82
   John 82
MULLEN William 82
MULLET Peter 82
MULLIN Charles 82
   John 82
   Thomas 82
   William 82
MULLINS Jonathan 82
MULLON Thomas 82
MULLOT Peter 82
MULSEY Priscilla 86
MUNFORD Peter 82
MUNKS James 82
MUNS Benjamin 78
MURPHEY Edward 82
   Francis 82
   John 83
   Thomas 83
MURPHY Edward 82
   Francis 82
   John 83
   Joseph 83
   Thomas 83
MURRAY Alexander 83
MUSE Walker 83
MYERS Temperance 35

NALEY Sarah 49
NASH George 83
   John 83
NEAD John 83

NEEDS James 83
NEIGHBOURS Joseph 83
NEILER Rebecca 14
NEILL Thomas 83
NELSON John 83
NESBOT Alec 65
NESBIT Robert 84
NEWEL Richard 83
  Stephen 83
  Thomas 83
NEWELL Thomas 83
NEWLAN Nathan 84
NEY Michael 99
NICHOLAS John 83
NICKELSON John 83
NIGLE Jacob 83
NISBETT James 83
  John 83
  Joseph, Jr. 84
  Joseph, Sr. 84
  Robert 84
NOBLE Philemon 84
NOLAND Elias 84
  John 84
NORTON Edward 84
  Nathan 84
NOWELL James 84
NOWLAN Nathan 84
NOWLAND Alias 51
  Alias 84
  Benoni 84
  Elias 84
  Elizabeth 18
  Gilbert 84
  John 84
  Rebecca 81
  Richard 51, 84
NUGENT Silvester 84
NURNER Mary 16
NUTT William 84

O'FLINN Patrick 84
O'NAIL Felix 85
OAR Robert 84
OBOURN James 84
OGELBY John 84
OGLE Elizabeth 44
OGLESBY John 5
OGLEVEE John 84
OGLEVIE John 4, 7, 9, 10, 14, 15, 21, 22, 23, 27, 29, 30, 31, 34, 39, 41, 47, 49, 55, 56, 57, 60, 73, 75, 76, 77, 79, 81, 82, 83, 84, 89, 91, 93, 97, 98, 101, 105, 106, 108, 109, 110, 112, 113, 119, 123
OLDHAM Ann 85
  Augustine H. 85
  Charles 85
  Edward 85
  Elizabeth 85, 106
  George W. 85
  Hamet 85
  Jeremiah 85
  Maria 85
  Moses 85
  Nathan 85
  Richard 85
  Robert 85
  Thomas 85
OLIVER Jane 79
ORRICK Catherine 44
  James 85
ORZIER Rachael 68
OSBORN James 84
OTHOSON Ann 78
  Garrett 85
  Garriot 88
  Mary 88
OWEN Stephen 85
OWENS David 85
  Elias 85
  Francis 85
  John 85
  Joseph 85
  Stephan 85
  Thomas 86
OWINGS Bartholomew 86
OWINS Thomas 86
OZIER Rachael 68

PALMER Thomas 86
PARKER Edmond 86
  Edward 34, 67, 68, 79, 86, 106, 109
  Samuel 86
  Samuel, Jr. 86
PARKS David 86
  John 86
PARRY Edward 86
PARSLEY Ann 61
  Benjamin 86
  Edward 86
  Eleanor 100
  Thomas 86
  Thomas, Jr. 86
PARTRIDGE James 41, 50
PASSMORE William 86
PATTEN Thomas 86
  William 86
PATTERSON David, Jr. 86
  Elizabeth 46
  Esther 117
  Hugh 86
  John 87
  Joseph 87
  Robert 87
  Samuel 87
  William 87
PATTON David 87
  James 87
  Jean 16
  Michael 87
  Thomas 87
PAUL John 87
PAYENTER Samuel 87
PEALE James 87
  Margaret J. 93
PEARCE Ann 94
  Benjamin 87
  Benjamin, Jr. 87
  Gregry 87
  Henry Ward 87
  James 88
  Matthew 94
  Nathaniel 88
  Sarah 7
  Thomas 88
  William 88
  William, Jr. 88
PEDEN Henry C. 98
PEMBERTON John 88
PENNINGTON
  Barthomolew 88
  Elizabeth 103, 118
  Hosannah 113
  Hyland 88
  James 88
  Jemima 82
  John 88, 123
  John, Sr. 88
  Margaret 88
  Mary 123

Mary Ann 106
Robert 88
Samuel 88
Sarah 96
Thomas 88
William 53
William D. 88
PERREY Anne 111
PERRY David 88
  Elizabeth 91
  James 89
  Lewellen 89
  Lewin 89
PETTIT Ann 76
PEW Mary 71
PHELAND Margaret 5
PHELPS Joseph 89
PHILBERT Joseph 89
PHILIPS Joseph 89
PHILLIPS Hesten 64
  John 89
  Nathan 89
  Samuel 89
  William 89
  Zebulon 89
PIERCE Jesse 91
PINKNEY William 98
PLEXCO George 89
  Henry 89
PLOW Annacart 33
PLUMLEY George 89
POALK Barkley W. 89
  David 89
  David, Sr. 89
  Samuel 90
  Thomas 90
POGUE George 90
POLK Elizabeth 20
POLLOCK David 89
POLSON John 90
PORTER Andrew 44
  Andrew, Jr. 90
  Andrew, Sr. 90
  Ann 44
  Benjamin 90
  Edward 90
  Elizabeth 34, 90
  James 23, 24, 90, 101
  Jesse 90
  Joseph 90
  Patrick 90
  Robert 3, 29, 57, 87, 90, 121

Robert, Jr. 91
William 91
PORTERFIELD Josiah 91
PRICE Andrew 91
  Ann 81
  Benjamin 91
  Catherine 51
  Eliakim 91
  Ephraim 91
  Francina 4
  Hannah 78
  Hyland 91
  Hylant 91
  James 68, 91
  James K. 91
  Jesse 91
  John 68, 91
  John H. 91
  Joseph 91
  Kazia 62
  Lewis 91
  Nicholas H. 92
  Noble 92
  Rebecca 52, 88
  Sarah 54
  Thomas 92
  William 51, 92
  William, Jr. 92
PRITCHARD James 23, 24, 92, 120
PUGH John 92
PULLIN John 92
PUNTELEY Priscilla 36
PURDY Edward 92
  Henery 92
  John 92
PYCKLIN William 92

QUAIL Thomas 92
QUIDLEY Charles 92
QUIGLEY Charles 92
  James 92

RAIN Isaac 92
RALSTON Hugh 92
  Joseph 93
RAMSAY James 93
  Nathaniel 67, 93
  Thomas 93
  William W. 93
RAMSEY Charles 93
  Thomas 93
RANDALL John 93

141

RANKIN Alexander 93
  George 93
  John 93
RATLIFF James 93
  Robert 93
RAWLINGS Joseph 94
  Sealy 94
  Thomas 94
RAY Robert 94
REA Andrew 94
  George 94
  James 94
READ Alexander 94
  Andrew 94
  Charles 94
  George 94
  John 94
  John, Jr. 94
  Mary 94, 95
  William 94
READE Charles 94
READGRAVE Samuel 95
REAH James 94
REDMAN James 95
REED Alexander 1
  Ann 41
  Elizabeth 22
  John 94
  Margaret 74
  Sarah E. 41
REES Charity 56
  Margaret 56
REILEY Davis 95
  John 95
  Jonathan 95
  Margaret 95
  Mary 95
  Michael 95
  Rebecca 95
  Robert 95
  Smith 95
  William 95
RENNOLDS George 95
REY James 95
REYLEY Mathew 95
REYNOLDS Elizabeth 98
  Frederick D. 2
  Henry 95
  John 56
  Mary 15, 64
  Prudence 61
  Rachel 11
  William 95
RHEA George 94

RICE Millicent 87
  Robert 95
  William 95
RICHARDSON James 95
  Jonathan 95
  Josiah 96
  Mary 20, 96
  Rebecca 96
  Robert 96
  Sarah 12
  Thomas 96
  William 44, 66, 96
RICKETTS Benjamin 96
  David 96
  John 96
  John T. 96
  John, Jr. 96
  Rachel 118
  Reubin 96
  Rulif 96
  Sarah 91
  Thomas 91
RIDDELL John 96
RIDDLE Samuel 96
RIDER Joseph 97
RIDLE Humphrey 97
RIELY Margaret 16
RIGHT John 60, 97
  Stephen 97
RILEY Mary 119
RING William 60, 97
RITTER William 97
ROACH James 97
  Phillip 97
ROBB Jacob 97
ROBERTS John 92, 97
  Mary 92
  Morgan John 97
  Robert 97
  Ruth 12
  Samuel 97
  Sarah 61
  Thomas 97
ROBERTSON Henry 97
ROBINSON John 98
  Margaret 12
  Patrick 98
ROBISON John 98
  Patrick 98
ROCK Mary 116

William 98
ROCKHOLD Asel 98
RODGERS Alexander 98
  Elisha 98
  Elizabeth 98
  George W. 98
  John 98
  Maria Ann 98
  Mary 98
  Rebecca 98
  Thomas R. 98
ROFF John 98
ROGERS Elisha 98
  Michael 98
  Rowland 98
  Samuel 98
  Thomas 98
  William 98
ROSE Henry 99
ROSS David 99
  Joseph 99
ROWLAND Anne 89
  Ester 72
  Jacob 99
  James 99
  Margaret 35
  Robert 99
  William 99
RUDULPH Jacob 99, 100
  John 99
  Michael 42, 99, 100
  Nicholas 99
  Rachael 99
  Thomas 99, 100
  Tobias 99, 100
  Tobias, Jr. 100
RULEY Ann 87
  Anthony 100
  Seth 100
RUMSEY Benjamin 100
  Charles 40, 52, 86, 100, 109, 113
  Elizabeth 14
  Thomas 100
  William 100
RUSSELL Abraham 100
RUTEN Rebecca 58
RUTHERFORD Joseph 100
RUTLEDGE
  Christopher 100

RUTTER Isaac 101
  Mary 34, 96
  Sarah 17
RYAN Eleanor 91
  John 101
RYLAND Fredus 101
  Jehu 101
  John 101
  John, Jr. 101
  John, Sr. 101
  Mary 92
  Sarah 97

SAMON Daniel 101
SAMPSON James 101
SANDERS William 101
SANDS Alexander 101
  James 101
  John 101
  Wiliam 101
SANNER Joseph 101
SAPPINGTON Benjamin 101
  Elizabeth 97
  James 101
  Mary 20
  Rebecca 8
SAVIN Edward 101
  Joshua 101
  Peregrine 101
  Polly 106
  Richard 101
  Thomas 19, 66, 92, 102
  William 102
SAYER George 102
SCANLAN John 102
SCHAEFFER William A. 54
SCOTT Alexander 102
  Capt. 6
  Elizabeth 89
  Isaac 102
  James 102
  John 102
  John, Jr. 102
  Martha 7
  Moses 102
  Robert 102
  Thomas 102
  William 102
  William, Jr. 102
SCURY Robert 102
SEARS John 102
  Mary 102

William 103
SEGER Joseph 103
SERVICE William 103
SEVERSON Ann 97, 123
  Benjamin 103
  Elizabeth 88
  Joseph 103
SEWELL James 103
  Thomas 103
SHANNON John 103
SHARP Araminta 103
  Bathia 103
  Jehu 103
  Lavinia 103
  Ledia 103
  Ruth 107
  Samuel 103
  Sinah 103
  Sophia 103
  Thomas 103
SHARPE Sarah 1
SHARPLESS Robert 103
SHEHEE Edward 103
SHELL Charles P. 103
SHELLEY John 103
SHEPARD Ann 56
SHEPHERD Samuel 103
SHEPPERD Nathaniel 103
SHERIDINE Daniel 103
SHIELDS Archibald 103
  Edmond 104
  Francis 104
  John 104
  Mary 78
  Thomas 104
SHIELS Patrick 104
SHIRKEY Charles 104
SHIRLEY John 104
SHOEMAKER John 104
SHORT Adam 104
  John 104
  Jonathan 104
  Sarah 57
  Thomas 104
  William 104
SILVER Samuel 104

SIMCO William 104
SIMCOE George 5
SIMISTER Thomas 104
SIMMONS Lawrence 104
SIMPERS Amey 91
  Ann 16
  George 104
  Jacob 104
  Jesse 104
  John 104
  Mary 39
  Rebecca 50
  Sarah 91
  Thomas 104
SIMPSON Alexander 105
SINGLETON Thomas 105
SINNO Elizabeth 1
SIRE John 105
SLEATOR Richard 105
SLOOP Joseph 105
SLUYTER Elizabeth 101
SLYCER Hannah 85
SMALLWOOD Col. 68
  Gen. 65, 81
  William 93
SMART Stephen 105
SMITH Barbary 4
  Catherine 110
  David 105
  Dinish 105
  Fergus 105
  Henry 105
  Hugh 105
  James 105
  John 105
  Joseph 105
  Joshua 105
  Margaret 92
  Michael 105, 106
  Nathan 106
  Robert 106
  Ruth 51
  Samuel 106
  Sarah 51
  Thomas 106
  Thomas L. 106
  William 51, 106
SOMERVILLE Capt. 43
SOPER Robert 106
SOUTH Hezekiah 21, 105, 106

143

SPEER John 106
SPENCER Edward 106
SPLANE William 106
SPRINGER Peter 106
SPROUL Mary 62
STACKHOUSE John 106
STALCOB Henry 106
STALCUP Rachel 37
STANLEY Michael 106
STARN Frederick 106
  John 107
  Joseph 107
STARNES George 107
  Mary 107
  Nicholas 107
STEEL Alexander 107
  Allen 107
  Ann 107
  Hugh 107
  James 107
  James, Jr. 107
  James, Sr. 107
  Jane 107
  John 107
  Mary 107
  Ruth 107
  Sara 107
  William 107
STEEN John 107
STEPHENSON Alexander 107
  Joseph 107
  Margaret 12
  William 107
STERLING Ephraim 107
  Jacob 107
  William 107
STERRETT John 107
  Samuel 107
STETT Thomas 108
STEUART William 108
STEVENSON James 108
  John 108
STEWARD George 108
STEWART Robert 108
  William 108
STIDHAM Henry 108
STILES Lawrence 108
  Michael 108
STITT Thomas 108
STOCKTON John 108
  John, Jr. 108
  Joseph 108
STOGDEN Elizabeth 28
STONE John H. 44

STONESTREET
  William 108
STOOPS John 108
  Philip 108
  William 109
STORMONT Nathaniel
  109
STRAGHIN William
  109
STRAHAN John 109
STRAWBRIDGE James
  109
  John 109
STREAN William 109
STRIKEINGBURG John
  A. 109
STRONGE Leonard
  109
STUART Alexander
  109
STUDSILL
  Christopher 109
STIMM George 109
STUMP George 109
  Hannah 109
  John 109
  John, Jr. 109
  William, Jr. 109
STURGIS Job 109
SUGARS Peter 109
SUMMERS John 109
SUTTON Abraham 110
  Ashberry 110
  Sarah 10
SWAN Bazel 110
SWINK Abraham 110
  George 110
  Jacob 110

TAGART John 110
TALANDIER Jeanne
  51
TALEN Joseph 110
TALER Amelia 88
TALLUM Adam 110
  John 110
TALLY John 50
TANNER Joseph 110
TATE John 110
TAYLOR Benjamin
  110
  Edward 110
  Elizabeth 25
  Hannah 19, 114
  James 110

Jeremiah 110
John 110
Joseph 110
Margaret 12
Marlow 110
Mary 110
Matthew 111
Rebecca 124
Richard 111
Richard, Jr. 111
Robert 111
Samuel 111
Thomas 111
William 111
TEADLY Edward 111
TENKINS Samuel 111
TERRY Joseph 111
THACKERY Ann 97
  Elizabeth 54
  Hannah 5
  James 111
  Rachel 14
THACKRAY James 111
THISTLOW George 111
THOMAS Ann 100
  Aquila 111
  Benjamin 111
  Christain 111
  Ensign 111
  Henry 111
  Isaac 112
  James 112
  John 112
  John G. 112
  Joseph 112
  Samuel 112
  Sarah 70
  William 112
THOMPSON Abraham
  112
  Alex. 112
  Andrew 112
  Deborah 71
  Edward 112
  Elizabeth 40
  Ephraim 80, 112
  Jane 14
  John 14. 112
  John D. 25, 36,
  40, 47, 49, 61,
  90, 101, 113,
  115, 116, 118
  Mary 80, 94, 116
  Richard 113
  Richard, Jr. 113

Robert 113
Samuel 113
Thomas 113
William 113
THOMSON William 113
TIBBS John 113
TIDBALL Abraham 113
TIGNER James 113
TILDEN Martha 54
  Rebecca 54
TILEDON Mary M. 17
TILGHMAN Matthew 33
TILL Gertrude R. 94
TILLEY William 113
TILYARD William 113
TOMB Sinah 103
TOOLE Andrew 113
  John 113
TOUCHSTONE Chris.
  114
  Rachel 69
  Samson 114
TOULSON John 114
TOWER John 114
TOWLAND James 114
TOWLIN John 114
TOWNSEND Granville
  S. 62
TREMBLE Hance 114
  Jacob 114
  Joseph 114
TREW James 38
TRIMBELL David 68
TRIMBLE James 56
TROATTLE Alexander
  114
TUCKER James 114
TULL Thomas 114
TUMBEL William 114
TUNSTILL John 114
TURNBEL William 114
TURNER Margaret 20
  Matthew 114
TUTON George 114
TYLER Joanna 12
TYSON Beulah 114
  Eliza 114
  Elizabeth 114
  Mathias 114
  Tacy 114
  Thomas 114
  William 114

VAIL John 114
VANDEVEARE Catherine

57
VANHORN Elizabeth 117
  Hester 33
  Nicholas 33
VANLEAR Ann 73
VANSANT John 114
  Susannah 47
VEAZEY Ann 118
  Araminta 81
  Capt. 46. 68
  Edward 2, 9, 76, 77, 114, 115
  Eli 115
  Elisha 115
  Hester 115
  J. W. 116
  James 115
  John 25, 114, 115
  John 114, 115
  John W. 22, 80, 90, 103
  John Ward 115
  John, III 115
  John, Jr. 25, 115, 118
  Joseph 115
  Mary 65
  Noble 115
  Rebecca 115
  Robert 116
  Samuel 7, 111, 116, 123
  Sarah 115
  Thomas 116
  Thomas B. 116
  William 46, 54, 70, 116
  William, 3rd 116
VICKERS Benjamin 116
  George 116
VOIYNLN Jacob 82, 83
Von COVENHOVEN Gertrude 44

WAGONER John 116
WAKEFIELD William 116
WALKER Andrew 116
  Hannah 63
  John 116
  Robert 116
  William 116
WALLACE Adam 116, 117
  Adam, Jr. 117
  Andrew 1, 117
  Catherine 117
  David 117
  Elizabeth 117
  George 117
  Hugh 117
  James 117
  John 117
  Michael 117
  Rachel 117
  Samuel 117
  Sarah 67
  Thomas 117
WALLIS Thomas 117
WALMSLEY Benjamin 117
  Catherine 45, 92
  John 117
  Rachel 118
  Rebecca 86
  Robert 117
  Robert, Jr. 118
  Sarah 118
  Susannah 63
  William 118
WALTER Christopher 118
WARAM James 118
WARD Alice 88
  Deborah 118
  Elizabeth 118
  George 118
  Henry 87, 118
  John 118
  John, Sr. 118
  Joshua 118
  Margarett 87
  Pereg. 118
  Robert 118
  Sarah 118
  Susannah 108
  William 118
  William, Jr. 118
WARE Sarah 33
WASHINGTON Gen. 55, 56, 95
  George 1, 93, 98
WATERS Allen 118
WATKINS Sally 12
WATSON Elizabeth 123

145

Isaac 5
  Isaac D. 119
  Joseph 119
  William 119
WATT John 119
WEIR Andrew 119
  Edward 119
  Robert 119
WELCH George, Jr. 119
  George, Sr. 119
  James 119
  John 119
  Robert 119
  Robert, Sr. 119
WELDON Lydia 84
WELLS James 44
  John 119
WELSH Andrew 119
  James 119
WENNER Jacob 119
WESTWOOD William 119
WETZLER Dan 34
WHAN James 119
  Samuel, Jr. 119
  William 119
WHATTSON Joseph 119
WHEATLEY Elizabeth 73
WHITE Abner 119
  Hannah 19
  John 120
  Jonathan 120
  Peter 120
  Sarah 120
  William 120
WHITEACRE Ralph 120
  William 120
WHITELOCK Charles, Jr. 120
  Charles, Sr. 120
  Elizabeth 55
  Patrick 120
WHITESIER William 120
WHITTAM Benjamin 120
  Peregrine 120
  William 120
WILCOX Joseph 120
WILEY John 120
WILKINSON John 120
WILLCOX Rachel 39
WILLCROFT James 120
WILLIAMS Baruch 1, 2, 15, 16, 18,

19, 24, 30, 39,
40, 57, 58, 59,
60, 72, 73, 74,
76, 77, 78, 81,
83, 101, 103,
106, 107, 108,
110, 112, 116,
120, 121, 122
  Basil 120, 121
  Benjamin 121
  Capt. 42-45, 48
  Charles 121
  Eliot 121
  Joseph 121
  Lidia 61
  Nancy 46
  Richard 121
  Robert 121
  Sarah 55
  Thomas 46, 121
WILLIAMSON
  Alexander 121
WILLIAMSON Daniel
  121
WILLOCK Andrew 121
  James 121
WILLSON Andrew 121
  George 121
  John 121
  Peter 121
  Samuel 121
WILMER Mary 115
WILSON Abigal 108
  Alexander 53,
    121
  Andrew 121
  Daniel 122
  Elizabeth 79
  George 122
  James 122
  John 122
  Margaret 105
  Mary 36, 66
  Robert C. 53
  Thomas 122
  William 122
WINCHESTER
  Elizabeth 9
  Mary 76
  William 122
WINDLE Jona. 122
WINGATE Charlotte
  5 Sarah 61
WINKELES George
  122

WINKERT Samuel 122
WINKET Samuel 122
  Thomas 122
WINTERS Elisha 122
WINTGAGE Hezekiah
  122
WIREY Michael 122
WIRTS Thomas 122
WISHAM John 122
WOOD John 123
  William 123
WORAM James 118
WORK Alexander 123
  Andrew 123
  James 123
  Samuel 123
  William 123
WORLEY Mary 39
WRIGHT James 123
  John 123
WROTH Ann 97, 103
  Elizabeth 101
  James 123
  James, Jr. 123
  Thomas 123

YARDLEY Joyce 5
  William 123
YELEFRAU John 68
  Mary 68
  Polly 68
  Rachael 68
  Sarah 68
YEOMAN Thomas 123
YEOMANS Joshua 123
  Samuel 123
  Thomas 123
YOUNG Godfrey 124
  John 124
  Robert 124
  Samuel 124
  William 124

# Heritage Books by Henry C. Peden, Jr.:

*A Closer Look at St. John's Parish Registers [Baltimore County, Maryland], 1701–1801*

*A Collection of Maryland Church Records*

*A Guide to Genealogical Research in Maryland: 5th Edition, Revised and Enlarged*

*Abstracts of Marriages and Deaths in
Harford County, Maryland, Newspapers, 1837–1871*

*Abstracts of the Ledgers and Accounts of the Bush Store and Rock Run Store, 1759–1771*

*Abstracts of the Orphans Court Proceedings of Harford County, 1778–1800*

*Abstracts of Wills, Harford County, Maryland, 1800–1805*

*Anne Arundel County, Maryland, Marriage References 1658–1800*
Henry C. Peden, Jr. and Veronica Clarke Peden

*Baltimore City [Maryland] Deaths and Burials, 1834–1840*

*Baltimore County, Maryland, Overseers of Roads, 1693–1793*

*Bastardy Cases in Baltimore County, Maryland, 1673–1783*

*Bastardy Cases in Harford County, Maryland, 1774–1844*

*More Bastardy Cases in Harford County, Maryland, 1773–1893*

*Bible and Family Records of Harford County, Maryland, Families: Volume V*

*Biographical Dictionary of Harford County, Maryland, 1774–1974:
Over 1,200 Sketches of Prominent Citizens during the First 200 years of the County's
History with Seventeen Appendices Listing Public Officials from 1774 to 2020*
Henry C. Peden, Jr. and William O. Carr

*Cecil County, Maryland Marriage References, 1674–1824*
Henry C. Peden, Jr. and Veronica Clarke Peden

*Children of Harford County: Indentures and Guardianships, 1801–1830*

*Colonial Delaware Soldiers and Sailors, 1638–1776*

*Colonial Families of the Eastern Shore of Maryland
Volumes 5, 6, 7, 8, 9, 11, 12, 13, 14, 16, and 19*
Henry C. Peden, Jr. and F. Edward Wright

*Colonial Families of the Eastern Shore of Maryland: Volume 21 and Volume 23*

*Colonial Maryland Soldiers and Sailors, 1634–1734*

*Colonial Tavern Keepers of Maryland and Delaware, 1634–1776*

*Dorchester County, Maryland, Marriage References, 1669–1800*
Henry C. Peden, Jr. and Veronica Clarke Peden

*Dr. John Archer's First Medical Ledger, 1767–1769, Annotated Abstracts*

*Early Anglican Records of Cecil County*

*Early Harford Countians, Individuals Living in
Harford County, Maryland in Its Formative Years
Volume 1: A to K, Volume 2: L to Z, and Volume 3: Supplement*

*Family Cemeteries and Grave Sites in Harford County, Maryland*

*First Presbyterian Church Records, Baltimore, Maryland, 1840–1879*

*Frederick County, Maryland, Marriage References and Family Relationships, 1748–1800*
Henry C. Peden, Jr. and Veronica Clarke Peden

*Genealogical Gleanings from Harford County, Maryland, Medical Records, 1772–1852*
Winner of the Norris Harris Prize from MHS for
the best genealogical reference book in 2016!

*Harford County Taxpayers in 1870, 1872 and 1883*

*Harford County, Maryland Death Records, 1849–1899*

*Harford County, Maryland Deponents, 1775–1835*

*Harford County, Maryland Divorces and Separations, 1823–1923*

*Harford County, Maryland, Death Certificates, 1898–1918: An Annotated Index*

*Harford County, Maryland, Divorce Cases, 1827–1912: An Annotated Index*

*Harford County, Maryland, Inventories, 1774–1804*

*Harford County, Maryland, Marriage References and Family Relationships, 1774–1824*
Henry C. Peden, Jr. and Veronica Clarke Peden

*Harford County, Maryland, Marriage References and Family Relationships, 1825–1850*

*Harford County, Maryland, Marriage References and Family Relationships, 1851–1860*
Henry C. Peden, Jr. and Veronica Clarke Peden

*Harford County, Maryland, Marriage References and Family Relationships, 1861–1870*
Henry C. Peden, Jr. and Veronica Clarke Peden

*Harford County, Maryland, Marriage References and Family Relationships, 1871–1875*

*Harford County, Maryland, Marriage References and Family Relationships, 1876–1880*

*Harford (Maryland) Homicides: Cases of Murder and Attempted Murder:
Committed by Men and Women Who Were "Seduced by the Instigation of the Devil"
in Harford County, Maryland During the 18th and 19th Centuries*

*Harford (Maryland) Suicides: Cases of Self-killings and Attempted Suicides
Committed by Men and Women Who Suffered from an "Aberration of the Mind"
in Harford County, Maryland, 1817–1947*

*Harford (Old Brick Baptist) Church,
Harford County, Maryland, Records and Members (1742–1974),
Tombstones, Burials (1775–2009) and Family Relationships*

*Heirs and Legatees of Harford County, Maryland, 1774–1802*

*Heirs and Legatees of Harford County, Maryland, 1802–1846*

*Inhabitants of Baltimore County, Maryland, 1763–1774*

*Inhabitants of Cecil County, Maryland 1774–1800*

*Inhabitants of Cecil County, Maryland, 1649–1774*

*Inhabitants of Harford County, Maryland, 1791–1800*

*Inhabitants of Kent County, Maryland, 1637–1787*

*Insolvent Debtors in 19th Century Harford County, Maryland:*
*A Legal and Genealogical Digest*

*Joseph A. Pennington & Co., Havre De Grace, Maryland, Funeral Home Records:*
*Volume II, 1877–1882, 1893–1900*

*Kent County, Maryland Marriage References, 1642–1800*
Henry C. Peden, Jr. and Veronica Clarke Peden

*Marriages and Deaths from Baltimore Newspapers, 1817–1824*

*Maryland Bible Records, Volume 1: Baltimore and Harford Counties*

*Maryland Bible Records, Volume 2: Baltimore and Harford Counties*

*Maryland Bible Records, Volume 3: Carroll County*

*Maryland Bible Records, Volume 4: Eastern Shore*

*Maryland Bible Records, Volume 5: Harford, Baltimore and Carroll Counties*

*Maryland Bible Records, Volume 7: Baltimore, Harford and Frederick Counties*

*Maryland Deponents, 1634–1799*

*Maryland Deponents: Volume 3, 1634–1776*

*Maryland Prisoners Languishing in Goal, Volume 1: 1635–1765*

*Maryland Prisoners Languishing in Goal, Volume 2: 1766–1800*

*Maryland Public Service Records, 1775–1783: A Compendium of Men and Women of Maryland Who Rendered Aid in Support of the American Cause against Great Britain during the Revolutionary War*

*Marylanders and Delawareans in the French and Indian War, 1756–1763*

*Marylanders to Carolina: Migration of Marylanders to*
*North Carolina and South Carolina prior to 1800*

*Marylanders to Kentucky, 1775–1825*

*Marylanders to Ohio and Indiana, Migration Prior to 1835*

*Marylanders to Tennessee*

*Methodist Records of Baltimore City, Maryland: Volume 1, 1799–1829*

*Methodist Records of Baltimore City, Maryland: Volume 2, 1830–1839*

*Methodist Records of Baltimore City, Maryland: Volume 3, 1840–1850*
*(East City Station)*

*More Maryland Deponents, 1716–1799*

*More Marylanders to Carolina:*
*Migration of Marylanders to North Carolina and South Carolina prior to 1800*

*More Marylanders to Kentucky, 1778–1828*

*More Marylanders to Ohio and Indiana: Migrations Prior to 1835*

*Orphans and Indentured Children of Baltimore County, Maryland, 1777–1797*

*Outpensioners of Harford County, Maryland, 1856–1896*

*Presbyterian Records of Baltimore City, Maryland, 1765–1840*
*Quaker Records of Baltimore and Harford Counties, Maryland, 1801–1825*
*Quaker Records of Northern Maryland, 1716–1800*
*Quaker Records of Southern Maryland, 1658–1800*
*Revolutionary Patriots of Anne Arundel County, Maryland, 1775–1783*
*Revolutionary Patriots of Baltimore Town and Baltimore County, 1775–1783*
*Revolutionary Patriots of Calvert and St. Mary's Counties, Maryland, 1775–1783*
*Revolutionary Patriots of Caroline County, Maryland, 1775–1783*
*Revolutionary Patriots of Cecil County, Maryland, 1775–1783*
*Revolutionary Patriots of Charles County, Maryland, 1775–1783*
*Revolutionary Patriots of Delaware, 1775–1783*
*Revolutionary Patriots of Dorchester County, Maryland, 1775–1783*
*Revolutionary Patriots of Frederick County, Maryland, 1775–1783*
*Revolutionary Patriots of Harford County, Maryland, 1775–1783*
*Revolutionary Patriots of Kent and Queen Anne's Counties, 1775–1783*
*Revolutionary Patriots of Lancaster County, Pennsylvania, 1775–1783*
*Revolutionary Patriots of Maryland, 1775–1783: A Supplement*
*Revolutionary Patriots of Maryland, 1775–1783: Second Supplement*
*Revolutionary Patriots of Montgomery County, Maryland, 1776–1783*
*Revolutionary Patriots of Prince George's County, Maryland, 1775–1783*
*Revolutionary Patriots of Talbot County, Maryland, 1775–1783*
*Revolutionary Patriots of Washington County, Maryland, 1776–1783*
*Revolutionary Patriots of Worcester and Somerset Counties, Maryland, 1775–1783*
*St. George's (Old Spesutia) Parish Harford County, Maryland Church and Cemetery Records, 1820–1920*
*St. John's and St. George's Parish Registers, 1696–1851*
*Survey Field Book of David and William Clark in Harford County, Maryland, 1770–1812*
*Talbot County, Maryland Marriage References, 1662–1800*
Henry C. Peden, Jr. and Veronica Clarke Peden
*The Crenshaws of Kentucky, 1800–1995*
*The Delaware Militia in the War of 1812*
*Union Chapel United Methodist Church Cemetery Tombstone Inscriptions, Wilna, Harford County, Maryland*

www.ingramcontent.com/pod-product-compliance
Lightning Source LLC
Chambersburg PA
CBHW051841090426
42736CB00011B/1909